Fast Peyote Stitch Jewelry

Josie Fabre

KB
Kalmbach Books

WAUKESHA, WI

Kalmbach Books
21027 Crossroads Circle
Waukesha, Wisconsin 53186
www.JewelryAndBeadingStore.com

© 2016 Josie Fabre

Numbered step-by-step photos and illustrations by the author. Author photo by Julie Wood, Paul Wood Photography. All other photography © 2016 Kalmbach Books except where otherwise noted.

Published in 2016
19 18 17 16 15   1 2 3 4 5

Manufactured in China.

ISBN: 978-1-62700-239-4
EISBN: 978-1-62700-240-0

Editor: Dianne Wheeler
Book Design: Lisa Bergman
Photographer: William Zuback

Library of Congress Control Number: 2015941330

Contents

PROJECTS

INTRODUCTION

W hen I was learning bead weaving, I admired beautiful peyote pieces made from patterns and I tried making them, but gave up for two reasons. First, it took so long to make a piece, picking up one bead at a time. Second, I got frustrated and confused following the patterns back and forth and stopping to mark my spot after only a few beads—often making mistakes and having to backtrack or start over.

When my bead society decided to participate in the Bead-It-Forward Project with a bird theme, I decided to try my hand at converting one of my photographs into a peyote pattern, and then, of course, I had to stitch up the square! I meticulously picked up one bead at a time, following the many-colored pattern, back and forth, backing up when I followed the pattern in the wrong direction and, starting over when I got too far off track. After more than a week (!) and several do-overs, I finished one, roughly one-inch square. The result is shown below. I stitched up one more of the pattern I made and I loved the results, but swore I would never do it again.

Later, I admired all the beautiful bead squares and resolved to find a way to make it easier and quicker for me to use peyote stitch. This resulted in designs with fewer colors and more than one bead per step (multiple-drop). My first attempts were simple two-color, three-drop fleur-de-lis bracelet patterns. I stitched up a bracelet with traditional peyote and was pretty happy with the results, but it still didn't meet my standards for speed of creation.

While conferring with some fellow beaders at my local bead shop (Meme's Beads and Things), the owner pulled out a back issue of *Bead&Button* Magazine describing fast peyote and showed several of us how to do it (thanks, Michelle!). By keeping my patterns to a minimum of colors, using a multi-drop stitch, and stitching them with fast peyote, I have been able to speed up the creation of beautiful peyote-stitched pieces. And now, so can you!

Josie

How to Use This Book

Each *Project* contains: 1) a short introduction; 2) a list of materials and tools; 3) finished measurements; 4) tips for adjusting the pattern to fit; 5) specific directions; and, 6) a bead pattern with the corresponding word chart.

The *Materials List* contains the type of thread and needle to use, plus a list of beads required to make the project. For each of the beads you will find: 1) size; 2) the manufacturer's bead number; 3) a description of the bead, including its specific color; and, 4) the quantity. The quantities are rounded up to the nearest gram or count based on the amount needed to complete the project.

I've spent more than two years designing and modifying the bracelet, necklace, and pendant patterns. I have organized them into the following categories: Natural Wonders, Wonderful Wings, Wild Side, Colorful Classics, Modern Marvels, and Bonus Projects.

I've included a variety of colors and styles—in other words— something for everyone! If you want to start with a quick project, try a pendant first. The smaller the piece, the less time it takes to complete.

In this book, my goal is to not only teach you how to use the Fast Peyote technique to make my jewelry pieces, but also to provide you with tips on how to modify the designs to truly make each one of them your very own.

BASICS

Materials

Beautiful handmade jewelry starts with a number of quality items. At a minimum, all the projects here require beads, thread, needle, and scissors or cutters. Other items are discussed below and each project description provides a specific, detailed supply list.

Seed beads

Since seed beads come in many sizes, manufacturers use a sizing system that allows buyers to select the correct beads for their project. Keep in mind that the sizes vary depending on how the beads are made and that the bead can be longer than it is wide or vice versa. The sizes are referred to as *aught* sizes and they indicate approximately how many beads of that size will fit in an inch. For example, 11 aught (11º) beads will be about an inch long if lined up side by side (not strung). The bigger the "aught" number, the smaller the bead.

Cylinder beads such as Miyuki Delicas or Toho cylinder beads are a popular choice for peyote because they are cylindrical and consistent in size. Cylinder beads or seed beads that are consistent in size, such as Japanese or Preciosa seed beads are recommended, but there are many options. Cube beads, bugle beads, and even triangle beads can be a fun option for peyote as well. I prefer Miyuki Delicas because of their consistency and wide variety of color options and finishes.

Very rounded beads can be a little difficult to work with because they do not lie next to each other as nicely as the cylinder beads and your thread tension must be kept a little tighter. Beware of round beads that are inconsistent in size. If using them, try to select the individual beads that are consistent in size or the piece will warp. 15º round seed beads are also used for fringe and trim in many projects in this book as they come in a wide variety of colors and finishes.

The finish on the beads can make a difference in how a piece is made and in how it looks and feels. The beads used in this book are primarily glass and can have different properties: transparent, opaque, and/or finished. Beads without a finish are shiny, smooth, and easy to work with. Matte or frost finish beads absorb light and are not as smooth, so they can hang onto each other a little as the piece is constructed, making it more difficult to straighten out tilted beads or get the needle between two beads.

Aurora borealis (AB) or iris finishes have a multi-colored or rainbow coating over the base color. Ceylon, Duracoat, or luster finishes give a shiny, durable coating to the beads. Transparent beads let light through and can show thread. Transparent beads can be smooth, have finishes, or can be lined with color or metal (silver, gold, copper), which adds a nice depth to the bead. Galvanized beads have a metallic finish and the flat sides of hex cut beads give added sparkle.

matte

luster

galvanized

opaque

silver-lined

transparent

AB

Beading thread

My preference is smoke-colored Fireline, 4 or 6 pound (lb). Four lb. is recommended for lower (1–2) drop peyote, with smaller than 11° beads or for a supple bracelet. Six lb. is recommended for a higher (3 or more) drop or with larger beads (e.g. 6° or 8°), or for a little stiffer piece. If adding trim or fringe, the 4 lb. is preferable, as it is easier to pass through the beads multiple times, especially with knots. 4 lb. also tends to hang straighter with fringe. Braided Fireline thread is a good option because it is strong, not flexible, and doesn't fray easily.

Fireline doesn't have a lot of stretch to it, which makes it perfect for peyote. While the smoke coloring on Fireline will come off on your fingers a bit, it washes off easily with soap and water. If the coloring gets on a bead (usually the ones with matte finish), it wipes off. Crystal-colored thread can be used for lighter colored or transparent beads.

Chain

Finished chains are widely available in a number of options. You can also make your own using unfinished chain, a clasp, jump rings, or wire.

Wire

I like to use wrapped wire loops for many projects. My preferred wire is 24-gauge, round, tarnish-resistant Artistic Wire; however, many options are available.

Embellishments

Small items other than beads or buttons can be added to peyote pieces to give them a different look. The Geared Up project uses small decorative metal gears as embellishment. Additional embellishments include filigree pieces, charms, found objects, chain, or just about anything that can be sewn onto the piece. Use the same techniques as adding buttons, beaded fringe, or trim to secure.

Leather, ribbon, and other cords

Finished leather and other cords are widely available. If buying finished cords, check for quality closures—that is, jump rings that are not easily stretched and are fully closed, and a good clasp. You can also make your own cord ends using cord ends, glue, a clasp, jump rings, or wire.

Peyote bracelet closures

A wide variety of closure options are available. A toggle/loop is used on most of the bracelets in this book. Toggles can easily be made from peyote stitch—a peyote tube is used frequently, and a peyote shape can also make a fun option. A button, a bead, or group of beads can be used as toggles to complement your beadwork nicely. Any pre-made clasp can also be sewn onto the ends of the bracelet.

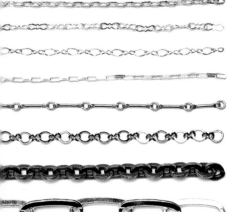

Clasps

Clasps come in many sizes, styles, and metals. For necklace chains and cords, I generally use a 12x6mm lobster claw clasp, but other options include toggle and bar, hook and eye, magnetic clasp, "S" clasp, and spring ring tube bar clasp.

Jump rings

Jump rings come in many sizes, weights, and metals. It is best to select the jump ring size to be consistent with the clasp, for example with a 12x6mm lobster claw, a 21-gauge, 5mm or 6mm jump ring works well.

Beads and buttons

There are an infinite variety of beads and buttons available for use in a closure, for trim or fringe, or for embellishing the chain or cord of a necklace. Specific options are discussed with each project, but in general, for closures, a large (8mm or larger) crystal, glass, or metal bead, button, or combination can be used

with a loop to form a toggle. Czech glass fire-polished round beads are used in a number of the projects for embellishment, as they have a nice shape and finish and are very smooth.

Bicone crystals or rondelles are also used for embellishments and provide a lovely sparkle. The edges on crystal beads can be sharp and over time, can wear on the thread. To minimize the risk of breakage, use a seed bead next to each crystal edge. Don't pull the thread too tightly along the edges of the crystals, and reinforce thread through crystals that will get a lot of movement in the finished piece. (The projects in this book are planned to minimize any breakage, but it can happen.)

Slide end tube

A slide end tube is useful for sliding onto the end of a peyote piece for a pendant or even bracelet ends. Slide end tubes were created for loom or square stitch pieces, but can be used on a peyote piece.

awl

Tools

Quality tools make any task easier. The projects in this book require very few tools. When shopping for a tool, read reviews or examine them carefully to make sure they will last; for example, a pair of good cutters or scissors should have sharp, consistent edges. Once you have purchased tools, follow the manufacturers' instructions on taking care of them so they will last.

bead scoops

Awl

A fine beading awl is useful for moving or straightening beads, untangling threads, and loosening knots.

Bead scoops

If you've ever tried to pick up a pile of beads with your fingernails or scooch them around to get them back into their bag, tube, or box,

you will recognize the genius of the inventor of the bead scoop. A bead scoop is a contraption with a thin flat edge that is used to scoop up beads and deposit them into their containers. There are many shapes and sizes available. I use a long thin one because it is easier to pour the beads into small boxes, bags, and tubes with minimal spillage.

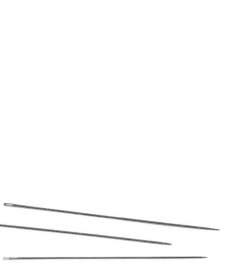

Cutters

The simplest option for cutting thread is a pair of sharp scissors. Other options, such as thread cutters and shears, are also available.

Needles

As with most tools, needle size and style (length, flexibility) is a personal preference. Size 10 or 12 is typical for the types of projects shown in this book. I prefer 2 in. long, size 12 Tulip brand English beading needles, as they are thin enough for 11° and 15° beads. English beading needles have a long, narrow eye so that the needle is not thicker at the eye. In addition, they have a rounded tip and are flexible, strong, and easy to thread.

As with wire and beads, the smaller the size, the thicker the needle. Size 10 is sturdier if you tend to snap needles, but it can get hung up on a knot, and may not work as easily as a smaller needle with smaller beads or multiple passes. I recommend buying good quality needles, as they tend to be more sturdy and last longer.

Needle threader

If you have trouble threading needles, a standard sewing needle threader can be used. The most common consists of a very thin loop of wire with an aluminum or plastic handle. The thin wire loop is inserted into the head of the needle; the thread is passed through the wire loop and the loop is pulled back through the head of the needle, thus threading the needle as it is pulled through the eye.

Chainnose pliers

Chainnose pliers are used for wirework, cord ends, and other similar tasks. Occasionally, in a moment of distraction or fatigue, if too many beads are strung into a row of peyote, rather than unstringing the row, a chainnose pliers can be used to gently crack the offending bead and remove it from the piece.

Pens/pencils

I write all over my beading patterns, primarily to keep my place, but also to note start and stop times at the appropriate locations (so I know how fast it's going). I also mark where thread was added, color changes, and any notes for future projects. A fairly thick marker or roller pen with a bright color will stand out on the colored pattern.

Thread conditioner

With some threads, like those with a little stretch or with a tendency to fray, a thread conditioner can be used to make the thread less likely to tangle, fray, and wear. It also adds a bit of stiffness and stickiness, which can be helpful for some stitches. (However, I typically do not use thread conditioner.)

Glue

I, along with many beaders, use E6000, but my preferred glue for cord ends is Locktite Control Gel Super Glue in the .14 ounce bottle, which has rubber ridged edges for holding and squeezing out the gel.

Preparing a workspace

This book teaches *Fast Peyote,* but no matter how fast you become, with many projects you will sit at your workspace for a significant length of time, so you should try to be as comfortable as possible. Creating a comfortable workspace is a very personal choice. If you are just starting out, sit at a table with your tools in a well-lit room and decide later whether or not to set up a special workspace. A good task lamp can help avoid lighting problems that can cause eyestrain. An adjustable arm is very helpful so that it can be moved closer or further from the work, depending on the light in the room, your level of fatigue, and colors you are working with. If like me, you need reading glasses for close work, choose a pair that gives you a clear view of your beads at a comfortable distance from the work surface so you are not bending toward or leaning away from your beads, thus creating neck strain.

I have found that sitting as straight as possible, with the table fairly close to my lap so I'm not reaching up for beads has worked well for me. Experiment with various chair / table setups so you are as comfortable as possible. Your work surface should be large enough to hold the items needed nearby, such as cutters, thread, and beads. Beads tend to bounce and roll, so a bead mat is essential. I have tried a number of options and the best I've found is a velour bead mat. Be sure to choose a light, neutral color so your beads stand out against it.

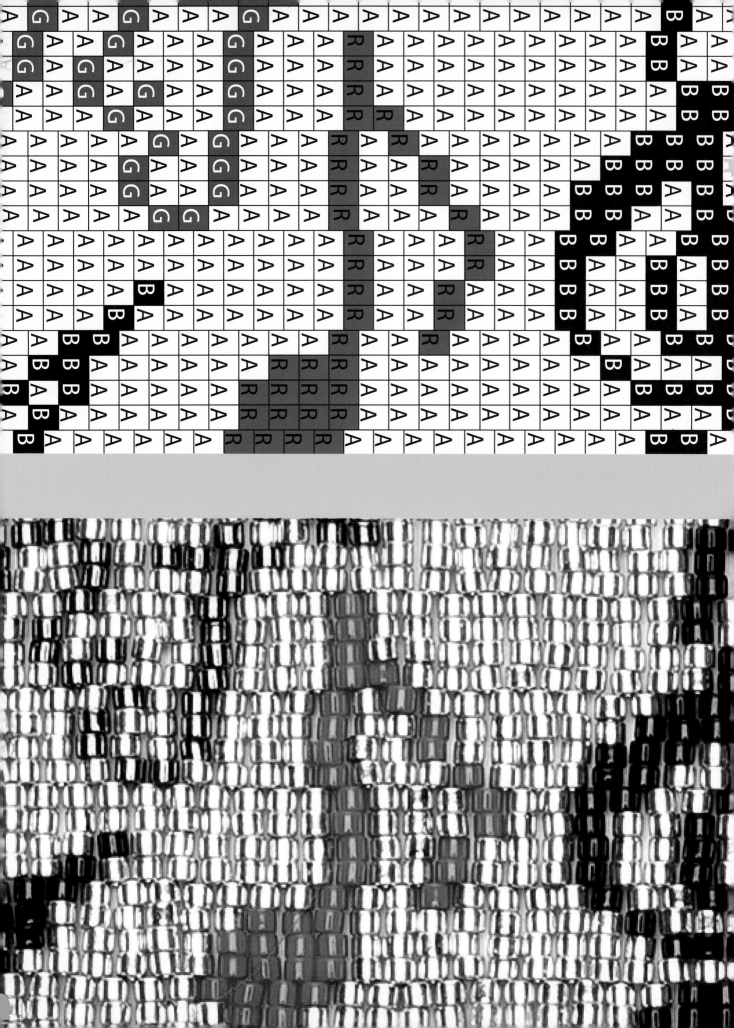

PROJECTS

Roses

For one of our wedding anniversaries, my
husband sent me a bouquet of roses. Since it was
a beautiful, clear, blue-sky day, I took them outside
and shot photos of them. Later, I turned a couple of
those photos into a bracelet pattern.

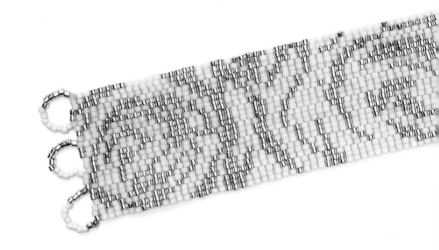

MATERIALS

- 11º Delica beads:
  - 6g (1045) DB0035 metallic silver (color S)
  - 8g (1475) DB0352 matte cream (color C)
- **3** 8mm cream Swarovski crystal pearls
- Fireline, 4-lb. or 6-lb. test

TOOLS

- #10 or #12 beading needle
- Thread cutters or scissors

MEASUREMENTS

1¼ in. wide and 7¼ in. long

To shorten, leave off the first several rows.

Instructions

1 Refer to the *Roses* three-drop pattern and word chart on pages 14 and 15. Follow the instructions for Fast Peyote (Techniques, p. 94) to create the peyote band. Add thread (Techniques, p. 97) as needed throughout the project.

Create loops for the closure

2 *The closure for this project consists of three simple loops and three 8mm crystal pearls.* Reinforce the end of the bracelet (Techniques, p. 96, step 11). Exit at the location on the pattern marked by the first black dot.

3 *Pick up 14 beads of either color or a mix of colors and sew into the piece at the next black dot. Exit the piece at the following black dot and repeat from * to create three loops across the end of the bracelet.

4 Weave back through each loop. To reinforce, use finishing knots to secure (Techniques, p. 97), then trim the thread and weave in the tail.

5 Remove the stop bead and add thread to the original tail at the opposite end of the piece. Weave into the piece, tucking the knot into a bead. Reinforce the end of the bracelet.

Add the crystal pearls

6 Exit at one of the black dots at the opposite end of the pattern, then pick up a color C bead, a crystal pearl, and a color S bead. Sew back through the crystal pearl and the C, then weave back into the piece. Exit at the next black dot marked on the pattern.

7 Repeat step 6, picking up a C, a crystal pearl, and an S. Repeat to add the third pearl.

8 Weave back into the piece using finishing knots to secure, then trim the thread, and weave in the tail.

Roses
three-drop peyote

Row 1&2 (L) (24)C
Row 3&4 (R) (14)C, (2)S, (8)C
Row 5&6 (R) (16)C, (2)S, (6)C
Row 7&8 (R) (3)C, (3)S, (1)C, (5)S, (6)C, (1)S, (5)C
Row 9&10 (R) (18)S, (1)C, (4)S, (1)C
Row 11&12 (R) (9)S, (4)C, (11)S
Row 13&14 (R) (4)S, (14)C, (6)S
Row 15&16 (R) (3)S, (1)C, (1)S, (7)C, (1)S, (3)C, (2)S, (6)C
Row 17&18 (R) (2)S, (1)C, (2)S, (4)C, (5)S, (3)C, (5)S, (2)C
Row 19&20 (R) (3)C, (1)S, (3)C, (4)S, (7)C, (5)S, (1)C
Row 21&22 (R) (1)C, (2)S, (1)C, (5)S, (10)C, (4)S, (1)C
Row 23&24 (R) (3)C, (1)S, (1)C, (5)S, (10)C, (3)S, (1)C
Row 25&26 (R) (4)C, (3)S, (1)C, (1)S, (5)C, (3)S, (4)C, (3)S
Row 27&28 (R) (1)C, (1)S, (2)C, (2)S, (2)C, (1)S, (7)C, (2)S, (4)C, (2)S
Row 29&30 (R) (1)C, (1)S, (1)C, (2)S, (1)C, (3)S, (6)C, (1)S, (2)C, (1)S, (3)C, (1)S, (1)C
Row 31&32 (R) (2)S, (1)C, (1)S, (2)C, (1)S, (8)C, (2)S, (1)C, (2)S, (2)C, (1)S, (1)C
Row 33&34 (R) (2)S, (1)C, (1)S, (2)C, (1)S, (2)C, (2)S, (3)C, (1)S, (1)C, (1)S, (1)C, (3)S, (1)C, (1)S, (1)C
Row 35&36 (R) (1)C, (3)S, (1)C, (2)S, (3)C, (1)S, (3)C, (1)S, (1)C, (2)S, (1)C, (2)S, (1)C, (2)S
Row 37&38 (R) (1)C, (3)S, (1)C, (2)S, (3)C, (2)S, (2)C, (1)S, (1)C, (2)S, (1)C, (1)S, (1)C, (1)S, (1)C, (1)S
Row 39&40 (R) (2)C, (2)S, (2)C, (1)S, (4)C, (2)S, (3)C, (2)S, (1)C, (1)S, (2)C, (2)S
Row 41&42 (R) (3)C, (2)S, (1)C, (2)S, (8)C, (1)S, (2)C, (1)S, (2)C, (2)S
Row 43&44 (R) (4)C, (2)S, (1)C, (5)S, (10)C, (2)S
Row 45&46 (R) (2)C, (3)S, (2)C, (8)S, (6)C, (3)S
Row 47&48 (R) (1)S, (1)C, (4)S, (4)C, (2)S, (9)C, (3)S
Row 49&50 (R) (1)S, (2)C, (4)S, (13)C, (3)S, (1)C
Row 51&52 (R) (2)S, (3)C, (1)S, (1)C, (1)S, (10)C, (3)S, (3)C
Row 53&54 (R) (3)S, (1)C, (8)S, (3)C, (4)S, (5)C
Row 55&56 (R) (5)S, (1)C, (11)S, (7)C
Row 57&58 (R) (2)C, (4)S, (1)C, (2)S, (3)C, (2)S, (8)C, (2)S
Row 59&60 (R) (21)C, (3)S
Row 61&62 (R) (17)C, (7)S
Row 63&64 (R) (6)S, (5)C, (6)S, (2)C, (2)S, (3)C
Row 65&66 (R) (6)C, (5)S, (13)C
Row 67&68 (R) (3)C, (3)S, (3)C, (8)S, (7)C
Row 69&70 (R) (3)C, (14)S, (7)C
Row 71&72 (R) (1)C, (3)S, (10)C, (1)S, (1)C, (3)S, (5)C
Row 73&74 (R) (3)S, (1)C, (10)S, (3)C, (3)S, (4)C
Row 75&76 (R) (2)S, (1)C, (13)S, (3)C, (3)S, (2)C
Row 77&78 (R) (2)C, (7)S, (3)C, (6)S, (2)C, (3)S, (1)C
Row 79&80 (R) (5)S, (11)C, (3)S, (3)C, (2)S
Row 81&82 (R) (3)S, (2)C, (2)S, (2)C, (3)S, (6)C, (2)S, (4)C
Row 83&84 (R) (1)S, (2)C, (1)S, (4)C, (1)S, (3)C, (2)S, (6)C, (1)S, (3)C
Row 85&86 (R) (1)C, (2)S, (4)C, (1)S, (6)C, (3)S, (5)C, (1)S, (1)C
Row 87&88 (R) (1)S, (4)C, (2)S, (12)C, (1)S, (3)C, (1)S
Row 89&90 (R) (3)C, (2)S, (5)C, (5)S, (5)C, (1)S, (3)C
Row 91&92 (R) (3)C, (1)S, (5)C, (1)S, (11)C, (1)S, (2)C
Row 93&94 (R) (6)C, (3)S, (6)C, (3)S, (4)C, (1)S, (1)C
Row 95&96 (R) (2)C, (1)S, (6)C, (10)S, (4)C, (1)S
Row 97&98 (R) (2)C, (1)S, (4)C, (13)S, (4)C
Row 99&100 (R) (1)C, (2)S, (3)C, (4)S, (4)C, (5)S, (1)C, (1)S, (3)C

Row 101&102 (R) (1)C, (2)S, (2)C, (4)S, (2)C, (3)S, (7)C, (1)S, (2)C
Row 103&104 (R) (1)C, (1)S, (2)C, (5)S, (1)C, (1)S, (10)C, (2)S, (1)C
Row 105&106 (R) (1)C, (1)S, (2)C, (4)S, (1)C, (1)S, (8)C, (1)S, (3)C, (1)S, (1)C
Row 107&108 (R) (1)C, (1)S, (2)C, (3)S, (2)C, (1)S, (6)C, (3)S, (3)C, (1)S, (1)C
Row 109&110 (R) (1)C, (1)S, (2)C, (3)S, (1)C, (1)S, (2)C, (2)S, (2)C, (4)S, (2)C, (2)S, (1)C
Row 111&112 (R) (1)C, (1)S, (2)C, (3)S, (1)C, (1)S, (2)C, (2)S, (1)C, (4)S, (2)C, (2)S, (2)C
Row 113&114 (R) (2)S, (2)C, (3)S, (1)C, (1)S, (2)C, (2)S, (1)C, (2)S, (4)C, (2)S, (2)C
Row 115&116 (R) (2)C, (1)S, (1)C, (3)S, (4)C, (3)S, (5)C, (2)S, (3)C
Row 117&118 (R) (2)C, (1)S, (2)C, (2)S, (5)C, (4)S, (2)C, (1)S, (5)C
Row 119&120 (R) (2)C, (2)S, (2)C, (1)S, (6)C, (4)S, (7)C
Row 121&122 (R) (2)C, (2)S, (2)C, (2)S, (4)C, (3)S, (9)C
Row 123&124 (R) (3)C, (2)S, (15)C, (1)S, (3)C
Row 125&126 (R) (1)S, (3)C, (2)S, (13)C, (1)S, (4)C
Row 127&128 (R) (1)C, (1)S, (3)C, (5)S, (5)C, (4)S, (5)C
Row 129&130 (R) (2)C, (1)S, (3)C, (9)S, (9)C
Row 131&132 (R) (2)C, (1)S, (7)C, (3)S, (9)C, (2)S
Row 133&134 (R) (8)C, (1)S, (12)C, (3)S
Row 135&136 (R) (6)S, (9)C, (9)S
Row 137&138 (R) (3)S, (21)C
Row 139&140 (R) (1)S, (5)C, (2)S, (11)C, (2)S, (3)C
Row 141&142 (R) (3)S, (5)C, (2)S, (4)S, (5)C
Row 143&144 (R) (5)S, (5)C, (2)S, (11)C, (1)S
Row 145&146 (R) (4)C, (2)S, (6)C, (3)S, (6)C, (2)S, (1)C
Row 147&148 (R) (1)S, (5)C, (1)S, (10)C, (1)S, (1)C, (3)S, (2)C
Row 149&150 (R) (6)S, (3)C, (3)S, (3)C, (6)S, (3)C
Row 151&152 (R) (5)S, (3)C, (11)S, (5)C
Row 153&154 (R) (2)S, (1)C, (1)S, (1)C, (2)S, (1)C, (1)S, (4)C, (2)S, (9)C
Row 155&156 (R) (1)S, (1)C, (4)S, (11)C, (1)S, (6)C
Row 157&158 (R) (1)C, (3)S, (14)C, (4)S, (2)C
Row 159&160 (R) (6)S, (3)C, (7)S, (4)C, (4)S
Row 161&162 (R) (3)S, (2)C, (19)S
Row 163&164 (R) (4)C, (5)S, (4)C, (2)S, (1)C, (1)S, (1)C, (6)S
Row 165&166 (R) (3)C, (3)S, (3)C, (4)S, (4)C, (1)S, (6)C
Row 167&168 (R) (5)S, (3)C, (1)S, (3)S, (1)S, (5)C, (5)S, (1)C
Row 169&170 (R) (3)S, (3)C, (2)S, (3)C, (2)S, (2)C, (1)S, (4)C, (4)S
Row 171&172 (R) (3)S, (2)C, (2)S, (1)C, (4)S, (1)C, (2)S, (2)C, (1)S, (4)C, (2)S
Row 173&174 (R) (2)S, (2)C, (3)S, (1)C, (5)S, (2)C, (1)S, (2)C, (1)S, (4)C, (1)S
Row 175&176 (R) (1)S, (3)C, (2)S, (1)C, (7)S, (2)C, (1)S, (2)C, (1)S, (4)C
Row 177&178 (R) (4)C, (3)S, (1)C, (1)S, (2)C, (1)S, (1)C, (1)S, (3)C, (1)S, (2)C, (1)S, (3)C
Row 179&180 (R) (4)C, (2)S, (1)C, (2)S, (5)C, (1)S, (3)C, (1)S, (2)C, (1)S, (2)C
Row 181&182 (R) (4)C, (1)S, (1)C, (2)S, (3)C, (1)S, (3)C, (1)S, (2)C, (2)S, (1)C, (2)S, (1)C
Row 183&184 (R) (3)C, (2)S, (1)C, (1)S, (3)C, (2)S, (4)C, (4)S, (1)C, (3)S
Row 185&186 (R) (3)C, (2)S, (1)C, (1)S, (2)C, (2)S, (1)C, (1)S, (4)C, (1)S, (1)C, (1)S, (2)C, (2)S
Row 187&188 (R) (1)S, (2)C, (2)S, (1)C, (1)S, (1)C, (2)S, (3)C, (1)S, (3)C, (1)S, (1)C, (2)S, (1)C, (2)S
Row 189&190 (R) (1)S, (3)C, (3)S, (1)C, (2)S, (2)C, (3)S, (3)C, (3)S, (1)C, (1)S, (1)C
Row 191&192 (R) (2)S, (3)C, (2)S, (2)C, (2)S, (1)C, (6)S, (2)C, (1)S, (1)C, (1)S, (1)C
Row 193&194 (R) (2)S, (4)C, (2)S, (2)C, (2)S, (9)C, (2)S, (1)C
Row 195&196 (R) (3)S, (4)C, (3)S, (2)C, (2)S, (6)C, (1)S, (3)C

Cool Waves

The ocean is a powerful and fascinating thing. The constant motion and soothing sound of the waves are an infinite paradox of calm and exhilaration. Inspired by *The Great Wave* painting by Hokusai in the early 1800s, this piece combines cool shades of blue to make a lovely piece of wearable art.

MATERIALS
- 11º Delica beads:
  1g (182) DB0798 matte opaque capri (color A)
  2g (382) DB0351 matte white (color B)
  2g (237) DB0741 matte transparent crystal (color C)
  2g (300) DB0608 blue zircon silver-lined (color D)
  2g (257) DB1269 matte transparent ocean blue (color E)
  5g (898) DB0377 matte metallic dark gray blue (color F)
- Fireline, 4-lb. or 6-lb. test (I recommend crystal Fireline due to the light-colored transparent beads used in this project.)

TOOLS
- #10 or #12 beading needle
- Thread cutters or scissors

MEASUREMENTS
1¼ in. wide and 6½ in. long

To shorten, remove rows from the toggle end of the pattern. To lengthen, adjust the toggle tail for the desired drape.

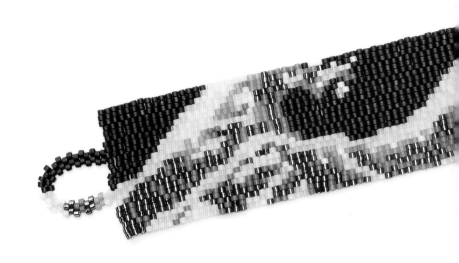

Instructions

1 Refer to the *Cool Waves* three-drop pattern and word chart on pages 18 and 19. Follow the instructions for Fast Peyote (Techniques, p. 94) to create the peyote band. Add thread (Techniques, p. 97) as needed throughout the project.

Create the round peyote loop
2 *The closure for this project consists of a round peyote loop and a peyote toggle.* Reinforce the end of the bracelet (Techniques, p. 96, step 11). Exit at the location on the pattern marked by the black dot that is closest to the edge.

3 Add a simple round loop of 27 beads to the end of the bracelet (Techniques, p. 99). If desired, the following bead order can be used for the loop. To create the curvature of the loop, two-drop peyote is used near the center of row four; these two beads are shown in bold.

Peyote row 1 & 2:   BCEEDDAADDBBCC, (14)F
Peyote row 3:   (7)F, BCDADEC
Peyote row 4:   BEDDB **CB** B **FF** (5)F

Use finishing knots to secure (Techniques, p. 97), trim the thread, and weave into the tail.

Create a peyote toggle
4 On a new 3-ft. length of Fireline, create the toggle referring to the pattern and word chart on page 19. Then zip up the six-row band to create a peyote tube (Techniques, p. 103).

5 Remove the stop bead and add thread to the original tail at the opposite end of the piece. Weave into the piece, tucking the knot into a bead. Reinforce the end of the bracelet. Exit at the black dot marked on the pattern. Add the toggle tail (Techniques, p. 103), making it five rows long.

6 Add the peyote tube (toggle) to the tail (Techniques, p. 103). Sew back into the tail to reinforce. Weave back into the piece and reinforce using finishing knots to secure, then trim the thread, and tuck into the piece.

Cool Waves
three-drop peyote

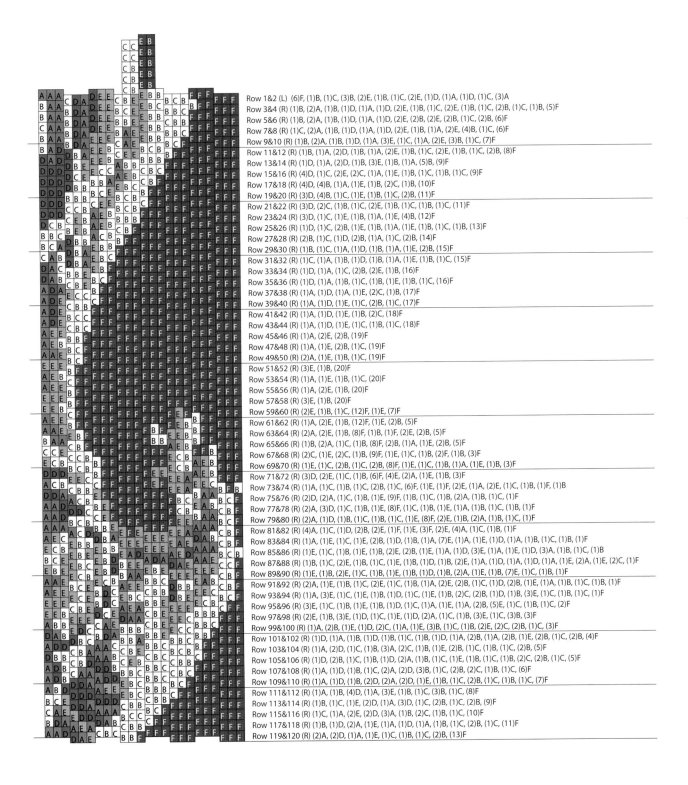

Row 1&2 (L) (6)F, (1)B, (1)C, (3)B, (2)E, (1)B, (1)C, (2)E, (1)D, (1)A, (1)D, (1)C, (3)A
Row 3&4 (R) (1)B, (2)A, (1)B, (1)D, (1)A, (1)D, (2)E, (1)B, (1)C, (2)E, (1)B, (1)C, (2)B, (1)C, (1)B, (5)F
Row 5&6 (R) (1)B, (2)A, (1)B, (1)D, (1)A, (1)D, (2)E, (2)B, (2)E, (2)B, (1)C, (2)B, (6)F
Row 7&8 (R) (1)C, (2)A, (1)B, (1)D, (1)A, (1)D, (2)E, (1)B, (1)A, (2)E, (4)B, (1)C, (6)F
Row 9&10 (R) (1)B, (2)A, (1)B, (1)D, (1)A, (3)E, (1)C, (1)A, (2)E, (3)B, (1)C, (7)F
Row 11&12 (R) (1)B, (1)A, (2)D, (1)B, (1)A, (2)E, (1)B, (1)C, (2)E, (1)B, (1)C, (2)B, (8)F
Row 13&14 (R) (1)D, (1)A, (2)D, (1)B, (3)E, (1)B, (1)A, (5)B, (9)F
Row 15&16 (R) (4)D, (1)C, (2)E, (2)C, (1)A, (1)E, (1)B, (1)C, (1)B, (1)C, (9)F
Row 17&18 (R) (4)D, (4)B, (1)A, (1)E, (1)B, (2)C, (1)B, (10)F
Row 19&20 (R) (3)D, (4)B, (1)C, (1)E, (1)B, (1)C, (2)B, (11)F
Row 21&22 (R) (3)D, (2)C, (1)B, (1)C, (2)E, (1)B, (1)C, (1)B, (1)C, (11)F
Row 23&24 (R) (3)D, (1)C, (1)E, (1)B, (1)A, (1)E, (4)B, (12)F
Row 25&26 (R) (1)D, (1)C, (2)B, (1)E, (1)B, (1)A, (1)E, (1)B, (1)C, (1)B, (13)F
Row 27&28 (R) (2)B, (1)C, (1)D, (2)B, (1)A, (1)C, (2)B, (14)F
Row 29&30 (R) (1)B, (1)C, (1)A, (1)D, (1)B, (1)A, (1)E, (2)B, (15)F
Row 31&32 (R) (1)C, (1)A, (1)B, (1)D, (1)B, (1)A, (1)E, (1)B, (1)C, (15)F
Row 33&34 (R) (1)D, (1)A, (1)C, (2)B, (2)E, (1)B, (16)F
Row 35&36 (R) (1)D, (1)A, (1)B, (1)C, (1)B, (1)E, (1)B, (1)C, (16)F
Row 37&38 (R) (1)A, (1)D, (1)A, (1)E, (2)C, (1)B, (17)F
Row 39&40 (R) (1)A, (1)D, (1)E, (1)C, (2)B, (1)C, (17)F
Row 41&42 (R) (1)A, (1)D, (1)E, (1)B, (2)C, (18)F
Row 43&44 (R) (1)A, (1)D, (1)E, (1)C, (1)B, (1)C, (18)F
Row 45&46 (R) (1)A, (2)E, (2)B, (19)F
Row 47&48 (R) (1)A, (1)E, (2)B, (1)C, (19)F
Row 49&50 (R) (2)A, (1)E, (1)B, (1)C, (19)F
Row 51&52 (R) (3)E, (1)B, (20)F
Row 53&54 (R) (1)A, (1)E, (1)B, (1)C, (20)F
Row 55&56 (R) (1)A, (2)E, (1)B, (20)F
Row 57&58 (R) (3)E, (1)B, (20)F
Row 59&60 (R) (2)E, (1)B, (1)C, (12)F, (1)E, (7)F
Row 61&62 (R) (1)A, (2)E, (1)B, (12)F, (1)E, (2)B, (5)F
Row 63&64 (R) (2)A, (2)E, (1)B, (8)F, (1)B, (1)F, (2)E, (2)B, (5)F
Row 65&66 (R) (1)B, (2)A, (1)C, (1)B, (8)F, (2)B, (1)A, (1)E, (2)B, (5)F
Row 67&68 (R) (2)C, (1)E, (2)C, (1)B, (9)F, (1)E, (1)C, (1)B, (2)F, (1)B, (3)F
Row 69&70 (R) (1)E, (1)C, (2)B, (1)C, (2)B, (8)F, (1)E, (1)C, (1)B, (1)A, (1)E, (1)B, (3)F
Row 71&72 (R) (3)D, (2)C, (1)C, (1)B, (6)F, (4)E, (2)A, (1)E, (1)B, (3)F
Row 73&74 (R) (1)A, (1)C, (1)B, (1)C, (2)B, (1)C, (6)F, (1)E, (1)F, (2)E, (1)A, (2)E, (1)C, (1)B, (1)F, (1)B
Row 75&76 (R) (2)D, (2)A, (1)C, (1)B, (1)E, (9)F, (1)B, (1)C, (1)B, (2)A, (1)B, (1)C, (1)F
Row 77&78 (R) (2)A, (3)D, (1)C, (1)B, (1)E, (8)F, (1)C, (1)B, (1)A, (1)B, (1)C, (1)B, (1)F
Row 79&80 (R) (2)A, (1)D, (1)B, (1)C, (1)B, (1)C, (1)E, (8)F, (2)E, (1)B, (2)A, (1)B, (1)C, (1)F
Row 81&82 (R) (4)A, (1)C, (1)D, (2)B, (2)E, (1)F, (1)E, (3)F, (2)E, (4)A, (1)C, (1)B, (1)F
Row 83&84 (R) (1)A, (1)E, (1)C, (1)B, (2)E, (2)D, (1)B, (1)A, (7)E, (1)A, (1)D, (1)A, (1)B, (1)C, (1)B, (1)F
Row 85&86 (R) (1)E, (1)C, (1)B, (1)E, (1)B, (2)D, (2)B, (1)A, (1)A, (1)D, (3)E, (1)A, (1)E, (1)D, (3)A, (1)B, (1)C, (1)B
Row 87&88 (R) (1)B, (1)C, (2)E, (1)B, (1)C, (1)E, (1)B, (1)D, (1)B, (2)E, (1)A, (1)D, (1)A, (1)D, (1)A, (1)E, (2)A, (1)E, (2)C, (1)F
Row 89&90 (R) (1)E, (1)B, (2)E, (1)C, (1)B, (1)E, (1)B, (1)D, (1)B, (2)A, (1)E, (1)B, (7)E, (1)C, (1)B, (1)F
Row 91&92 (R) (2)A, (1)E, (1)B, (1)C, (2)E, (1)C, (1)B, (1)A, (2)E, (2)B, (1)C, (1)D, (2)B, (1)E, (1)C, (1)B, (1)F
Row 93&94 (R) (1)A, (3)E, (1)C, (1)B, (1)E, (1)B, (1)D, (1)C, (1)A, (1)E, (1)A, (2)C, (2)B, (1)D, (1)B, (3)E, (1)C, (1)B, (1)F
Row 95&96 (R) (3)E, (1)C, (1)B, (1)E, (1)B, (1)D, (1)C, (1)A, (1)E, (1)A, (2)B, (5)E, (1)C, (1)B, (1)C, (2)F
Row 97&98 (R) (2)E, (1)B, (3)E, (1)D, (1)C, (1)E, (1)D, (2)A, (1)C, (1)B, (3)E, (1)C, (3)B, (3)F
Row 99&100 (R) (1)A, (2)E, (1)E, (1)D, (2)C, (1)A, (1)E, (3)B, (1)C, (1)B, (2)E, (2)C, (2)B, (1)C, (3)F
Row 101&102 (R) (1)D, (1)A, (1)B, (1)D, (1)B, (1)C, (1)B, (1)D, (1)A, (2)B, (1)A, (2)B, (1)E, (2)B, (1)C, (2)B, (4)F
Row 103&104 (R) (1)A, (2)D, (1)C, (1)B, (3)A, (2)C, (1)B, (1)E, (2)B, (1)C, (1)B, (1)C, (2)B, (5)F
Row 105&106 (R) (1)D, (2)B, (1)C, (1)B, (1)D, (2)A, (1)B, (1)C, (1)E, (1)B, (1)C, (1)B, (2)C, (2)B, (1)C, (5)F
Row 107&108 (R) (1)A, (1)D, (1)B, (1)C, (2)A, (2)D, (3)B, (1)C, (2)B, (2)C, (1)B, (1)C, (6)F
Row 109&110 (R) (1)A, (1)D, (1)B, (2)D, (2)A, (1)D, (1)C, (1)B, (1)C, (1)B, (1)C, (7)F
Row 111&112 (R) (1)A, (1)B, (4)D, (1)A, (3)E, (1)B, (1)C, (3)B, (1)C, (8)F
Row 113&114 (R) (1)B, (1)C, (1)E, (2)D, (1)A, (3)D, (1)C, (2)B, (1)C, (2)B, (9)F
Row 115&116 (R) (1)C, (1)A, (2)E, (2)D, (3)A, (1)B, (2)C, (1)B, (1)C, (10)F
Row 117&118 (R) (1)B, (1)D, (2)A, (1)E, (1)A, (1)D, (1)A, (1)B, (1)C, (2)B, (1)C, (11)F
Row 119&120 (R) (2)A, (2)D, (1)A, (1)E, (1)C, (1)B, (2)B, (13)F

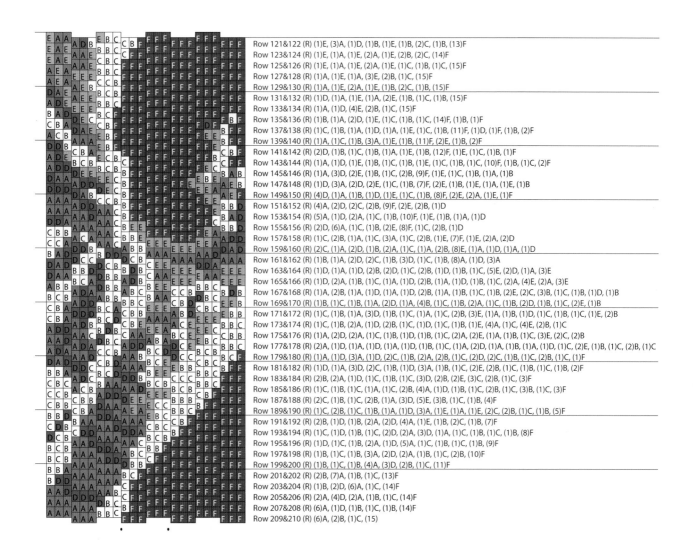

Row 121&122 (R) (1)E, (3)A, (1)D, (1)B, (1)E, (1)B, (2)C, (1)B, (13)F
Row 123&124 (R) (1)E, (1)A, (1)E, (2)A, (1)E, (2)B, (2)C, (14)F
Row 125&126 (R) (1)E, (1)A, (1)E, (2)A, (1)E, (1)C, (1)B, (1)C, (15)F
Row 127&128 (R) (1)A, (1)E, (1)A, (3)E, (2)B, (1)C, (15)F
Row 129&130 (R) (1)A, (1)E, (2)A, (1)E, (1)B, (2)C, (1)B, (15)F
Row 131&132 (R) (1)D, (1)A, (1)E, (1)A, (2)E, (1)B, (1)C, (1)B, (15)F
Row 133&134 (R) (1)A, (1)D, (4)E, (2)B, (1)C, (15)F
Row 135&136 (R) (1)B, (1)A, (2)D, (1)E, (1)C, (1)B, (1)C, (14)F, (1)B, (1)F
Row 137&138 (R) (1)C, (1)B, (1)A, (1)D, (1)A, (1)E, (1)C, (1)B, (11)F, (1)D, (1)F, (1)B, (2)F
Row 139&140 (R) (1)A, (1)C, (1)B, (3)A, (1)E, (1)B, (11)F, (2)E, (1)B, (2)F
Row 141&142 (R) (2)D, (1)B, (1)C, (1)B, (1)A, (1)E, (1)B, (12)F, (1)E, (1)C, (1)B, (1)F
Row 143&144 (R) (1)A, (1)D, (1)E, (1)B, (1)C, (1)B, (1)E, (1)C, (1)B, (10)F, (1)B, (1)C, (2)F
Row 145&146 (R) (1)A, (3)D, (2)E, (1)C, (2)B, (9)F, (1)E, (1)C, (1)B, (1)A, (1)B
Row 147&148 (R) (1)D, (3)A, (2)D, (2)E, (1)C, (1)B, (7)F, (2)E, (1)B, (1)E, (1)A, (1)E, (1)B
Row 149&150 (R) (4)D, (1)A, (1)B, (1)D, (1)E, (1)C, (1)B, (8)F, (2)E, (2)A, (1)E, (1)F
Row 151&152 (R) (4)A, (2)D, (2)C, (2)B, (9)F, (2)E, (2)B, (1)D
Row 153&154 (R) (5)A, (1)D, (2)A, (1)C, (1)B, (10)F, (1)E, (1)B, (1)A, (1)D
Row 155&156 (R) (2)D, (6)A, (1)C, (1)B, (2)E, (8)F, (1)C, (2)B, (1)D
Row 157&158 (R) (1)C, (2)B, (1)A, (1)C, (3)A, (1)C, (2)B, (1)E, (7)F, (1)E, (2)A, (2)D
Row 159&160 (R) (2)C, (1)A, (2)D, (1)B, (2)A, (1)C, (1)A, (2)B, (8)E, (1)A, (1)D, (1)A, (1)D
Row 161&162 (R) (1)B, (1)A, (2)D, (2)C, (1)B, (3)D, (1)C, (1)B, (8)A, (1)D, (3)A
Row 163&164 (R) (1)D, (1)A, (1)D, (2)B, (2)D, (1)C, (2)B, (1)D, (1)B, (1)C, (5)E, (2)D, (1)A, (3)E
Row 165&166 (R) (1)D, (2)A, (1)B, (1)C, (1)A, (1)D, (2)B, (1)A, (1)D, (1)B, (1)C, (2)A, (4)E, (2)A, (3)E
Row 167&168 (R) (1)A, (2)B, (1)A, (1)D, (1)A, (1)D, (2)B, (1)A, (1)B, (1)C, (1)B, (2)E, (2)C, (3)B, (1)C, (1)B, (1)D, (1)B
Row 169&170 (R) (1)C, (1)B, (1)B, (1)A, (2)D, (1)A, (4)B, (1)C, (1)B, (2)A, (1)C, (1)B, (2)D, (1)B, (1)C, (2)E, (1)B
Row 171&172 (R) (1)C, (1)B, (1)A, (3)D, (1)B, (1)C, (1)A, (1)C, (2)B, (3)E, (1)A, (1)B, (1)D, (1)C, (1)B, (1)C, (1)E, (2)B
Row 173&174 (R) (1)C, (1)B, (2)A, (1)D, (2)B, (1)C, (1)D, (1)C, (1)B, (1)E, (4)A, (1)C, (4)E, (2)B, (1)C
Row 175&176 (R) (1)A, (2)D, (2)A, (1)C, (1)B, (1)D, (1)B, (1)C, (2)A, (2)E, (1)A, (1)B, (1)C, (3)E, (2)C, (2)B
Row 177&178 (R) (2)A, (1)D, (1)A, (1)D, (1)D, (1)A, (1)D, (1)B, (1)C, (1)A, (2)D, (1)A, (1)B, (1)D, (1)C, (1)E, (1)B, (1)C, (2)B, (1)C
Row 179&180 (R) (1)A, (1)D, (3)A, (1)D, (2)C, (1)B, (2)A, (2)B, (1)C, (2)D, (2)C, (1)B, (1)C, (1)B, (1)C, (1)F
Row 181&182 (R) (1)D, (1)A, (3)D, (2)C, (1)B, (1)D, (3)A, (1)B, (1)C, (2)E, (2)B, (1)C, (1)B, (1)C, (1)B, (2)F
Row 183&184 (R) (2)B, (2)A, (1)D, (1)C, (1)B, (1)C, (3)D, (2)B, (2)E, (3)C, (2)B, (1)C, (3)F
Row 185&186 (R) (1)C, (1)B, (1)C, (1)A, (1)C, (2)B, (4)A, (1)D, (1)B, (1)C, (2)B, (1)C, (3)B, (1)C, (3)F
Row 187&188 (R) (2)C, (1)B, (1)C, (2)B, (1)A, (3)D, (5)E, (3)B, (1)C, (1)B, (4)F
Row 189&190 (R) (1)C, (2)B, (1)C, (1)B, (1)A, (1)D, (3)A, (1)A, (1)E, (1)C, (2)B, (1)C, (1)B, (5)F
Row 191&192 (R) (2)B, (1)D, (1)B, (2)A, (2)D, (4)A, (1)E, (1)B, (2)C, (1)B, (7)F
Row 193&194 (R) (1)C, (1)D, (1)B, (1)C, (2)D, (2)A, (3)D, (1)A, (1)C, (1)B, (1)C, (1)B, (8)F
Row 195&196 (R) (1)C, (1)B, (2)A, (1)D, (5)A, (1)C, (1)B, (1)C, (1)B, (9)F
Row 197&198 (R) (1)B, (1)C, (1)B, (3)A, (2)D, (2)A, (1)B, (1)C, (2)B, (10)F
Row 199&200 (R) (1)B, (1)C, (1)B, (4)A, (3)D, (2)B, (1)C, (11)F
Row 201&202 (R) (2)B, (7)A, (1)B, (1)C, (13)F
Row 203&204 (R) (1)B, (2)D, (6)A, (1)C, (14)F
Row 205&206 (R) (2)A, (4)D, (2)A, (1)B, (1)C, (14)F
Row 207&208 (R) (6)A, (1)D, (1)B, (1)C, (1)B, (14)F
Row 209&210 (R) (6)A, (2)B, (1)C, (15)

Cool Waves toggle
three-drop peyote

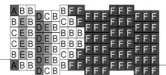

Row 1&2 (L) (11)F, (2)B, (1)C, (1)D, (2)B, (1)A
Row 3&4 (R) (1)B, (1)E, (1)B, (1)D, (1)E, (1)B, (1)C, (10)F
Row 5&6 (R) (1)C, (1)E, (1)B, (1)D, (1)E, (1)B, (3)B, (9)F
Row 7&8 (R) (1)C, (1)E, (1)B, (1)D, (1)E, (1)B, (3)B, (9)F
Row 9&10 (R) (1)B, (1)E, (1)B, (1)D, (1)E, (1)B, (1)C, (1)B, (10)F
Row 11&12 (R) (1)A, (2)B, (1)D, (1)C, (2)B, (11)F

Magnetic Berries

This pattern is based on some plots of magnetic fields modified in shades of pink that make an interesting abstract bracelet. It brings to mind berries and cream in a blender.

MATERIALS
- 11º Delica beads:
  - 2g (399) DB0778 matte transparent cranberry (color A)
  - 4g (742) DB0355 matte rose (color B)
  - 2g (324) DB1849 galvanized magenta (color C)
  - 2g (201) DB0116 transparent luster red metallic (color D)
  - 2g (291) DB1705 copper rust (color E)
  - 2g (347) DB2137 opaque hydrangea (color F)
- Fireline, 4-lb. or 6-lb. test

TOOLS
- #10 or #12 beading needle
- Thread cutters

MEASUREMENTS
1¼ in. wide and 6¾ in. long

To shorten, simply leave off rows at either end. To lengthen, adjust the toggle tail for the desired drape.

Instructions

1 Refer to the *Magnetic Berries* four-drop pattern and word chart on pages 22 and 23. Follow the instructions for Fast Peyote (Techniques, p. 94) to create the peyote band. Add thread (Techniques, p. 97) as needed throughout the project.

Create a flat peyote loop

2 *The closure for this project consist of a flat peyote loop and a peyote tube toggle.* Reinforce the end of the bracelet (Techniques, p. 96, step 11). Exit at the location on the pattern marked by one of the two black dots.

3 Follow the instructions to create the flat loop (Techniques, p. 98) using 19 rows of a mixture of beads. Secure the other end of the loop at the second location marked on the pattern with a black dot.

4 Weave back into the piece and reinforce using finishing knots to secure (Techniques, p. 97), trim the thread, and tuck into the piece.

Create a peyote tube (toggle)

5 On a new 3-ft. length of Fireline, create a two-drop peyote band that is six rows long and 16 columns wide using color C beads. Zip up the six-row band to create a peyote tube (Techniques, p. 103).

6 Remove the stop bead and add thread to the original tail at the opposite end of the piece. Weave into the piece, tucking the knot into a bead. Reinforce the end of the bracelet. Exit at the black dot marked at the center of the pattern and add a two-drop tail that is six rows long.

7 Add the peyote tube to the tail. Sew back into the tail to reinforce. Weave into the piece using finishing knots to secure, then trim the thread, and tuck into the piece.

Magnetic Berries
four-drop peyote

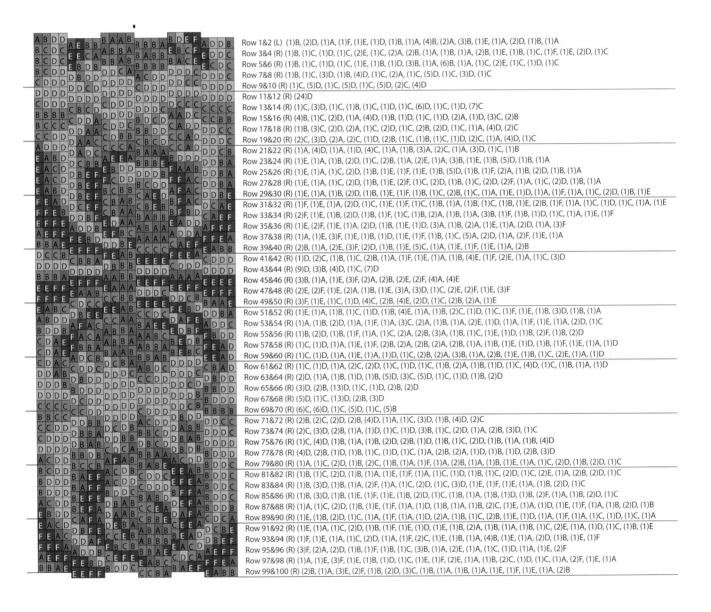

Row 1&2 (L) (1)B, (2)D, (1)A, (1)F, (1)E, (1)D, (1)B, (1)A, (4)B, (2)A, (3)B, (1)E, (1)A, (2)D, (1)B, (1)A

Row 3&4 (R) (1)B, (1)C, (1)D, (1)C, (2)E, (1)C, (2)A, (2)B, (1)A, (1)B, (1)A, (2)B, (1)E, (1)B, (1)C, (1)F, (1)E, (2)D, (1)C

Row 5&6 (R) (1)B, (1)C, (1)D, (1)C, (1)E, (1)B, (1)D, (3)B, (1)A, (6)B, (1)A, (1)C, (2)E, (1)C, (1)D, (1)C

Row 7&8 (R) (1)B, (1)C, (3)D, (1)B, (4)D, (1)C, (2)A, (1)C, (5)D, (1)C, (3)D, (1)C

Row 9&10 (R) (1)C, (5)D, (1)C, (5)D, (1)C, (5)D, (2)C, (4)D

Row 11&12 (R) (24)D

Row 13&14 (R) (1)C, (3)D, (1)C, (1)B, (1)C, (1)D, (1)C, (6)D, (1)C, (1)D, (7)C

Row 15&16 (R) (4)B, (1)C, (2)D, (1)A, (4)D, (1)B, (1)D, (1)C, (1)D, (2)A, (1)D, (3)C, (2)B

Row 17&18 (R) (1)B, (3)C, (2)D, (2)A, (1)C, (2)D, (1)C, (2)B, (2)D, (1)C, (1)A, (4)D, (2)C

Row 19&20 (R) (2)C, (3)D, (2)A, (2)C, (1)D, (2)B, (1)C, (1)B, (1)C, (1)D, (2)C, (1)A, (4)D, (1)C

Row 21&22 (R) (1)A, (4)D, (1)A, (1)D, (4)C, (1)A, (1)B, (3)A, (2)C, (1)A, (3)D, (1)C, (1)B

Row 23&24 (R) (1)E, (1)A, (1)B, (2)D, (1)C, (2)B, (1)A, (2)E, (1)A, (3)B, (1)E, (1)B, (5)D, (1)B, (1)A

Row 25&26 (R) (1)E, (1)A, (1)C, (2)D, (1)B, (1)E, (1)F, (1)E, (1)B, (5)D, (1)B, (1)F, (2)A, (1)B, (2)D, (1)B, (1)A

Row 27&28 (R) (1)E, (1)A, (1)C, (2)D, (1)B, (1)E, (2)F, (1)C, (2)D, (1)B, (1)C, (2)D, (2)F, (1)A, (1)C, (2)D, (1)B, (1)A

Row 29&30 (R) (1)E, (1)A, (1)B, (2)D, (1)B, (1)E, (1)B, (1)C, (2)B, (1)C, (1)A, (1)E, (1)D, (1)A, (1)F, (1)A, (1)C, (2)D, (1)B, (1)E

Row 31&32 (R) (1)F, (1)E, (1)A, (2)D, (1)C, (1)E, (1)F, (1)C, (1)B, (1)A, (1)B, (1)C, (1)B, (1)E, (2)B, (1)F, (1)A, (1)C, (1)D, (1)C, (1)A, (1)E

Row 33&34 (R) (2)F, (1)E, (1)B, (2)D, (1)B, (1)F, (1)C, (1)B, (2)D, (1)B, (3)B, (1)F, (1)B, (1)D, (1)C, (1)A, (1)E, (1)F

Row 35&36 (R) (1)E, (2)F, (1)E, (1)A, (2)D, (1)B, (1)E, (1)D, (3)A, (1)B, (2)A, (1)E, (1)A, (2)D, (1)A, (3)F

Row 37&38 (R) (1)A, (1)E, (3)F, (1)E, (1)B, (1)D, (1)E, (1)F, (1)B, (1)C, (5)A, (2)D, (1)A, (2)F, (1)E, (1)A

Row 39&40 (R) (2)B, (1)A, (2)E, (3)F, (2)D, (1)B, (1)E, (5)C, (1)A, (1)E, (1)F, (1)E, (1)A, (2)B

Row 41&42 (R) (1)D, (2)C, (1)B, (1)C, (2)B, (1)A, (1)F, (1)E, (1)A, (1)B, (4)E, (1)F, (2)E, (1)A, (1)C, (3)D

Row 43&44 (R) (9)D, (3)B, (4)D, (1)C, (7)D

Row 45&46 (R) (3)B, (1)A, (1)E, (3)F, (2)A, (2)B, (2)E, (2)F, (4)A, (4)E

Row 47&48 (R) (2)E, (2)F, (1)E, (2)A, (1)B, (1)E, (3)A, (3)D, (1)C, (2)E, (2)F, (1)E, (3)F

Row 49&50 (R) (3)F, (1)E, (1)C, (1)D, (4)C, (2)B, (4)E, (2)D, (1)C, (2)B, (2)A, (1)E

Row 51&52 (R) (1)E, (1)A, (1)B, (1)C, (1)D, (1)B, (4)E, (1)A, (1)B, (2)C, (1)D, (1)C, (1)F, (1)E, (1)B, (3)D, (1)B, (1)A

Row 53&54 (R) (1)A, (1)B, (2)D, (1)A, (1)F, (1)A, (3)C, (2)A, (1)B, (1)A, (2)E, (1)D, (1)A, (1)F, (1)E, (1)A, (2)D, (1)C

Row 55&56 (R) (1)B, (2)D, (1)B, (1)F, (1)A, (1)C, (2)A, (2)B, (3)A, (1)B, (1)C, (1)E, (1)D, (1)B, (2)F, (1)B, (2)D

Row 57&58 (R) (1)C, (1)D, (1)A, (1)E, (1)F, (2)B, (2)A, (2)B, (2)A, (2)B, (1)A, (1)B, (1)E, (1)D, (1)B, (1)F, (1)E, (1)A, (1)D

Row 59&60 (R) (1)E, (1)D, (1)A, (1)E, (1)A, (1)D, (1)C, (2)B, (2)A, (3)B, (1)F, (1)B, (2)B, (1)F, (1)B, (1)C, (2)E, (1)A, (1)D

Row 61&62 (R) (1)C, (1)D, (1)A, (2)C, (2)D, (1)C, (1)D, (1)C, (1)B, (2)A, (1)B, (1)D, (1)C, (4)D, (1)C, (1)B, (1)A, (1)D

Row 63&64 (R) (2)D, (1)A, (1)B, (1)D, (1)B, (5)D, (3)C, (5)D, (1)C, (1)D, (1)B, (2)D

Row 65&66 (R) (3)D, (2)B, (13)D, (1)C, (1)D, (2)B, (2)D

Row 67&68 (R) (5)D, (1)C, (13)D, (2)B, (3)D

Row 69&70 (R) (6)C, (6)D, (1)C, (5)D, (1)C, (5)B

Row 71&72 (R) (2)B, (2)C, (2)D, (2)B, (4)D, (1)A, (1)C, (3)D, (1)B, (4)D, (2)C

Row 73&74 (R) (2)C, (3)D, (2)B, (1)A, (1)D, (1)C, (1)D, (3)B, (1)C, (2)D, (1)A, (2)B, (3)D, (1)C

Row 75&76 (R) (1)C, (4)D, (1)B, (1)A, (1)B, (2)D, (2)B, (1)D, (1)B, (1)C, (2)D, (1)B, (1)A, (1)B, (4)D

Row 77&78 (R) (4)D, (2)B, (1)D, (1)B, (1)A, (1)C, (1)A, (2)B, (2)A, (1)D, (1)B, (1)D, (2)B, (3)D

Row 79&80 (R) (1)A, (1)C, (2)D, (1)B, (2)C, (1)B, (1)A, (1)F, (1)A, (2)B, (1)A, (1)B, (1)E, (1)A, (1)C, (2)D, (1)B, (2)D, (1)C

Row 81&82 (R) (1)B, (1)C, (2)D, (1)B, (1)A, (1)E, (1)F, (1)A, (1)C, (1)D, (1)B, (1)C, (2)D, (1)C, (2)E, (1)A, (2)B, (2)D, (1)C

Row 83&84 (R) (1)B, (3)D, (1)B, (1)A, (2)F, (1)A, (1)C, (2)D, (1)C, (3)D, (1)E, (1)F, (1)E, (1)A, (1)B, (2)D, (1)C

Row 85&86 (R) (1)B, (3)D, (1)B, (1)E, (1)F, (1)E, (1)B, (2)D, (1)C, (1)B, (1)A, (1)B, (1)D, (1)B, (2)F, (1)B, (1)A, (1)B, (2)D, (1)C

Row 87&88 (R) (1)A, (1)C, (2)D, (1)B, (1)E, (1)F, (1)A, (1)D, (1)B, (1)A, (1)B, (2)C, (1)E, (1)A, (1)D, (1)E, (1)F, (1)A, (1)B, (2)D, (1)B

Row 89&90 (R) (1)E, (1)B, (2)D, (1)C, (1)A, (1)F, (1)A, (1)D, (2)A, (1)B, (1)C, (2)B, (1)E, (1)D, (1)A, (1)F, (1)A, (1)C, (1)D, (1)C, (1)A

Row 91&92 (R) (1)E, (1)A, (1)C, (2)D, (1)B, (1)F, (1)E, (1)D, (1)E, (1)B, (2)A, (1)B, (1)A, (1)B, (1)C, (2)E, (1)A, (1)D, (1)C, (1)B, (1)E

Row 93&94 (R) (1)F, (1)E, (1)A, (1)C, (2)D, (1)A, (1)F, (2)C, (1)E, (1)B, (1)A, (4)B, (1)E, (1)A, (2)D, (1)B, (1)E, (1)F

Row 95&96 (R) (3)F, (2)A, (2)D, (1)B, (1)F, (1)B, (1)C, (3)B, (1)A, (2)B, (2)C, (1)D, (1)A, (1)E, (2)F

Row 97&98 (R) (1)A, (1)E, (3)F, (1)E, (1)B, (1)D, (1)E, (1)F, (2)E, (1)A, (1)B, (2)C, (1)D, (1)C, (1)A, (2)F, (1)E, (1)A

Row 99&100 (R) (2)B, (1)A, (3)E, (2)F, (1)B, (2)D, (3)C, (1)B, (1)A, (1)B, (1)A, (1)E, (1)F, (1)E, (1)A, (2)B

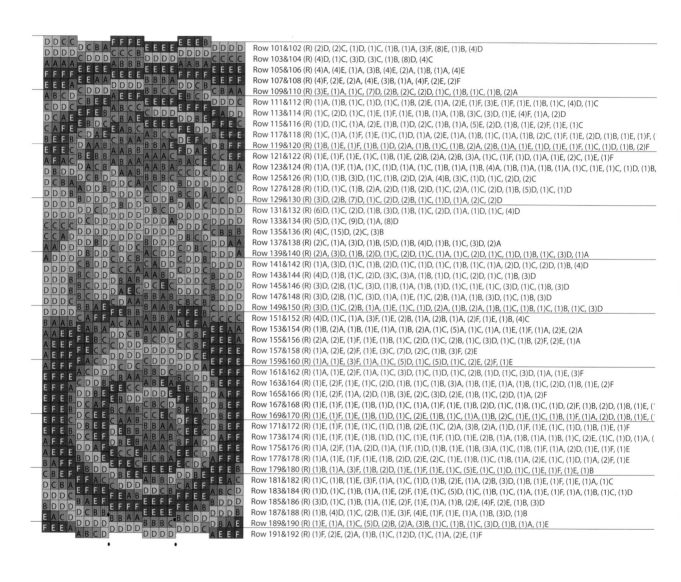

Row 101&102 (R) (2)D, (2)C, (1)D, (1)C, (1)B, (1)A, (3)F, (8)E, (1)B, (4)D
Row 103&104 (R) (4)D, (1)C, (3)D, (3)C, (1)B, (8)D, (4)C
Row 105&106 (R) (4)A, (4)E, (1)A, (3)B, (4)E, (2)A, (1)B, (1)A, (4)E
Row 107&108 (R) (4)F, (2)E, (2)A, (4)E, (3)B, (1)A, (4)F, (2)E, (2)F
Row 109&110 (R) (3)E, (1)A, (1)C, (7)D, (2)B, (2)C, (2)D, (1)C, (1)B, (1)C, (1)B, (2)A
Row 111&112 (R) (1)A, (1)B, (1)C, (1)D, (1)C, (1)B, (2)E, (1)A, (2)E, (1)F, (3)E, (1)F, (1)E, (1)B, (1)C, (4)D, (1)C
Row 113&114 (R) (1)C, (2)D, (1)C, (1)E, (1)F, (1)E, (1)B, (1)A, (1)B, (3)C, (3)D, (1)E, (4)F, (1)A, (2)D
Row 115&116 (R) (1)D, (1)C, (1)A, (2)E, (1)B, (1)D, (2)C, (1)B, (1)A, (5)E, (2)D, (1)B, (1)E, (2)F, (1)E, (1)C
Row 117&118 (R) (1)C, (1)A, (1)F, (1)E, (1)C, (1)D, (1)A, (2)E, (1)A, (1)B, (1)C, (1)A, (1)B, (2)C, (1)F, (1)E, (2)D, (1)B, (1)E, (1)F, (
Row 119&120 (R) (1)B, (1)E, (1)F, (1)B, (1)D, (2)A, (1)B, (1)C, (1)B, (2)A, (2)B, (1)A, (1)E, (1)D, (1)E, (1)F, (1)C, (1)D, (1)B, (2)F
Row 121&122 (R) (1)E, (1)F, (1)E, (1)C, (1)B, (1)E, (2)B, (2)A, (2)B, (3)A, (1)C, (1)F, (1)D, (1)A, (1)E, (2)C, (1)E, (1)F
Row 123&124 (R) (1)A, (1)F, (1)A, (1)C, (1)D, (1)A, (1)C, (1)B, (1)A, (1)B, (4)A, (1)B, (1)A, (1)B, (1)A, (1)C, (1)E, (1)C, (1)D, (1)B,
Row 125&126 (R) (1)D, (1)B, (3)D, (1)C, (1)B, (2)D, (2)A, (4)B, (3)C, (1)D, (1)C, (2)D, (2)C
Row 127&128 (R) (1)D, (1)C, (1)B, (2)A, (2)D, (1)B, (2)D, (1)C, (2)A, (1)C, (2)D, (1)B, (5)D, (1)C, (1)D
Row 129&130 (R) (3)D, (2)B, (7)D, (1)C, (2)D, (2)B, (1)C, (1)D, (1)A, (2)C, (2)D
Row 131&132 (R) (6)D, (1)C, (2)D, (1)B, (3)D, (1)B, (1)C, (2)D, (1)A, (1)D, (1)C, (4)D
Row 133&134 (R) (5)D, (1)C, (9)D, (1)A, (8)D
Row 135&136 (R) (4)C, (15)D, (2)C, (3)B
Row 137&138 (R) (2)C, (1)A, (3)D, (1)B, (5)D, (1)B, (4)D, (1)B, (1)C, (3)D, (2)A
Row 139&140 (R) (2)A, (3)D, (1)B, (2)D, (1)C, (2)D, (1)C, (1)A, (1)C, (2)D, (1)C, (1)D, (1)B, (1)C, (3)D, (1)A
Row 141&142 (R) (1)A, (3)D, (1)C, (1)B, (2)D, (1)C, (1)D, (1)C, (1)B, (1)C, (1)A, (2)D, (1)C, (2)D, (1)B, (4)D
Row 143&144 (R) (4)D, (1)B, (1)C, (2)D, (3)C, (3)A, (1)B, (1)D, (1)C, (2)D, (1)C, (1)B, (3)D
Row 145&146 (R) (3)D, (2)B, (1)C, (3)D, (1)B, (1)A, (1)B, (1)D, (1)C, (1)E, (1)C, (3)D, (1)C, (1)B, (3)D
Row 147&148 (R) (3)D, (2)B, (1)C, (3)D, (1)A, (1)E, (1)C, (1)D, (2)A, (1)B, (1)A, (3)D, (1)C, (1)B, (3)D
Row 149&150 (R) (3)D, (1)C, (2)B, (1)A, (1)E, (1)C, (1)D, (2)A, (1)B, (2)A, (1)B, (1)C, (1)B, (1)A, (1)B, (1)C, (3)D
Row 151&152 (R) (4)D, (1)C, (1)A, (3)F, (1)E, (2)B, (1)A, (2)B, (1)A, (2)F, (1)E, (1)B, (4)C
Row 153&154 (R) (1)B, (2)A, (1)B, (1)E, (1)A, (1)B, (2)A, (1)C, (5)A, (1)C, (1)A, (1)E, (1)F, (1)A, (2)E, (2)A
Row 155&156 (R) (2)A, (2)E, (1)F, (1)E, (1)B, (1)C, (2)D, (1)C, (2)B, (1)C, (3)D, (1)C, (1)B, (2)F, (2)E, (1)A
Row 157&158 (R) (1)A, (2)E, (2)F, (1)E, (3)C, (7)D, (2)C, (1)B, (3)F, (2)E
Row 159&160 (R) (1)A, (1)E, (3)F, (1)A, (1)C, (5)D, (1)C, (5)D, (1)C, (2)E, (2)F, (1)E
Row 161&162 (R) (1)A, (1)E, (2)F, (1)A, (1)C, (3)D, (1)C, (1)D, (1)C, (2)B, (1)D, (1)C, (3)D, (1)A, (1)E, (3)F
Row 163&164 (R) (1)E, (2)F, (1)E, (1)C, (2)D, (1)B, (1)C, (1)B, (3)A, (1)B, (1)E, (1)A, (1)B, (1)C, (2)D, (1)B, (1)E, (2)F
Row 165&166 (R) (1)E, (2)F, (1)A, (2)D, (1)B, (3)E, (2)C, (3)D, (2)E, (1)B, (1)C, (2)D, (1)C, (1)A, (2)F
Row 167&168 (R) (1)E, (1)F, (1)E, (1)B, (1)D, (1)C, (1)A, (1)E, (1)B, (2)D, (1)C, (1)C, (1)D, (2)F, (1)B, (2)D, (1)B, (1)E, (
Row 169&170 (R) (1)E, (1)F, (1)E, (1)B, (1)D, (1)C, (2)E, (1)B, (1)C, (1)A, (1)B, (2)C, (1)E, (1)C, (1)B, (1)F, (1)A, (2)D, (1)B, (1)E, (
Row 171&172 (R) (1)E, (1)F, (1)E, (1)C, (1)D, (1)B, (2)E, (1)C, (2)A, (3)B, (2)A, (1)D, (1)F, (1)E, (1)C, (1)D, (1)B, (1)E, (1)F
Row 173&174 (R) (1)E, (1)F, (1)E, (1)B, (1)D, (1)C, (1)E, (1)F, (1)D, (1)E, (2)B, (1)A, (1)B, (1)A, (1)B, (1)C, (2)E, (1)C, (1)D, (1)A, (
Row 175&176 (R) (1)A, (2)F, (1)A, (2)D, (1)A, (1)F, (1)D, (1)B, (1)E, (1)B, (3)A, (1)C, (1)B, (1)F, (1)A, (2)D, (1)B, (1)F, (1)E
Row 177&178 (R) (1)A, (1)E, (1)F, (1)E, (1)B, (2)D, (2)C, (1)E, (1)B, (1)C, (1)B, (1)A, (2)E, (1)C, (1)D, (1)A, (2)F, (1)E
Row 179&180 (R) (1)B, (1)A, (3)F, (1)B, (2)D, (1)E, (1)F, (1)E, (1)C, (5)E, (1)C, (1)D, (1)C, (1)E, (1)F, (1)E, (1)B
Row 181&182 (R) (1)C, (1)B, (1)E, (3)F, (1)A, (1)C, (1)D, (1)B, (2)E, (1)A, (2)B, (3)D, (1)B, (1)E, (1)F, (1)E, (1)A, (1)C
Row 183&184 (R) (1)D, (1)C, (1)B, (1)A, (1)E, (2)F, (1)E, (1)C, (5)D, (1)C, (1)B, (1)C, (1)A, (1)E, (1)F, (1)A, (1)B, (1)C, (1)D
Row 185&186 (R) (3)D, (1)C, (1)B, (1)A, (1)E, (2)F, (1)E, (1)A, (1)B, (2)E, (4)F, (2)E, (1)B, (3)D
Row 187&188 (R) (1)B, (4)D, (1)C, (2)B, (1)E, (3)F, (4)E, (1)F, (1)E, (1)A, (1)B, (3)D, (1)B
Row 189&190 (R) (1)E, (1)A, (1)C, (5)D, (2)B, (2)A, (3)B, (1)C, (1)B, (1)C, (3)D, (1)B, (1)A, (1)E
Row 191&192 (R) (1)F, (2)E, (2)A, (1)B, (1)C, (12)D, (1)C, (1)A, (2)E, (1)F

Serene Silhouette Pendants

These little beauties are very quick to make and fun to wear. Use leather or cotton cord, chain, or ribbon to hold your pendant.

MATERIALS

TULIP
- 11º Delica beads:
  - 1g (184) DB0310 matte black (color B)
  - 1g (135) DB2111 opaque flesh (mix to make color M)
  - 1g (135) DB2112 opaque salmon (mix to make color M)
  - 1g (135) DB2114 opaque light watermelon (mix to make color M)

TULIP FRINGE
- Remaining M Beads
- 15º rocaille silver-lined clear seed beads
- 11 4mm vintage rose Swarovski bicones

PALM BRANCH
- 11º Delica beads:
  - 1g (194) DB0310 matte black (color B)
  - 1g (132) DB0658 opaque turquoise green (mix to make color M)
  - 1g (132) DB0878 matte opaque turquoise AB (mix to make color M)
  - 1g (132) DB0793 matte opaque turquoise (mix to make color M)

PALM BRANCH FRINGE
- Remaining M Beads
- 15º rocaille black seed beads
- 24 3mm black Swarovski bicones
- 6 12mm black twisted bugle beads

FLAMINGO
- 11º Delica beads:
  - 1g (134) DB0310 matte black (Bead B)
  - 1g (152) DB2137 opaque hydrangea (mix to make Bead M)
  - 1g (152) DB0355 matte rose (mix to make Bead M)
  - 1g (152) DB0800 matte opaque rose (mix to make Bead M)

FLAMINGO FRINGE
- Remaining M Beads
- 15º rocaille silver-lined clear seed beads
- 13 4mm rose Swarovski bicones

ADDITIONAL MATERIALS
- Fireline, 4-lb. or 6-lb. test
- Finished leather or cotton cord, ribbon, or chain of desired length

TOOLS
- #10 or #12 beading needle
- Thread cutters or scissors

MEASUREMENTS
½ in. wide and 3–4-in. long, depending on the fringe.

Instructions

1 Refer to the *Serene Silhouette Pendants* three-drop patterns and word charts on pages 26 and 27. Follow the instructions for Fast Peyote (Techniques, p. 94) to create each peyote band. Add thread (Techniques, p. 97) as needed throughout each project.

2 Reinforce the bottom of the pendant (Techniques, p. 96, step 11).

Add fringe to Palm or Tulip pendant

3(a) Starting at point **a** marked on the pattern, follow the instructions for adding inverted V fringe (Techniques, p. 106) for the Palm and Tulip pendants. Follow the bead lists below:

Palm fringe
Column 1: 1 M bead, 1 bicone, 1 M bead, 1 bugle bead, 1 M bead, 1 bicone, 1 M bead, 1 bicone, 1 M bead, 1 bicone, 1 seed bead
Column 2: 1 bicone, 2 M beads, 1 bugle bead, 2 M beads, 1 bicone, 1 M bead, 1 bicone, 1 M bead, 1 bicone, 1 seed bead
Column 3: 1 M bead, 1 bicone, 3 M beads, 1 bugle bead, 3 M beads, 1 bicone, 1 M bead, 1 bicone, 1 M bead, 1 bicone, 1 seed bead
Column 4: 1 bicone, 3 M beads, 1 bugle bead, 3 M beads, 1 bicone, 1 M bead, 1 bicone, 1 M bead, 1 bicone, 1 seed bead
Column 5: 1 M bead, 1 bicone, 2 M beads, 1 bugle bead, 2 M beads, 1 bicone, 1 M bead, 1 bicone, 1 M bead, 1 bicone, 1 seed bead
Column 6: 1 bicone, 1 M bead, 1 bugle bead, 3 M beads, 1 bicone, 1 M bead, 1 bicone, 1 M bead, 1 bicone, 1 seed bead

Tulip fringe
Column 1: 9 M beads, 1 bicone, 1 seed bead
Column 2: 6 M beads, 1 bicone, 1 seed bead
Column 3: 3 M beads, 1 bicone, 1 seed bead
Column 4: 3 M beads, 1 bicone, 1 seed bead
Column 5: 6 M beads, 1 bicone, 1 seed bead
Column 6: 9 M beads, 1 bicone, 1 seed bead

Tulip fringe: step 2
Turn back, start at point **c**. Follow the bead list below:
Column 1: 6 M beads, 1 bicone, 1 seed bead
Column 2: 3 M beads, 1 bicone, 1 seed bead
Column 3: 1 M beads, 1 bicone, 1 seed bead
Column 4: 3 M beads, 1 bicone, 1 seed bead
Column 5: 6 M beads, 1 bicone, 1 seed bead

Add fringe to the Flamingo pendant

3(b) Starting at point **a** marked on the pattern, follow the instructions for adding tufted fringe (Techniques, p. 107). Follow the bead list below:

Flamingo fringe
Column 1: 1 seed bead, 1 bicone, 1 seed bead
Column 2: 2 seed beads, 1 bicone, 1 seed bead
Column 3: 3 seed beads, 1 bicone, 1 seed bead
Column 4: 4 seed beads, 1 bicone, 1 seed bead
Column 5: 3 seed beads, 1 bicone, 1 seed bead
Column 6: 2 seed beads, 1 bicone, 1 seed bead
Column 7: 1 seed bead, 1 bicone, 1 seed bead

Go back into the piece and exit between two beads on the same level at point **c**. Follow the bead list below:

Flamingo fringe: step 2
Column 1: 1 bicone, 1 seed bead
Column 2: 1 bicone, 1 seed bead
Column 3: 1 seed bead, 1 bicone, 1 seed bead
Column 4: 1 seed bead, 1 bicone, 1 seed bead
Column 5: 1 bicone, 1 seed bead
Column 6: 1 bicone, 1 seed bead

4 When the fringe is complete, sew back into the piece using finishing knots to secure (Techniques, p. 97), then trim the thread and weave into the piece.

5 Remove the stop bead and add thread to the original tail at the top of the piece. Fold the piece over so the end (or top) meets the line marked on the pattern with the notation "attach here for fold." Secure the end of the piece to the main piece in order to make a "fold over" loop for the cord.

6 *With the thread that is exiting the end of the piece at the edge, sew into the two beads marked on the pattern at the base of the piece and then back into the next two beads on the edge. Do this until the loop is secured. Exit from the opposite edge.

7 Repeat from *, sewing in the opposite direction in order to secure the end to the base of the piece. Weave back into the piece and reinforce using finishing knots to secure, then trim the thread, and weave the tail into a neighboring bead.

Tulip
two-drop peyote

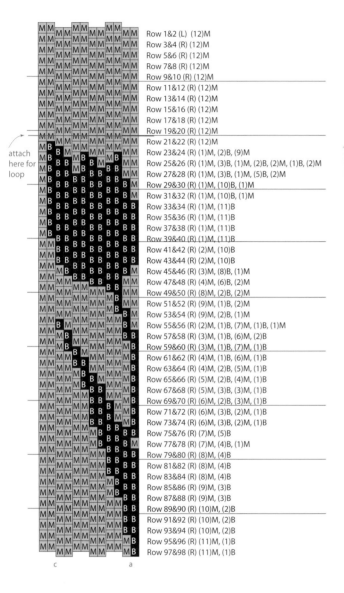

Row 1&2 (L) (12)M
Row 3&4 (R) (12)M
Row 5&6 (R) (12)M
Row 7&8 (R) (12)M
Row 9&10 (R) (12)M
Row 11&12 (R) (12)M
Row 13&14 (R) (12)M
Row 15&16 (R) (12)M
Row 17&18 (R) (12)M
Row 19&20 (R) (12)M
Row 21&22 (R) (12)M
Row 23&24 (R) (1)M, (2)B, (9)M
Row 25&26 (R) (1)M, (3)B, (1)M, (2)B, (2)M, (1)B, (2)M
Row 27&28 (R) (1)M, (3)B, (1)M, (5)B, (2)M
Row 29&30 (R) (1)M, (10)B, (1)M
Row 31&32 (R) (1)M, (10)B, (1)M
Row 33&34 (R) (1)M, (11)B
Row 35&36 (R) (1)M, (11)B
Row 37&38 (R) (1)M, (11)B
Row 39&40 (R) (1)M, (11)B
Row 41&42 (R) (2)M, (10)B
Row 43&44 (R) (2)M, (10)B
Row 45&46 (R) (3)M, (8)B, (1)M
Row 47&48 (R) (4)M, (6)B, (2)M
Row 49&50 (R) (5)M, (5)B, (2)M
Row 51&52 (R) (9)M, (1)B, (2)M
Row 53&54 (R) (9)M, (2)B, (1)M
Row 55&56 (R) (2)M, (1)B, (7)M, (1)B, (1)M
Row 57&58 (R) (3)M, (1)B, (6)M, (2)B
Row 59&60 (R) (3)M, (1)B, (7)M, (1)B
Row 61&62 (R) (4)M, (1)B, (6)M, (1)B
Row 63&64 (R) (4)M, (2)B, (5)M, (1)B
Row 65&66 (R) (5)M, (2)B, (4)M, (1)B
Row 67&68 (R) (5)M, (3)B, (3)M, (1)B
Row 69&70 (R) (6)M, (2)B, (3)M, (1)B
Row 71&72 (R) (6)M, (3)B, (2)M, (1)B
Row 73&74 (R) (6)M, (3)B, (2)M, (1)B
Row 75&76 (R) (7)M, (5)B
Row 77&78 (R) (7)M, (4)B, (1)M
Row 79&80 (R) (8)M, (4)B
Row 81&82 (R) (8)M, (4)B
Row 83&84 (R) (8)M, (4)B
Row 85&86 (R) (9)M, (3)B
Row 87&88 (R) (9)M, (3)B
Row 89&90 (R) (10)M, (2)B
Row 91&92 (R) (10)M, (2)B
Row 93&94 (R) (10)M, (2)B
Row 95&96 (R) (11)M, (1)B
Row 97&98 (R) (11)M, (1)B

attach here for loop

c   a

Palm
two-drop peyote

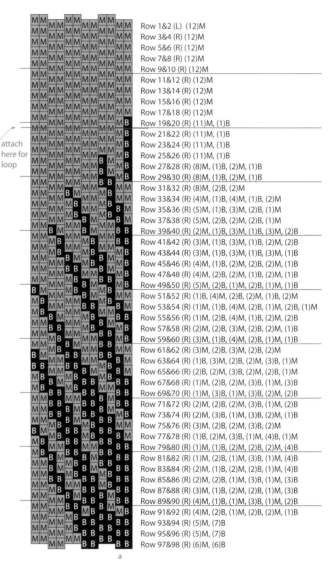

Row 1&2 (L) (12)M
Row 3&4 (R) (12)M
Row 5&6 (R) (12)M
Row 7&8 (R) (12)M
Row 9&10 (R) (12)M
Row 11&12 (R) (12)M
Row 13&14 (R) (12)M
Row 15&16 (R) (12)M
Row 17&18 (R) (12)M
Row 19&20 (R) (11)M, (1)B
Row 21&22 (R) (11)M, (1)B
Row 23&24 (R) (11)M, (1)B
Row 25&26 (R) (11)M, (1)B
Row 27&28 (R) (8)M, (1)B, (2)M, (1)B
Row 29&30 (R) (8)M, (1)B, (2)M, (1)B
Row 31&32 (R) (8)M, (2)B, (2)M
Row 33&34 (R) (4)M, (1)B, (4)M, (1)B, (2)M
Row 35&36 (R) (5)M, (1)B, (3)M, (2)B, (1)M
Row 37&38 (R) (5)M, (2)B, (2)M, (2)B, (1)M
Row 39&40 (R) (2)M, (1)B, (3)M, (1)B, (3)M, (2)B
Row 41&42 (R) (1)M, (1)B, (3)M, (1)B, (2)M, (2)B
Row 43&44 (R) (3)M, (1)B, (3)M, (1)B, (3)M, (1)B
Row 45&46 (R) (4)M, (1)B, (2)M, (2)B, (2)M, (1)B
Row 47&48 (R) (4)M, (2)B, (2)M, (1)B, (2)M, (1)B
Row 49&50 (R) (5)M, (2)B, (1)M, (2)B, (1)M, (1)B
Row 51&52 (R) (1)B, (4)M, (2)B, (2)M, (1)B, (2)M
Row 53&54 (R) (1)M, (1)B, (4)M, (2)B, (1)M, (2)B, (1)M
Row 55&56 (R) (1)M, (2)B, (4)M, (1)B, (2)M, (2)B
Row 57&58 (R) (2)M, (2)B, (3)M, (2)B, (2)M, (1)B
Row 59&60 (R) (5)M, (2)B, (1)M, (4)M, (2)B, (1)M, (1)B
Row 61&62 (R) (3)M, (2)B, (3)M, (2)B, (2)M
Row 63&64 (R) (1)B, (3)M, (2)B, (2)M, (3)B, (1)M
Row 65&66 (R) (2)B, (2)M, (3)B, (2)M, (2)B, (1)M
Row 67&68 (R) (1)M, (2)B, (3)M, (2)B, (1)M, (3)B
Row 69&70 (R) (1)M, (3)B, (1)M, (3)B, (2)M, (2)B
Row 71&72 (R) (2)M, (2)B, (2)M, (3)B, (1)M, (2)B
Row 73&74 (R) (2)M, (3)B, (1)M, (3)B, (2)M, (1)B
Row 75&76 (R) (3)M, (2)B, (2)M, (3)B, (2)M
Row 77&78 (R) (1)B, (2)M, (3)B, (1)M, (4)B, (1)M
Row 79&80 (R) (1)M, (1)B, (2)M, (2)B, (2)M, (4)B
Row 81&82 (R) (1)M, (2)B, (1)M, (3)B, (1)M, (4)B
Row 83&84 (R) (2)M, (1)B, (2)M, (2)B, (1)M, (4)B
Row 85&86 (R) (2)M, (2)B, (1)M, (3)B, (1)M, (3)B
Row 87&88 (R) (3)M, (1)B, (2)M, (2)B, (1)M, (3)B
Row 89&90 (R) (4)M, (1)B, (1)M, (3)B, (1)M, (2)B
Row 91&92 (R) (4)M, (2)B, (1)M, (2)B, (2)M, (1)B
Row 93&94 (R) (5)M, (7)B
Row 95&96 (R) (5)M, (7)B
Row 97&98 (R) (6)M, (6)B

attach here for loop

a

Flamingo
two-drop peyote

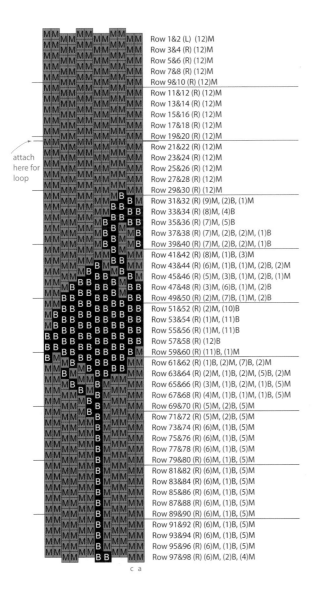

attach here for loop

Row 1&2 (L) (12)M
Row 3&4 (R) (12)M
Row 5&6 (R) (12)M
Row 7&8 (R) (12)M
Row 9&10 (R) (12)M
Row 11&12 (R) (12)M
Row 13&14 (R) (12)M
Row 15&16 (R) (12)M
Row 17&18 (R) (12)M
Row 19&20 (R) (12)M
Row 21&22 (R) (12)M
Row 23&24 (R) (12)M
Row 25&26 (R) (12)M
Row 27&28 (R) (12)M
Row 29&30 (R) (12)M
Row 31&32 (R) (9)M, (2)B, (1)M
Row 33&34 (R) (8)M, (4)B
Row 35&36 (R) (7)M, (5)B
Row 37&38 (R) (7)M, (2)B, (2)M, (1)B
Row 39&40 (R) (7)M, (2)B, (2)M, (1)B
Row 41&42 (R) (8)M, (1)B, (3)M
Row 43&44 (R) (6)M, (1)B, (1)M, (2)B, (2)M
Row 45&46 (R) (5)M, (3)B, (1)M, (2)B, (1)M
Row 47&48 (R) (3)M, (6)B, (1)M, (2)B
Row 49&50 (R) (2)M, (7)B, (1)M, (2)B
Row 51&52 (R) (2)M, (10)B
Row 53&54 (R) (1)M, (11)B
Row 55&56 (R) (1)M, (11)B
Row 57&58 (R) (12)B
Row 59&60 (R) (11)B, (1)M
Row 61&62 (R) (1)B, (2)M, (7)B, (2)M
Row 63&64 (R) (2)M, (1)B, (2)M, (5)B, (2)M
Row 65&66 (R) (3)M, (1)B, (2)M, (1)B, (5)M
Row 67&68 (R) (4)M, (1)B, (1)M, (1)B, (5)M
Row 69&70 (R) (5)M, (2)B, (5)M
Row 71&72 (R) (5)M, (2)B, (5)M
Row 73&74 (R) (6)M, (1)B, (5)M
Row 75&76 (R) (6)M, (1)B, (5)M
Row 77&78 (R) (6)M, (1)B, (5)M
Row 79&80 (R) (6)M, (1)B, (5)M
Row 81&82 (R) (6)M, (1)B, (5)M
Row 83&84 (R) (6)M, (1)B, (5)M
Row 85&86 (R) (6)M, (1)B, (5)M
Row 87&88 (R) (6)M, (1)B, (5)M
Row 89&90 (R) (6)M, (1)B, (5)M
Row 91&92 (R) (6)M, (1)B, (5)M
Row 93&94 (R) (6)M, (1)B, (5)M
Row 95&96 (R) (6)M, (1)B, (5)M
Row 97&98 (R) (6)M, (2)B, (4)M

c a

mix it up
To create the bead mixture, simply estimate the quantity of each of the three colors and mix them together with a bead scoop on a bead mat or stir them together in a small dish.

Oscar the Egret

Egrets are beautiful white birds we often see in southeast Louisiana. I have photographed this particular bird several times as he hunted and rested on my best friend's dock. The kids named him *Oscar*.

Instructions

1 Refer to the *Oscar the Egret* three-drop pattern and word chart below. Follow the instructions for Fast Peyote (Techniques, p. 94) to create the peyote band. Add thread (Techniques, p. 97) as needed throughout the project.

2 Reinforce the bottom of the pendant (Techniques, p. 96, step 11).

3 Starting at point **a** marked on the bottom of the pattern, follow the instructions for adding pendant fringe (Techniques, p. 106). Follow the bead list above right:

4 When the fringe is complete, sew back into the piece using finishing knots to secure (Techniques, p. 97), then trim the thread and weave into the piece.

5 Remove the stop bead and add thread to the original tail on the other end of the piece. Weave into the piece, tucking the knot into a bead. Reinforce along the end.

6 Exit at the edge. Pick up 24 color A beads and add the slide end tube (Techniques, p. 108). Finish the top following the instructions (Techniques, p. 96, step 11).

Add the chain

7 Construct the chain using wrapped wire loops, jump rings, and a clasp (Techniques, p. 109). If you wish, a simple chain or cord can be strung through the loops at either end of the bar. The bar loops can be opened and closed using chainnose pliers.

Oscar the Egret fringe

Column 1:	1 A bead, 1 brushed tube, 1 Czech bead, 2 seed beads, 1 drop bead, 2 seed beads
Column 2:	3 A beads, 1 brushed tube, 1 Czech bead, 2 seed beads, 1 drop bead, 2 seed beads
Column 3:	5 A beads, 1 brushed tube, 1 Czech bead, 2 seed beads, 1 drop bead, 2 seed beads
Column 4:	7 A beads, 1 brushed tube, 1 Czech bead, 2 seed beads, 1 drop bead, 2 seed beads
Column 5:	9 A beads, 1 brushed tube, 1 Czech bead, 2 seed beads, 1 drop bead, 2 seed beads
Column 6:	10 A beads, 1 brushed tube, 1 Czech bead, 2 seed beads, 1 drop bead, 2 seed beads
Column 7:	9 A beads, 1 brushed tube, 1 Czech bead, 2 seed beads, 1 drop bead, 2 seed beads
Column 8:	9 A beads, 1 brushed tube, 1 Czech bead, 2 seed beads, 1 drop bead, 2 seed beads
Column 9:	7 A beads, 1 brushed tube, 1 Czech bead, 2 seed beads, 1 drop bead, 2 seed beads
Column 10:	5 A beads, 1 brushed tube, 1 Czech bead, 2 seed beads, 1 drop bead, 2 seed beads
Column 11:	3 A beads, 1 brushed tube, 1 Czech bead, 2 seed beads, 1 drop bead, 2 seed beads
Column 12:	1 A bead, 1 brushed tube, 1 Czech bead, 2 seed beads, 1 drop bead, 2 seed beads

MATERIALS

- 11º Delica beads:
  - 3g (548) DB0465 metallic midnight blue (color A)
  - 1g (106) DB0351 matte white (color W)
  - 1g (13) DB0010 black (color B)
  - 1g (47) DB1518 matte opaque light smoke (color G)
  - 1g (4) DB1521 matte opaque yellow AB (color Y)
- **18** 3mm black Czech round beads
- 1g 15º black rocailles or seed beads
- 1g (12) 3.4mm gunmetal Miyuki drop beads (magatamas)
- 24-gauge tarnish-resistant silver artistic wire
- 26 in. 2mm silver-plated fine cable beading chain
- 12x6mm silver-plated lobster claw clasp
- **2** 5mm jump rings
- **14** 30x3mm silver-plated brushed satin tube beads
- 6x35mm Miyuki silver-plated 2-strand slide end tube
- Fireline, 4-lb. or 6-lb. test

TOOLS

- #10 or #12 beading needle
- Thread cutters or scissors
- Chainnose pliers

MEASUREMENTS

1¼ in. wide and 1¾ in. long without the fringe, and 3¾ in. long with the fringe.

To adjust the length of this necklace, simply lengthen or shorten the chain sections.

Oscar the Egret
three-drop peyote

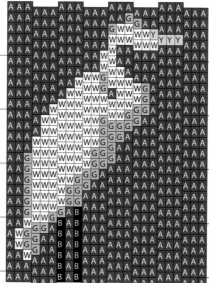

Row 1&2 (L) (24)A
Row 3&4 (R) (14)A, (2)G, (8)A
Row 5&6 (R) (12)A, (1)G, (4)W, (1)Y, (6)A
Row 7&8 (R) (12)A, (6)W, (3)Y, (3)A
Row 9&10 (R) (11)A, (2)W, (11)A
Row 11&12 (R) (11)A, (2)W, (11)A
Row 13&14 (R) (9)A, (2)W, (1)G, (2)W, (10)A
Row 15&16 (R) (8)A, (3)W, (1)G, (4)W, (1)G, (7)A
Row 17&18 (R) (7)A, (5)W, (1)A, (3)W, (1)G, (7)A
Row 19&20 (R) (5)A, (10)W, (2)G, (7)A
Row 21&22 (R) (4)A, (7)W, (1)G, (2)W, (2)G, (8)A
Row 23&24 (R) (4)A, (7)W, (4)G, (9)A
Row 25&26 (R) (3)A, (8)W, (3)G, (10)A
Row 27&28 (R) (3)A, (7)W, (3)G, (11)A
Row 29&30 (R) (2)A, (1)G, (7)W, (3)G, (11)A
Row 31&32 (R) (2)A, (1)G, (6)W, (2)G, (13)A
Row 33&34 (R) (2)A, (1)G, (5)W, (2)G, (14)A
Row 35&36 (R) (2)A, (1)G, (4)W, (2)G, (15)A
Row 37&38 (R) (2)A, (1)G, (4)W, (2)G, (15)A
Row 39&40 (R) (2)A, (1)G, (2)W, (2)G, (1)A, (1)B, (15)A
Row 41&42 (R) (2)A, (1)W, (2)G, (1)A, (1)B, (1)A, (1)B, (15)A
Row 43&44 (R) (1)A, (1)W, (2)G, (2)A, (1)B, (1)A, (1)B, (15)A
Row 45&46 (R) (1)A, (1)W, (2)G, (2)A, (1)B, (1)A, (1)B, (15)A
Row 47&48 (R) (2)A, (1)W, (3)A, (1)B, (1)A, (1)B, (15)A
Row 49&50 (R) (6)A, (1)B, (1)A, (1)B, (15)A
Row 51&52 (R) (6)A, (1)B, (1)A, (1)B, (15)A

a

Monarch Butterflies

Butterflies are symbols of, among other things, hope, rebirth, and freedom. Besides being beautiful, butterflies are fragile, yet strong little creatures. There are many species, but the monarch (possibly named in honor of a king) is perhaps the most common and recognizable.

MATERIALS
- 11º Delica beads:
  - 3g (438) DB0746 matte transparent kelly green (color A)
  - 1g (149) DB0351 matte white (color W)
  - 6g (1188) DB0310 matte black (color B)
  - 2g (259) DB0461 nickel-plated copper (color D)
  - 2g (255) DB0781 transparent matte light marmalade (color M)
  - 4g (1702) DB1702 copper pearl-lined marigold (color L)
- 2 8mm black Swarovski crystal pearls
- 2 15º black seed beads (Black B beads can be substituted.)
- Fireline, 4-lb. or 6-lb. test

ALTERNATE COLOR:
- 11º Delicas:
  - 3g (438) DB0861 matte transparent sky blue (color A)
  - 1g (149) DB0351 matte white (color W)
  - 6g (1188) DB0310 matte black (color B)
  - 2g (259) DB0420 metallic pink (color D)
  - 2g (255) DB0246 lined crystal dark pink (color M)
  - 4g (1702) DB0244 lined crystal light pink (color L)
- 2 8mm turquoise Swarovski crystals
- 2 15º silver lined seed beads (blue A beads can be substituted.)

TOOLS
- #10 or #12 beading needle
- Thread cutters or scissors

MEASUREMENTS
1¼ in. wide and 7¾ in. long

To shorten by approximately .3 inches, leave off the first two rows and the last four rows.

Instructions

1 Refer to the *Monarch Butterflies* three-drop pattern and word chart on pages 32 and 33. Follow the instructions for Fast Peyote (Techniques, p. 94) to create the peyote band. Add thread (Techniques, p. 97) as needed throughout the project.

Create loops for the closure

2 *The closure for this project consists of two flat peyote loops and two 10mm crystal beads.* Reinforce the end of the bracelet (Techniques, p. 96, step 11). *Exit at the location on the pattern marked by a pair of black dots.

3 Follow the instructions to create a flat peyote loop (Techniques, p. 98) using 14 rows of beads. Secure the other end of the loop at the next location marked by the second pair of black dots. Weave back through the loop to reinforce, using finishing knots to secure (Techniques, p. 97).

4 Repeat steps 2 and 3 from *. Trim the thread and tuck into the piece.

5 Remove the stop bead and add thread to the original tail at the opposite end of the piece. Weave into the piece, tucking the knot into a bead. Reinforce the end of the bracelet.

Add the crystal pearls

6 Exit at one of the black dots at the opposite end of the pattern, then pick up three color A beads, a crystal pearl, and a 15º black seed bead or a color B bead. Sew back through the crystal pearl and the three As, and then weave back into the piece.

7 Exit at the next black dot marked on the pattern. Repeat step 6.

8 Weave back into the piece and reinforce using finishing knots to secure, then trim the thread, and tuck into the piece.

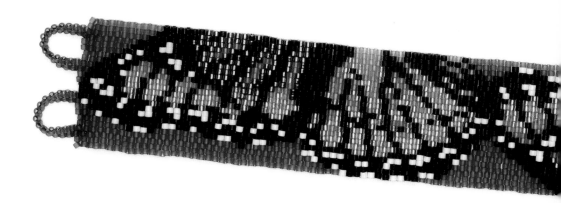

Monarch Butterflies
three-drop peyote

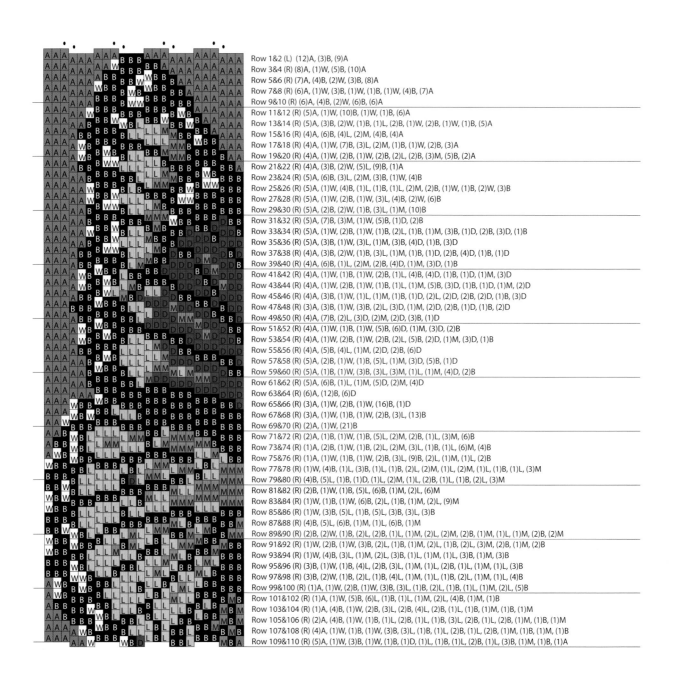

Row 1&2 (L) (12)A, (3)B, (9)A
Row 3&4 (R) (8)A, (1)W, (5)B, (10)A
Row 5&6 (R) (7)A, (4)B, (2)W, (3)B, (8)A
Row 7&8 (R) (6)A, (1)W, (3)B, (1)W, (1)B, (1)W, (4)B, (7)A
Row 9&10 (R) (6)A, (4)B, (2)W, (6)B, (6)A
Row 11&12 (R) (5)A, (1)W, (10)B, (1)W, (1)B, (6)A
Row 13&14 (R) (5)A, (3)B, (2)W, (1)B, (1)L, (2)B, (1)W, (2)B, (1)W, (1)B, (5)A
Row 15&16 (R) (4)A, (6)B, (4)L, (2)M, (4)B, (4)A
Row 17&18 (R) (4)A, (1)W, (7)B, (3)L, (2)M, (1)B, (1)W, (2)B, (3)A
Row 19&20 (R) (4)A, (1)W, (2)B, (1)W, (2)B, (2)L, (2)B, (3)M, (5)B, (2)A
Row 21&22 (R) (4)A, (3)B, (2)W, (5)L, (9)B, (1)A
Row 23&24 (R) (5)A, (6)B, (3)L, (2)M, (3)B, (1)W, (4)B
Row 25&26 (R) (5)A, (1)W, (4)B, (1)L, (1)B, (1)L, (2)M, (2)B, (1)W, (1)B, (2)W, (3)B
Row 27&28 (R) (5)A, (1)W, (2)B, (1)W, (3)L, (4)B, (2)W, (6)B
Row 29&30 (R) (5)A, (2)B, (2)W, (1)B, (3)L, (1)M, (10)B
Row 31&32 (R) (5)A, (7)B, (3)M, (1)W, (5)B, (1)D, (2)B
Row 33&34 (R) (5)A, (1)W, (2)B, (1)W, (1)B, (2)L, (1)B, (1)M, (3)B, (1)D, (2)B, (3)D, (1)B
Row 35&36 (R) (5)A, (3)B, (1)W, (3)L, (1)M, (3)B, (4)D, (1)B, (3)D
Row 37&38 (R) (4)A, (3)B, (2)W, (1)B, (3)L, (1)M, (1)B, (1)D, (2)B, (4)D, (1)B, (1)D
Row 39&40 (R) (4)A, (6)B, (1)L, (2)M, (2)B, (4)D, (1)M, (3)D, (1)B
Row 41&42 (R) (4)A, (1)W, (1)B, (1)W, (2)B, (1)L, (4)B, (4)D, (1)B, (1)D, (1)M, (3)D
Row 43&44 (R) (4)A, (1)W, (2)B, (1)W, (1)B, (1)L, (1)M, (5)B, (3)D, (1)B, (1)D, (1)M, (2)D
Row 45&46 (R) (4)A, (3)B, (1)W, (1)L, (1)M, (1)B, (1)D, (2)L, (2)D, (2)B, (2)D, (1)B, (3)D
Row 47&48 (R) (3)A, (3)B, (1)W, (3)B, (2)L, (3)D, (1)M, (2)D, (2)B, (1)D, (1)B, (2)D
Row 49&50 (R) (4)A, (7)B, (2)L, (3)D, (2)M, (2)D, (3)B, (1)D
Row 51&52 (R) (4)A, (1)W, (1)B, (1)W, (5)B, (6)D, (1)M, (3)D, (2)B
Row 53&54 (R) (4)A, (1)W, (2)B, (1)W, (2)B, (2)L, (5)B, (2)D, (1)M, (3)D, (1)B
Row 55&56 (R) (4)A, (5)B, (4)L, (1)M, (2)D, (2)B, (6)D
Row 57&58 (R) (5)A, (2)B, (1)W, (1)B, (5)L, (1)M, (3)D, (5)B, (1)D
Row 59&60 (R) (5)A, (1)B, (1)W, (3)B, (3)L, (1)W, (1)L, (1)M, (4)D, (2)B
Row 61&62 (R) (5)A, (6)B, (1)L, (1)M, (5)D, (2)M, (4)D
Row 63&64 (R) (6)A, (12)B, (6)D
Row 65&66 (R) (3)A, (1)W, (2)B, (1)W, (16)B, (1)D
Row 67&68 (R) (3)A, (1)W, (1)B, (1)W, (2)B, (3)L, (13)B
Row 69&70 (R) (2)A, (1)W, (21)B
Row 71&72 (R) (2)A, (1)B, (1)W, (1)B, (5)L, (2)M, (2)B, (1)L, (3)M, (6)B
Row 73&74 (R) (1)A, (2)B, (1)W, (1)B, (2)L, (2)M, (3)L, (1)B, (1)L, (6)M, (4)B
Row 75&76 (R) (1)A, (1)W, (1)B, (1)W, (2)B, (3)L, (9)B, (2)L, (1)M, (1)L, (2)B
Row 77&78 (R) (1)W, (4)B, (1)L, (3)B, (1)L, (3)B, (2)L, (2)M, (1)L, (2)M, (1)L, (1)B, (1)L, (3)M
Row 79&80 (R) (4)B, (5)L, (1)B, (1)D, (1)L, (2)M, (1)L, (2)B, (1)L, (1)B, (2)L, (3)M
Row 81&82 (R) (2)B, (1)W, (1)B, (5)L, (6)B, (1)M, (2)L, (6)M
Row 83&84 (R) (1)W, (1)B, (1)W, (6)B, (2)L, (1)B, (1)M, (2)L, (9)M
Row 85&86 (R) (1)W, (3)B, (5)L, (1)B, (5)L, (3)B, (3)L, (3)B
Row 87&88 (R) (4)B, (5)L, (6)B, (1)M, (1)L, (6)B, (1)M
Row 89&90 (R) (2)B, (2)W, (1)B, (2)L, (2)B, (1)L, (1)M, (2)L, (2)M, (2)B, (1)M, (1)L, (1)M, (2)B, (2)M
Row 91&92 (R) (1)W, (2)B, (1)W, (3)B, (2)L, (1)B, (1)M, (2)L, (1)B, (2)L, (3)M, (2)B, (1)M, (2)B
Row 93&94 (R) (1)W, (4)B, (3)L, (1)M, (2)L, (3)B, (1)L, (1)M, (1)L, (3)B, (1)M, (3)B
Row 95&96 (R) (3)B, (1)W, (1)B, (4)L, (2)B, (3)L, (1)M, (1)L, (2)B, (1)L, (1)M, (1)L, (3)B
Row 97&98 (R) (3)B, (2)W, (1)B, (2)L, (1)B, (4)L, (1)M, (1)L, (1)B, (2)L, (1)M, (1)L, (4)B
Row 99&100 (R) (1)A, (1)W, (2)B, (1)W, (3)B, (3)L, (1)B, (2)L, (1)B, (1)L, (1)M, (2)L, (5)B
Row 101&102 (R) (1)A, (1)W, (5)B, (6)L, (1)B, (1)L, (1)M, (2)L, (4)B, (1)M, (1)B
Row 103&104 (R) (1)A, (4)B, (1)W, (2)B, (3)L, (2)B, (4)L, (2)B, (1)L, (1)M, (1)L, (3)B, (1)M, (1)M
Row 105&106 (R) (2)A, (4)B, (1)W, (1)B, (1)L, (2)B, (1)L, (1)B, (3)L, (2)B, (1)L, (2)B, (1)M, (1)B, (1)M
Row 107&108 (R) (4)A, (1)W, (1)B, (1)W, (3)B, (3)L, (1)B, (1)L, (2)B, (1)L, (2)B, (1)M, (1)B, (1)M, (1)B
Row 109&110 (R) (5)A, (1)W, (3)B, (1)W, (1)B, (1)D, (1)L, (1)B, (1)L, (2)B, (1)L, (3)B, (1)M, (1)B, (1)A

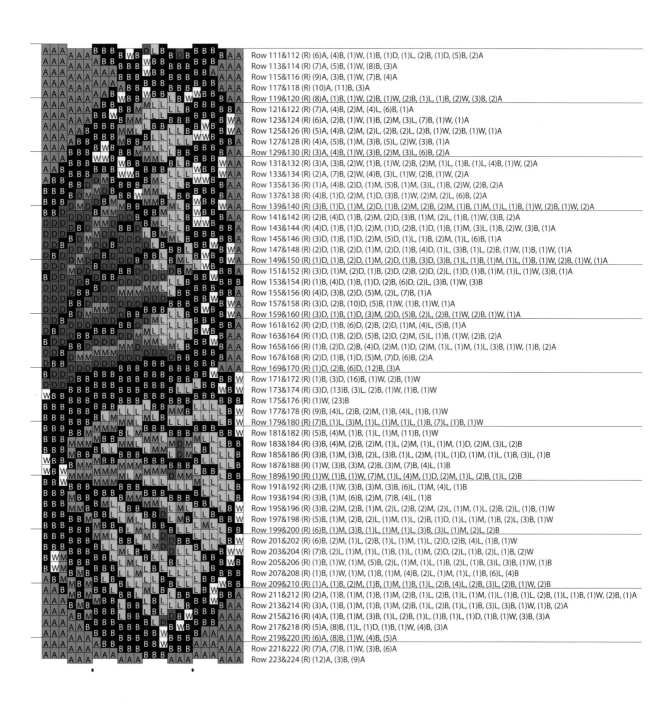

Row 111&112 (R) (6)A, (4)B, (1)W, (1)B, (1)D, (1)L, (2)B, (1)D, (5)B, (2)A
Row 113&114 (R) (7)A, (5)B, (1)W, (8)B, (3)A
Row 115&116 (R) (9)A, (3)B, (1)W, (7)B, (4)A
Row 117&118 (R) (10)A, (11)B, (3)A
Row 119&120 (R) (8)A, (1)B, (1)W, (2)B, (1)W, (2)B, (1)L, (1)B, (2)W, (3)B, (2)A
Row 121&122 (R) (7)A, (4)B, (2)M, (4)L, (6)B, (1)A
Row 123&124 (R) (6)A, (2)B, (1)W, (1)B, (2)M, (3)L, (7)B, (1)W, (1)A
Row 125&126 (R) (5)A, (4)B, (2)M, (2)L, (2)B, (2)L, (2)B, (1)W, (2)B, (1)W, (1)A
Row 127&128 (R) (4)A, (5)B, (1)M, (3)B, (5)L, (2)W, (3)B, (1)A
Row 129&130 (R) (3)A, (4)B, (1)W, (3)B, (2)M, (3)L, (6)B, (2)A
Row 131&132 (R) (3)A, (3)B, (2)W, (1)B, (1)W, (2)B, (2)M, (1)L, (1)B, (1)L, (4)B, (1)W, (2)A
Row 133&134 (R) (2)A, (7)B, (2)W, (4)B, (3)L, (1)W, (2)B, (1)W, (2)A
Row 135&136 (R) (1)A, (4)B, (2)D, (1)M, (5)B, (1)M, (3)L, (1)B, (2)W, (2)B, (2)A
Row 137&138 (R) (4)B, (1)D, (2)M, (1)D, (3)B, (1)W, (2)M, (2)L, (6)B, (2)A
Row 139&140 (R) (3)B, (1)D, (1)M, (2)D, (1)B, (2)M, (2)B, (2)M, (1)B, (1)M, (1)L, (1)B, (1)W, (2)B, (1)W, (2)A
Row 141&142 (R) (2)B, (4)D, (1)B, (2)M, (2)D, (3)B, (1)M, (2)L, (1)B, (1)W, (3)B, (2)A
Row 143&144 (R) (4)D, (1)B, (1)D, (2)M, (1)D, (2)B, (1)D, (1)B, (1)M, (3)L, (1)B, (2)W, (3)B, (1)A
Row 145&146 (R) (3)D, (1)B, (1)D, (2)M, (5)D, (1)L, (1)B, (2)M, (1)L, (6)B, (1)A
Row 147&148 (R) (2)D, (2)D, (1)M, (2)D, (1)B, (4)D, (1)L, (3)B, (1)L, (2)B, (1)W, (1)B, (1)W, (1)A
Row 149&150 (R) (1)D, (1)B, (2)D, (1)M, (2)D, (1)B, (3)D, (3)B, (1)L, (1)B, (1)M, (1)L, (1)B, (1)W, (2)B, (1)W, (1)A
Row 151&152 (R) (3)D, (1)M, (2)D, (1)B, (2)D, (2)B, (2)D, (2)L, (1)D, (1)B, (1)M, (1)L, (1)W, (3)B, (1)A
Row 153&154 (R) (1)B, (4)D, (1)B, (1)D, (2)B, (6)D, (2)L, (3)B, (1)W, (3)B
Row 155&156 (R) (4)D, (3)B, (2)D, (5)M, (2)L, (7)B, (1)A
Row 157&158 (R) (3)D, (2)B, (10)D, (5)B, (1)W, (1)B, (1)W, (1)A
Row 159&160 (R) (3)D, (1)B, (1)D, (3)M, (2)D, (5)B, (2)L, (2)B, (1)W, (2)B, (1)W, (1)A
Row 161&162 (R) (2)D, (1)B, (6)D, (2)B, (2)D, (1)M, (4)B, (5)B, (1)A
Row 163&164 (R) (1)D, (1)B, (2)D, (5)B, (2)D, (2)M, (5)L, (1)B, (1)W, (2)B, (2)A
Row 165&166 (R) (1)B, (2)D, (2)B, (4)D, (2)M, (1)D, (2)M, (1)L, (1)M, (1)L, (3)B, (1)W, (1)B, (2)A
Row 167&168 (R) (2)D, (1)B, (1)D, (5)M, (7)D, (6)B, (2)A
Row 169&170 (R) (1)D, (2)B, (6)D, (12)B, (3)A
Row 171&172 (R) (1)B, (3)D, (16)B, (1)W
Row 173&174 (R) (3)D, (13)B, (3)L, (2)B, (1)W, (1)B, (1)W
Row 175&176 (R) (1)W, (23)B
Row 177&178 (R) (9)B, (4)L, (2)B, (2)M, (1)B, (4)L, (1)B, (1)W
Row 179&180 (R) (7)B, (1)M, (1)L, (1)M, (1)L, (1)M, (11)B, (1)W
Row 181&182 (R) (5)B, (4)M, (1)B, (1)L, (1)M, (11)B, (1)W
Row 183&184 (R) (3)B, (4)M, (2)B, (2)M, (1)L, (2)M, (1)L, (1)M, (1)D, (2)M, (3)L, (2)B
Row 185&186 (R) (3)B, (1)M, (3)B, (2)L, (3)B, (1)L, (2)M, (1)L, (1)D, (1)M, (1)L, (1)B, (3)L, (1)B
Row 187&188 (R) (1)W, (3)B, (3)M, (2)B, (3)M, (7)B, (4)L, (1)B
Row 189&190 (R) (1)W, (1)B, (1)W, (7)M, (1)L, (4)M, (1)D, (2)M, (1)L, (2)B, (1)L, (2)B
Row 191&192 (R) (2)B, (1)W, (3)B, (3)M, (3)B, (6)L, (1)M, (4)L, (1)B
Row 193&194 (R) (3)B, (1)M, (6)B, (2)M, (7)B, (4)L, (1)B
Row 195&196 (R) (3)B, (2)M, (2)B, (1)M, (2)L, (2)B, (2)M, (2)L, (1)M, (1)L, (2)B, (2)L, (1)B, (1)W
Row 197&198 (R) (5)B, (1)M, (2)B, (2)L, (1)M, (1)L, (2)B, (1)D, (1)L, (1)M, (1)B, (2)L, (3)B, (1)W
Row 199&200 (R) (6)B, (1)M, (3)B, (1)L, (1)M, (1)L, (3)B, (3)L, (1)M, (2)L, (2)B
Row 201&202 (R) (6)B, (2)M, (1)L, (2)B, (1)L, (1)M, (1)L, (2)D, (2)B, (4)L, (1)B, (1)W
Row 203&204 (R) (7)B, (2)L, (1)M, (1)L, (1)B, (1)L, (1)M, (2)D, (2)L, (1)B, (2)L, (1)B, (2)W
Row 205&206 (R) (1)B, (1)W, (1)M, (5)B, (2)L, (1)M, (1)L, (1)B, (2)L, (1)B, (3)L, (3)B, (1)W, (1)B
Row 207&208 (R) (1)B, (1)W, (1)M, (1)B, (1)M, (4)B, (2)L, (1)M, (1)L, (1)B, (6)L, (4)B
Row 209&210 (R) (1)A, (1)B, (2)M, (1)B, (1)M, (1)B, (1)L, (2)B, (4)L, (2)B, (3)L, (2)B, (1)W, (2)B
Row 211&212 (R) (2)A, (1)B, (1)M, (1)B, (1)M, (2)B, (1)L, (2)B, (1)L, (1)M, (1)L, (1)B, (1)L, (2)B, (1)L, (1)B, (1)W, (2)B, (1)A
Row 213&214 (R) (3)A, (1)B, (1)M, (1)B, (1)M, (2)B, (1)L, (2)B, (1)L, (1)B, (3)L, (3)B, (1)W, (1)B, (2)A
Row 215&216 (R) (4)A, (1)B, (1)M, (3)B, (1)L, (1)B, (1)L, (1)B, (1)L, (1)D, (1)B, (1)W, (3)B, (3)A
Row 217&218 (R) (5)A, (8)B, (1)L, (1)D, (1)B, (1)W, (4)B, (3)A
Row 219&220 (R) (6)A, (8)B, (1)W, (4)B, (5)A
Row 221&222 (R) (7)A, (7)B, (1)W, (3)B, (6)A
Row 223&224 (R) (12)A, (3)B, (9)A

Penguin Colony

Penguins are very popular,
perhaps because they are so
cute, but also because they are
so interesting. They are hearty
animals that thrive in harsh
environments. This beaded colony of
king penguins with a single grey chick
on an Antarctic blue background
is a tribute to one of my favorite animals.

MATERIALS

- 11º Delica beads:
  - 5g (885) DB0266 opaque denim blue luster (color A)
  - 6g (1017) DB0010 black (color B)
  - 4g (670) DB0351 black (color W)
  - 1g (55) DB0761 matte opaque gray (color G)
  - 1g (61) DB0351 matte opaque canary (color Y)
- **2** 8mm black Swarovski crystal rounds
- Fireline, 4-lb. or 6-lb. test

TOOLS

- #10 or #12 beading needle
- Thread cutters or scissors

MEASUREMENTS

1½ in. wide and 6¾ in. long

To shorten, leave off the end rows that are just the background color; to lengthen, add rows of the background color or lengthen the toggle tails.

Instructions

1 Refer to the *Penguin Colony* two-drop pattern and word chart on pages 36 and 37. Follow the instructions for Fast Peyote (Techniques, p. 94) to create the peyote band. Add thread (Techniques, p. 97) as needed throughout the project.

Create the loops for the closure

2 *The closure for this project consists of two simple loops and two 8mm crystal rounds.* Reinforce the end of the bracelet (Techniques, p. 96, step 11). Exit at the location on the pattern marked by a black dot that is closest to the edge just exited.

3 *Pick up 20 color A beads and sew into the piece at the next black dot. Exit the piece at the following black dot and repeat from * to create two loops across the end of the bracelet.

4 Weave back through each loop to reinforce, then sew into the base of the piece using finishing knots to secure (Techniques, p. 97). Trim the thread and weave into the piece.

5 Remove the stop bead and add thread to the original tail at the opposite end of the piece. Weave into the piece, tucking the knot into a bead. Reinforce the end of the bracelet.

Add the crystal rounds

6 Exit at one of the two black dots. *Pick up three As, a crystal round, and an A. Sew back through the crystal round, the A, and then back into the piece.

7 Exit at the next black dot marked on the pattern. Repeat step 6 from *.

8 Weave back into the piece and reinforce using finishing knots to secure, then trim the thread, and weave into the piece.

Penguin Colony
two-drop peyote

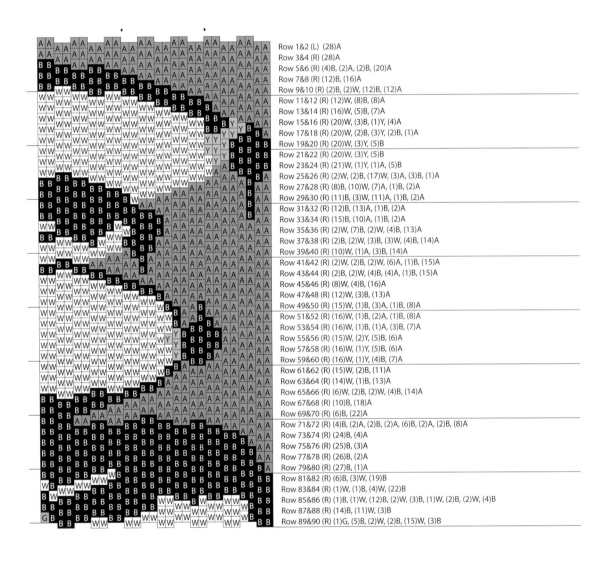

Row 1&2 (L) (28)A
Row 3&4 (R) (28)A
Row 5&6 (R) (4)B, (2)A, (2)B, (20)A
Row 7&8 (R) (12)B, (16)A
Row 9&10 (R) (2)B, (2)W, (12)B, (12)A
Row 11&12 (R) (12)W, (8)B, (8)A
Row 13&14 (R) (16)W, (5)B, (7)A
Row 15&16 (R) (20)W, (3)B, (1)Y, (4)A
Row 17&18 (R) (20)W, (2)B, (3)Y, (2)B, (1)A
Row 19&20 (R) (20)W, (3)Y, (5)B
Row 21&22 (R) (20)W, (3)Y, (5)B
Row 23&24 (R) (21)W, (1)Y, (1)A, (5)B
Row 25&26 (R) (2)W, (2)B, (17)W, (3)A, (3)B, (1)A
Row 27&28 (R) (8)B, (10)W, (7)A, (1)B, (2)A
Row 29&30 (R) (11)B, (3)W, (11)A, (1)B, (2)A
Row 31&32 (R) (12)B, (13)A, (1)B, (2)A
Row 33&34 (R) (15)B, (10)A, (1)B, (2)A
Row 35&36 (R) (2)W, (7)B, (2)W, (4)B, (13)A
Row 37&38 (R) (2)B, (2)W, (3)B, (3)W, (4)B, (14)A
Row 39&40 (R) (10)W, (1)A, (3)B, (14)A
Row 41&42 (R) (2)W, (2)B, (2)W, (6)A, (1)B, (15)A
Row 43&44 (R) (2)B, (2)W, (4)B, (4)A, (1)B, (15)A
Row 45&46 (R) (8)W, (4)B, (16)A
Row 47&48 (R) (12)W, (3)B, (13)A
Row 49&50 (R) (15)W, (1)B, (3)A, (1)B, (8)A
Row 51&52 (R) (16)W, (1)B, (2)A, (1)B, (8)A
Row 53&54 (R) (16)W, (1)B, (1)A, (3)B, (7)A
Row 55&56 (R) (15)W, (2)Y, (5)B, (6)A
Row 57&58 (R) (16)W, (1)Y, (5)B, (6)A
Row 59&60 (R) (16)W, (1)Y, (4)B, (7)A
Row 61&62 (R) (15)W, (2)B, (11)A
Row 63&64 (R) (14)W, (1)B, (13)A
Row 65&66 (R) (6)W, (2)B, (2)W, (4)B, (14)A
Row 67&68 (R) (10)B, (18)A
Row 69&70 (R) (6)B, (22)A
Row 71&72 (R) (4)B, (2)A, (2)B, (2)A, (6)B, (2)A, (2)B, (8)A
Row 73&74 (R) (24)B, (4)A
Row 75&76 (R) (25)B, (3)A
Row 77&78 (R) (26)B, (2)A
Row 79&80 (R) (27)B, (1)A
Row 81&82 (R) (6)B, (3)W, (19)B
Row 83&84 (R) (1)W, (1)B, (4)W, (22)B
Row 85&86 (R) (1)B, (1)W, (12)B, (2)W, (3)B, (1)W, (2)B, (2)W, (4)B
Row 87&88 (R) (14)B, (11)W, (3)B
Row 89&90 (R) (1)G, (5)B, (2)W, (2)B, (15)W, (3)B

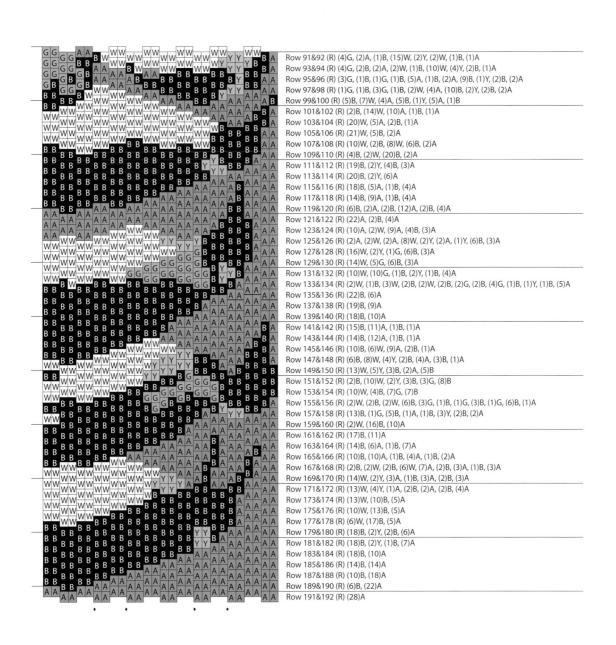

Row 91&92 (R) (4)G, (2)A, (1)B, (15)W, (2)Y, (2)W, (1)B, (1)A
Row 93&94 (R) (4)G, (2)B, (2)A, (2)W, (1)B, (10)W, (4)Y, (2)B, (1)A
Row 95&96 (R) (3)G, (1)B, (1)G, (1)B, (5)A, (1)B, (2)A, (9)B, (1)Y, (2)B, (2)A
Row 97&98 (R) (1)G, (1)B, (3)G, (1)B, (2)W, (4)A, (10)B, (2)Y, (2)B, (2)A
Row 99&100 (R) (5)B, (7)W, (4)A, (5)B, (1)Y, (5)A, (1)B
Row 101&102 (R) (2)B, (14)W, (10)A, (1)B, (1)A
Row 103&104 (R) (20)W, (5)A, (2)B, (1)A
Row 105&106 (R) (21)W, (5)B, (2)A
Row 107&108 (R) (10)W, (2)B, (8)W, (6)B, (2)A
Row 109&110 (R) (4)B, (2)W, (20)B, (2)A
Row 111&112 (R) (19)B, (2)Y, (4)B, (3)A
Row 113&114 (R) (20)B, (2)Y, (6)A
Row 115&116 (R) (18)B, (5)A, (1)B, (4)A
Row 117&118 (R) (14)B, (9)A, (1)B, (4)A
Row 119&120 (R) (6)B, (2)A, (2)B, (12)A, (2)B, (4)A
Row 121&122 (R) (22)A, (2)B, (4)A
Row 123&124 (R) (10)A, (2)W, (9)A, (4)B, (3)A
Row 125&126 (R) (2)A, (2)W, (2)A, (8)W, (2)Y, (2)A, (1)Y, (6)B, (3)A
Row 127&128 (R) (16)W, (2)Y, (1)G, (6)B, (3)A
Row 129&130 (R) (14)W, (5)G, (6)B, (3)A
Row 131&132 (R) (10)W, (10)G, (1)B, (2)Y, (1)B, (4)A
Row 133&134 (R) (2)W, (1)B, (3)W, (2)B, (2)W, (2)B, (2)G, (2)B, (4)G, (1)B, (1)Y, (1)B, (5)A
Row 135&136 (R) (22)B, (6)A
Row 137&138 (R) (19)B, (9)A
Row 139&140 (R) (18)B, (10)A
Row 141&142 (R) (15)B, (11)A, (1)B, (1)A
Row 143&144 (R) (14)B, (12)A, (1)B, (1)A
Row 145&146 (R) (10)B, (6)W, (9)A, (2)B, (1)A
Row 147&148 (R) (6)B, (8)W, (4)Y, (2)B, (4)A, (3)B, (1)A
Row 149&150 (R) (13)W, (5)Y, (3)B, (2)A, (5)B
Row 151&152 (R) (2)B, (10)W, (2)Y, (3)B, (3)G, (8)B
Row 153&154 (R) (10)W, (4)B, (7)G, (7)B
Row 155&156 (R) (2)W, (2)B, (2)W, (6)B, (3)G, (1)B, (1)G, (3)B, (1)G, (6)B, (1)A
Row 157&158 (R) (13)B, (1)G, (5)B, (1)A, (1)B, (3)Y, (2)B, (2)A
Row 159&160 (R) (2)W, (16)B, (10)A
Row 161&162 (R) (17)B, (11)A
Row 163&164 (R) (14)B, (6)A, (1)B, (7)A
Row 165&166 (R) (10)B, (10)A, (1)B, (4)A, (1)B, (2)A
Row 167&168 (R) (2)B, (2)W, (2)B, (6)W, (7)A, (2)B, (3)A, (1)B, (3)A
Row 169&170 (R) (14)W, (2)Y, (3)A, (1)B, (3)A, (2)B, (3)A
Row 171&172 (R) (13)W, (4)Y, (1)A, (2)B, (2)A, (2)B, (4)A
Row 173&174 (R) (13)W, (10)B, (5)A
Row 175&176 (R) (10)W, (13)B, (5)A
Row 177&178 (R) (6)W, (17)B, (5)A
Row 179&180 (R) (18)B, (2)Y, (2)B, (6)A
Row 181&182 (R) (18)B, (2)Y, (1)B, (7)A
Row 183&184 (R) (18)B, (10)A
Row 185&186 (R) (14)B, (14)A
Row 187&188 (R) (10)B, (18)A
Row 189&190 (R) (6)B, (22)A
Row 191&192 (R) (28)A

Hummingbird Dance

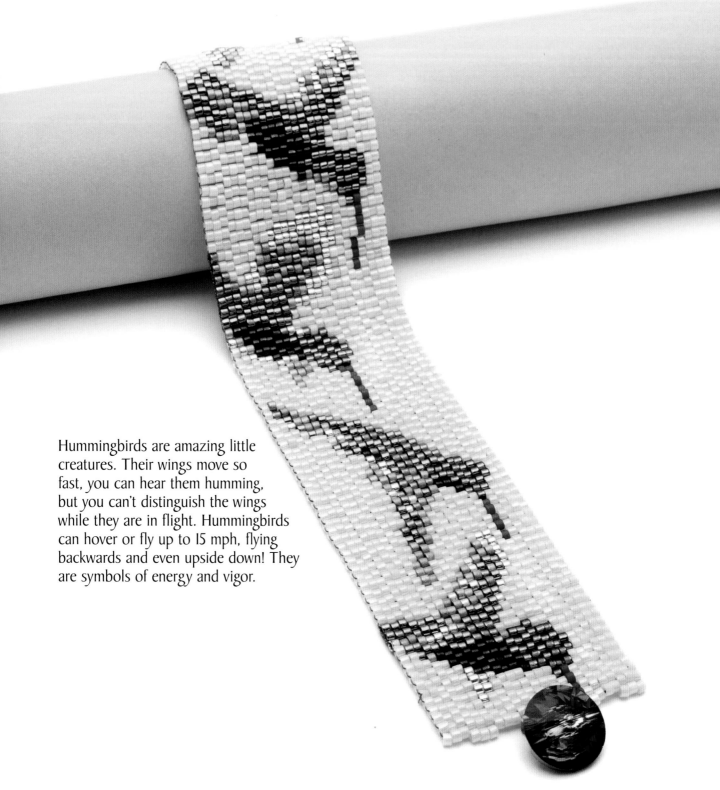

Hummingbirds are amazing little creatures. Their wings move so fast, you can hear them humming, but you can't distinguish the wings while they are in flight. Hummingbirds can hover or fly up to 15 mph, flying backwards and even upside down! They are symbols of energy and vigor.

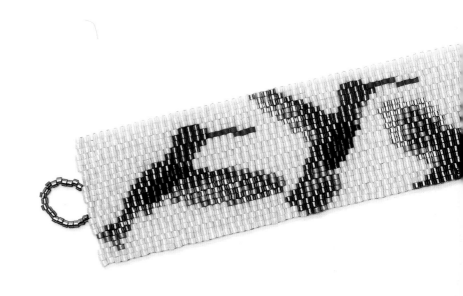

MATERIALS

- 11º Delica beads:
  - 9g (1683) DB0211 opaque alabaster luster (color A)
  - 2g (309) DB0021 nickel-plated (color B)
  - 1g (180) DB0180 galvanized pewter (color C)
  - 1g (138) DB0035 metallic silver (color D)
  - 1g (93) DB0609 silver-lined dark purple (color E)
  - 1g (132) DB0608 silver-lined blue zircon (color F)
  - 1g (33) DB0796 matte opaque maroon (color G)
- 12mm volcano Swarovski crystal rivoli button
- Fireline, 4-lb. or 6-lb. test

TOOLS

- #10 or #12 beading needle
- Thread cutters or scissors

MEASUREMENTS

1¼ in. wide and 7½ in. long

To lengthen, rows of the background color can be added at either end or the toggle tail can be lengthened. To shorten, rows can be removed from the loop end (from the last bird's tai).

Instructions

1 Refer to the *Hummingbird Dance* three-drop pattern and word chart on pages 40 and 41. Follow the instructions for Fast Peyote (Techniques, p. 94) to create the peyote band. Add thread (Techniques, p. 97) as needed throughout the project.

Create the loop for the closure

2 *The closure for this project consists of a simple loop and a 12mm Swarovski rivoli button.* Reinforce the end of the bracelet (Techniques, p. 96, step 11). Exit at the location on the pattern marked by one of two black dots.

3 Pick up 20 color F beads and sew into the piece at the next black dot. Secure the end of the loop at the remaining black dot marked on the pattern. Weave back through the loop.

4 Reinforce along the base using finishing knots to secure (Techniques, p. 97), then trim the thread and weave into the piece.

5 Remove the stop bead and add thread to the original tail at the opposite end of the piece. Weave into the piece, tucking the knot into a bead. Reinforce the end of the bracelet.

Add the rivoli button

6 Exit at the black dot marked on the pattern. Follow the instructions to add a button (Techniques, p. 101) using five color D beads, the rivoli button, and five Ds. Sew into the tail, through the button, and through the beads to reinforce.

7 Weave back into the piece and reinforce using finishing knots to secure, then trim the thread, and weave into the piece.

Hummingbird Dance
three-drop peyote

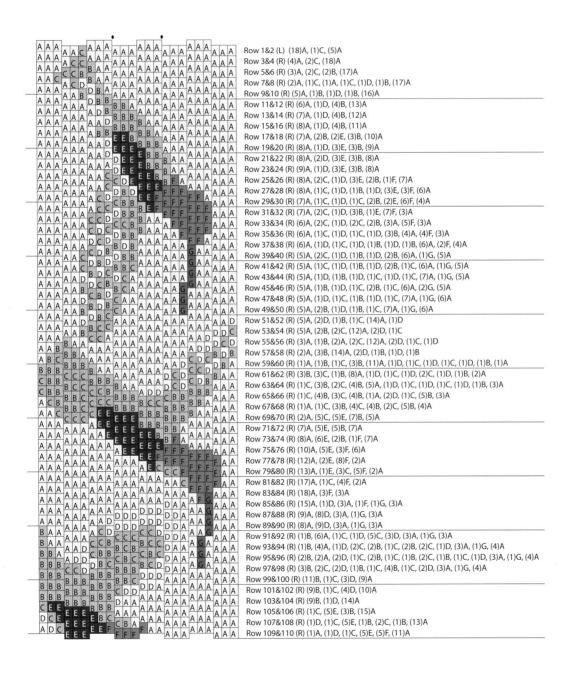

Row 1&2 (L) (18)A, (1)C, (5)A
Row 3&4 (R) (4)A, (2)C, (18)A
Row 5&6 (R) (3)A, (2)C, (2)B, (17)A
Row 7&8 (R) (2)A, (1)C, (1)A, (1)C, (1)D, (1)B, (17)A
Row 9&10 (R) (5)A, (1)B, (1)D, (1)B, (16)A
Row 11&12 (R) (6)A, (1)D, (4)B, (13)A
Row 13&14 (R) (7)A, (1)D, (4)B, (12)A
Row 15&16 (R) (8)A, (1)D, (4)B, (11)A
Row 17&18 (R) (7)A, (2)B, (2)E, (3)B, (10)A
Row 19&20 (R) (8)A, (1)D, (3)E, (3)B, (9)A
Row 21&22 (R) (8)A, (2)D, (3)E, (3)B, (8)A
Row 23&24 (R) (9)A, (1)D, (3)E, (3)B, (8)A
Row 25&26 (R) (8)A, (2)C, (1)D, (3)E, (2)B, (1)F, (7)A
Row 27&28 (R) (8)A, (1)C, (1)D, (1)B, (1)D, (3)E, (3)F, (6)A
Row 29&30 (R) (7)A, (1)C, (1)D, (1)C, (2)B, (2)E, (6)F, (4)A
Row 31&32 (R) (7)A, (2)C, (1)D, (3)B, (1)E, (7)F, (3)A
Row 33&34 (R) (6)A, (2)C, (1)D, (2)C, (2)B, (3)A, (5)F, (3)A
Row 35&36 (R) (6)A, (1)C, (1)D, (1)C, (1)D, (3)B, (4)A, (4)F, (3)A
Row 37&38 (R) (6)A, (1)D, (1)C, (1)D, (1)B, (1)D, (1)B, (6)A, (2)F, (4)A
Row 39&40 (R) (5)A, (2)C, (1)D, (1)B, (1)D, (2)B, (6)A, (1)G, (5)A
Row 41&42 (R) (5)A, (1)C, (1)D, (1)B, (1)D, (2)B, (1)C, (6)A, (1)G, (5)A
Row 43&44 (R) (5)A, (1)D, (1)B, (1)D, (1)C, (1)D, (1)C, (7)A, (1)G, (5)A
Row 45&46 (R) (5)A, (1)B, (1)D, (1)C, (2)B, (1)C, (6)A, (2)G, (5)A
Row 47&48 (R) (5)A, (1)D, (1)C, (1)B, (1)D, (1)C, (7)A, (1)G, (6)A
Row 49&50 (R) (5)A, (2)B, (1)D, (1)B, (1)C, (7)A, (1)G, (6)A
Row 51&52 (R) (5)A, (2)D, (1)B, (1)C, (14)A, (1)D
Row 53&54 (R) (5)A, (2)B, (2)C, (12)A, (2)D, (1)C
Row 55&56 (R) (3)A, (1)B, (2)A, (2)C, (12)A, (2)D, (1)C, (1)D
Row 57&58 (R) (2)A, (3)B, (14)A, (2)D, (1)B, (1)D, (1)B
Row 59&60 (R) (1)A, (1)B, (1)C, (3)B, (11)A, (1)D, (1)C, (1)D, (1)C, (1)D, (1)B, (1)A
Row 61&62 (R) (3)B, (3)C, (1)B, (8)A, (1)D, (1)C, (1)D, (2)C, (1)D, (1)B, (2)A
Row 63&64 (R) (1)C, (3)B, (2)C, (4)B, (5)A, (1)D, (1)C, (1)D, (1)C, (1)D, (1)B, (3)A
Row 65&66 (R) (1)C, (4)B, (3)C, (4)B, (1)A, (2)D, (1)C, (5)B, (3)A
Row 67&68 (R) (1)A, (1)C, (3)B, (4)C, (4)B, (2)C, (5)B, (4)A
Row 69&70 (R) (2)A, (5)C, (5)E, (7)B, (5)A
Row 71&72 (R) (7)A, (5)E, (5)B, (7)A
Row 73&74 (R) (8)A, (6)E, (2)B, (1)F, (7)A
Row 75&76 (R) (10)A, (5)E, (3)F, (6)A
Row 77&78 (R) (12)A, (2)E, (8)F, (2)A
Row 79&80 (R) (13)A, (1)E, (3)C, (5)F, (2)A
Row 81&82 (R) (17)A, (1)C, (4)F, (2)A
Row 83&84 (R) (18)A, (3)F, (3)A
Row 85&86 (R) (15)A, (1)D, (3)A, (1)F, (1)G, (3)A
Row 87&88 (R) (9)A, (8)D, (3)A, (1)G, (3)A
Row 89&90 (R) (8)A, (9)D, (3)A, (1)G, (3)A
Row 91&92 (R) (1)B, (6)A, (1)C, (1)D, (5)C, (3)D, (3)A, (1)G, (3)A
Row 93&94 (R) (1)B, (4)A, (1)D, (2)C, (2)B, (1)C, (2)B, (2)C, (1)D, (3)A, (1)G, (4)A
Row 95&96 (R) (2)B, (2)A, (2)D, (1)C, (2)B, (1)C, (1)B, (2)C, (1)B, (1)C, (1)D, (3)A, (1)G, (4)A
Row 97&98 (R) (3)B, (2)C, (2)D, (1)B, (1)C, (4)B, (1)C, (2)D, (3)A, (1)G, (4)A
Row 99&100 (R) (11)B, (1)C, (3)D, (9)A
Row 101&102 (R) (9)B, (1)C, (4)D, (10)A
Row 103&104 (R) (9)B, (1)D, (14)A
Row 105&106 (R) (1)C, (5)E, (3)B, (15)A
Row 107&108 (R) (1)D, (1)C, (5)E, (1)B, (2)C, (1)B, (13)A
Row 109&110 (R) (1)A, (1)D, (1)C, (5)E, (5)F, (11)A

Row 111&112 (R) (2)A, (3)D, (4)E, (5)F, (10)A
Row 113&114 (R) (5)A, (3)D, (1)E, (6)F, (9)A
Row 115&116 (R) (6)A, (3)C, (1)A, (5)F, (9)A
Row 117&118 (R) (6)A, (3)C, (2)A, (3)F, (10)A
Row 119&120 (R) (6)A, (2)C, (4)A, (2)G, (10)A
Row 121&122 (R) (6)A, (1)C, (6)A, (1)G, (10)A
Row 123&124 (R) (13)A, (1)G, (10)A
Row 125&126 (R) (1)A, (1)C, (11)A, (1)G, (10)A
Row 127&128 (R) (1)A, (1)B, (2)C, (9)A, (1)G, (10)A
Row 129&130 (R) (2)A, (1)B, (2)C, (1)B, (7)A, (1)G, (10)A
Row 131&132 (R) (2)A, (1)D, (1)B, (2)C, (2)B, (5)A, (1)G, (10)A
Row 133&134 (R) (4)A, (1)B, (2)C, (4)B, (13)A
Row 135&136 (R) (6)A, (1)D, (1)C, (4)B, (12)A
Row 137&138 (R) (7)A, (1)D, (5)B, (11)A
Row 139&140 (R) (6)A, (9)B, (9)A
Row 141&142 (R) (7)A, (2)B, (1)E, (6)B, (8)A
Row 143&144 (R) (9)A, (1)D, (1)E, (6)B, (7)A
Row 145&146 (R) (9)A, (1)C, (1)D, (7)B, (6)A
Row 147&148 (R) (8)A, (2)C, (1)D, (7)B, (6)A
Row 149&150 (R) (8)A, (3)C, (2)B, (1)C, (1)B, (5)F, (4)A
Row 151&152 (R) (9)A, (1)C, (1)D, (1)B, (1)C, (1)B, (1)C, (7)F, (2)A
Row 153&154 (R) (9)A, (1)D, (1)B, (1)B, (1)C, (1)B, (2)E, (5)F, (2)A
Row 155&156 (R) (9)A, (1)C, (1)B, (1)D, (1)C, (1)B, (1)C, (2)A, (1)E, (3)F, (3)A
Row 157&158 (R) (9)A, (1)B, (1)D, (1)B, (2)C, (4)A, (3)F, (3)A
Row 159&160 (R) (9)A, (2)B, (2)C, (6)A, (1)F, (4)A
Row 161&162 (R) (9)A, (2)B, (1)C, (7)A, (1)G, (4)A
Row 163&164 (R) (8)A, (2)B, (1)C, (8)A, (1)G, (4)A
Row 165&166 (R) (8)A, (2)B, (1)C, (8)A, (1)G, (4)A
Row 167&168 (R) (8)A, (2)C, (6)A, (2)D, (1)A, (1)G, (4)A
Row 169&170 (R) (8)A, (2)C, (5)A, (1)C, (2)D, (1)A, (1)G, (4)A
Row 171&172 (R) (7)A, (2)C, (5)A, (3)C, (1)D, (6)A
Row 173&174 (R) (7)A, (2)C, (4)A, (1)D, (1)C, (2)B, (1)D, (6)A
Row 175&176 (R) (7)A, (2)C, (2)A, (2)C, (1)D, (1)B, (1)C, (1)B, (1)D, (6)A
Row 177&178 (R) (10)A, (1)C, (1)D, (2)C, (2)B, (1)D, (7)A
Row 179&180 (R) (9)A, (1)D, (2)C, (1)D, (1)B, (1)C, (1)D, (8)A
Row 181&182 (R) (8)A, (2)C, (1)D, (2)C, (2)B, (9)A
Row 183&184 (R) (6)B, (1)A, (3)C, (4)B, (1)D, (9)A
Row 185&186 (R) (7)B, (2)C, (5)B, (10)A
Row 187&188 (R) (1)D, (3)C, (4)D, (5)B, (11)A
Row 189&190 (R) (1)A, (11)B, (3)A, (1)F, (8)A
Row 191&192 (R) (2)A, (1)B, (1)C, (2)E, (3)B, (2)E, (1)B, (1)C, (5)F, (6)A
Row 193&194 (R) (5)A, (7)E, (6)F, (6)A
Row 195&196 (R) (6)A, (6)E, (7)F, (5)A
Row 197&198 (R) (6)A, (1)D, (6)E, (6)F, (5)A
Row 199&200 (R) (6)A, (3)D, (3)A, (1)E, (5)F, (6)A
Row 201&202 (R) (6)A, (2)D, (7)A, (1)F, (1)G, (7)A
Row 203&204 (R) (6)A, (1)D, (9)A, (1)G, (7)A
Row 205&206 (R) (16)A, (1)G, (7)A
Row 207&208 (R) (16)A, (1)G, (7)A
Row 209&210 (R) (16)A, (1)G, (7)A
Row 211&212 (R) (16)A, (1)G, (7)A
Row 213&214 (R) (24)A

Safari Nights

This wild, abstract print in copper and
green brings to mind a lush jungle or rain
forest. Whip up the quick Safari Nights
earrings to complete the set.

MATERIALS

- 11º Delica beads:
  7g (1267) DB0040 metallic bright copper plated (color C)
  6g (1037) DB1786 white-lined light green AB (color G)
- **3** Swarovski crystal copper 8x6mm faceted rondelles
- **58** Swarovski crystal copper 4mm bicones
- **2g** 15º Miyuki color-lined fancy rose gold rocaille seed beads
- Fireline, 4-lb. or 6-lb. test

EARRING MATERIALS

- 11º Delica beads:
  1g (160) (color A)
  1g (178) (color B)
- **4** 4x3mm Swarovski crystal copper faceted rondelles
- **2** 2½ in. 26- or 28-gauge bright copper head pins
- **2** 11mm copper earring wires with front loop

TOOLS

- #10 or #12 beading needle
- Thread cutters or scissors

MEASUREMENTS

1¼ in. wide and 6¾ in. long

To shorten the pattern, leave off as many rows as necessary. To lengthen, the toggle tail can be made longer.

Bracelet Instructions

1 Refer to the *Safari Nights* three-drop pattern and word chart on pages 44 and 45. Follow the instructions for Fast Peyote (Techniques, p. 94) to create the peyote band. Add thread (Techniques, p. 97) as needed throughout the project.

Create loops for the closure

2 *The closure for this project consists of a flat peyote loop and a cluster of three 8x6mm Swarovski rondelle beads.* Reinforce the end of the bracelet (Techniques, p. 96, step 11). Exit at the location on the pattern marked by a black dot.

3 Follow the instructions to create a flat peyote loop (Techniques, p. 98) using 17 rows of color G beads. Secure the other end of the loop at the next location marked by a black dot. Sew back into the loop. Reinforce the base using finishing knots to secure (Techniques, p. 97).

4 Weave back into the piece using finishing knots to secure, trim the thread, and tuck into the piece.

Add toggle tail and beads

5 Remove the stop bead and add thread to the original tail at the opposite end of the piece. Weave into the piece, tucking the knot into a bead. Reinforce the end of the bracelet.

6 Exit at the black dot. Pick up 10 rose gold 15º seed beads (or color C beads), a rondelle, and a seed bead. Sew back into the rondelle and the tail (making the seed bead an anchor). Weave back into the piece using finishing knots to secure.

7 *Sew back into the tail and through five of the seed beads. Add four seed beads, a rondelle, and a seed bead. Sew back into

the tail and then through the end of the bracelet. Repeat from * for the last rondelle. Weave back into the base using finishing knots to secure, then trim the thread, and tuck into the piece.

Add the trim

8 Exit the piece at the end and along the edge. Follow the instructions for picot trim (Techniques, p. 104), using a 15º seed bead on either side of a 4mm Swarovski bicone. When the trim is complete along both edges, weave through the piece using finishing knots to secure, then trim the thread, and tuck into the piece.

Earring Instructions

1 Refer to the *Safari Nights Earrings* two-drop pattern and word chart on page 45. Follow the instructions for Fast Peyote (Techniques, p. 94) to create the peyote band. Add thread (Techniques, p. 97) as needed throughout the project.

2 Zip up the band to create a peyote tube (Techniques, p. 103). Weave back through the tube using finishing knots to secure, then trim the thread, and tuck into the piece

3. Repeat steps 1 and 2 to create a second peyote tube.

4 String a rondelle, a peyote tube, and another rondelle on a headpin. Follow the instructions (Techniques, p. 109) to make a wrapped-wire loop. Repeat to make the second earring.

5 Hook an earring wire to each loop. Slightly twist open the loop of the wire with pliers (Techniques, p. 109). Thread the open loop through the loop of the peyote tube earring. Gently close the loop.

Safari Nights
three-drop peyote

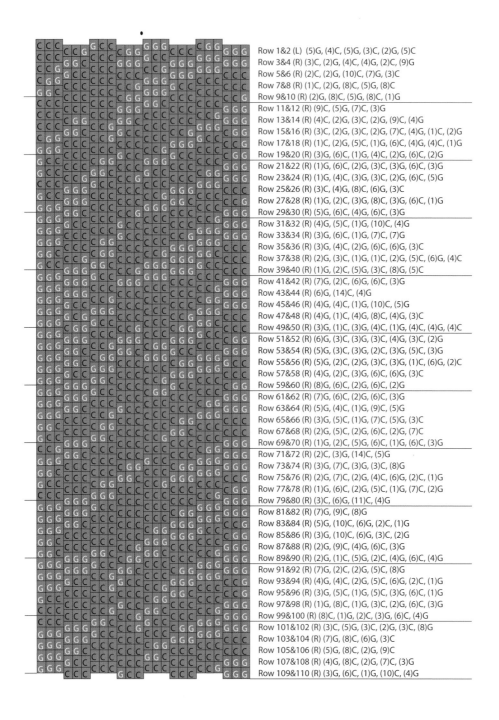

Row 1&2 (L) (5)G, (4)C, (5)G, (3)C, (2)G, (5)C
Row 3&4 (R) (3)C, (2)G, (4)C, (4)G, (2)C, (9)G
Row 5&6 (R) (2)C, (2)G, (10)C, (7)G, (3)C
Row 7&8 (R) (1)C, (2)G, (8)C, (5)G, (8)C
Row 9&10 (R) (2)G, (8)C, (5)G, (8)C, (1)G
Row 11&12 (R) (9)C, (5)G, (7)C, (3)G
Row 13&14 (R) (4)C, (2)G, (3)C, (2)G, (9)C, (4)G
Row 15&16 (R) (3)C, (2)G, (3)C, (2)G, (7)C, (4)G, (1)C, (2)G
Row 17&18 (R) (1)C, (2)G, (5)C, (1)G, (6)C, (4)G, (4)C, (1)G
Row 19&20 (R) (3)G, (6)C, (1)G, (4)C, (2)G, (6)C, (2)G
Row 21&22 (R) (1)G, (6)C, (2)G, (3)C, (3)G, (6)C, (3)G
Row 23&24 (R) (1)G, (4)C, (3)G, (3)C, (2)G, (6)C, (5)G
Row 25&26 (R) (3)C, (4)G, (8)C, (6)G, (3)C
Row 27&28 (R) (1)G, (2)C, (3)G, (8)C, (3)G, (6)C, (1)G
Row 29&30 (R) (5)G, (6)C, (4)G, (6)C, (3)G
Row 31&32 (R) (4)G, (5)C, (1)G, (10)C, (4)G
Row 33&34 (R) (3)G, (6)C, (1)G, (7)C, (7)G
Row 35&36 (R) (3)G, (4)C, (2)G, (6)C, (6)G, (3)C
Row 37&38 (R) (2)G, (3)C, (1)G, (1)C, (2)G, (5)C, (6)G, (4)C
Row 39&40 (R) (1)G, (2)C, (5)G, (3)C, (8)G, (5)C
Row 41&42 (R) (7)G, (2)C, (6)G, (6)C, (3)G
Row 43&44 (R) (6)G, (14)C, (4)G
Row 45&46 (R) (4)G, (4)C, (1)G, (10)C, (5)G
Row 47&48 (R) (4)G, (1)C, (4)G, (8)C, (4)G, (3)C
Row 49&50 (R) (3)G, (1)C, (3)G, (4)C, (1)G, (4)C, (4)G, (4)C
Row 51&52 (R) (6)G, (3)C, (3)G, (3)C, (4)G, (3)C, (2)G
Row 53&54 (R) (5)G, (3)C, (3)G, (2)C, (3)G, (5)C, (3)G
Row 55&56 (R) (5)G, (2)C, (2)G, (3)C, (3)G, (1)C, (6)G, (2)C
Row 57&58 (R) (4)G, (2)C, (3)G, (6)C, (6)G, (3)C
Row 59&60 (R) (8)G, (6)C, (2)G, (6)C, (2)G
Row 61&62 (R) (7)G, (6)C, (2)G, (6)C, (3)G
Row 63&64 (R) (5)G, (4)C, (1)G, (9)C, (5)G
Row 65&66 (R) (3)G, (5)C, (1)G, (7)C, (5)G, (3)C
Row 67&68 (R) (2)G, (5)C, (2)G, (6)C, (2)G, (7)C
Row 69&70 (R) (1)G, (2)C, (5)G, (6)C, (1)G, (6)C, (3)G
Row 71&72 (R) (2)C, (3)G, (14)C, (5)G
Row 73&74 (R) (3)G, (7)C, (3)G, (3)C, (8)G
Row 75&76 (R) (2)G, (7)C, (2)G, (4)C, (6)G, (2)C, (1)G
Row 77&78 (R) (1)G, (6)C, (2)G, (5)C, (1)G, (7)C, (2)G
Row 79&80 (R) (3)C, (6)G, (11)C, (4)G
Row 81&82 (R) (7)G, (9)C, (8)G
Row 83&84 (R) (5)G, (10)C, (6)G, (2)C, (1)G
Row 85&86 (R) (3)G, (10)C, (6)G, (3)C, (2)G
Row 87&88 (R) (2)G, (9)C, (4)G, (6)C, (3)G
Row 89&90 (R) (2)G, (1)C, (5)G, (2)C, (4)G, (6)C, (4)G
Row 91&92 (R) (7)G, (2)C, (2)G, (5)C, (8)G
Row 93&94 (R) (4)G, (4)C, (2)G, (5)C, (6)G, (2)C, (1)G
Row 95&96 (R) (3)G, (5)C, (1)G, (5)C, (3)G, (6)C, (1)G
Row 97&98 (R) (1)G, (8)C, (1)G, (3)C, (2)G, (6)C, (3)G
Row 99&100 (R) (8)C, (1)G, (2)C, (3)G, (6)C, (4)G
Row 101&102 (R) (3)C, (5)G, (3)C, (2)G, (3)C, (8)G
Row 103&104 (R) (7)G, (8)C, (6)G, (3)C
Row 105&106 (R) (5)G, (8)C, (2)G, (9)C
Row 107&108 (R) (4)G, (8)C, (2)G, (7)C, (3)G
Row 109&110 (R) (3)G, (6)C, (1)G, (10)C, (4)G

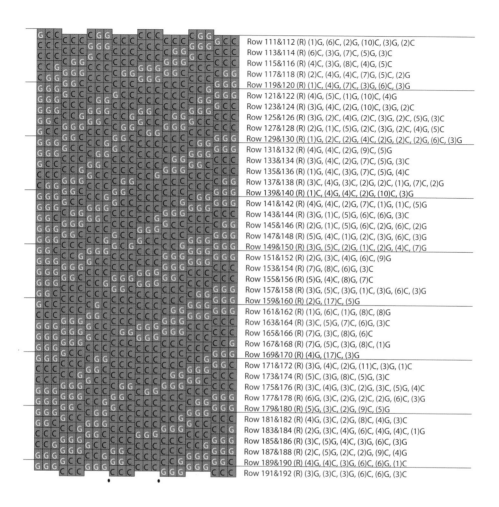

Row 111&112 (R) (1)G, (6)C, (2)G, (10)C, (3)G, (2)C
Row 113&114 (R) (6)C, (3)G, (7)C, (5)G, (3)C
Row 115&116 (R) (4)C, (3)G, (8)C, (4)G, (5)C
Row 117&118 (R) (2)C, (4)G, (4)C, (7)G, (5)C, (2)G
Row 119&120 (R) (1)C, (4)G, (7)C, (3)G, (6)C, (3)G
Row 121&122 (R) (4)G, (5)C, (1)G, (10)C, (4)G
Row 123&124 (R) (3)G, (4)C, (2)G, (10)C, (3)G, (2)C
Row 125&126 (R) (3)G, (2)C, (4)G, (2)C, (3)G, (2)C, (5)G, (3)C
Row 127&128 (R) (2)G, (1)C, (5)G, (2)C, (3)G, (2)C, (4)G, (5)C
Row 129&130 (R) (1)G, (2)C, (2)G, (4)C, (2)G, (2)C, (2)G, (6)C, (3)G
Row 131&132 (R) (4)G, (4)C, (2)G, (9)C, (5)G
Row 133&134 (R) (3)G, (4)C, (2)G, (7)C, (5)G, (3)C
Row 135&136 (R) (1)G, (4)C, (3)G, (7)C, (5)G, (4)C
Row 137&138 (R) (3)C, (4)G, (3)C, (2)G, (2)C, (1)G, (7)C, (2)G
Row 139&140 (R) (1)C, (4)G, (4)C, (2)G, (10)C, (3)G
Row 141&142 (R) (4)G, (4)C, (2)G, (7)C, (1)G, (1)C, (5)G
Row 143&144 (R) (3)G, (1)C, (5)G, (6)C, (6)G, (3)C
Row 145&146 (R) (2)G, (1)C, (5)G, (6)C, (2)G, (6)C, (2)G
Row 147&148 (R) (5)G, (4)C, (1)G, (2)C, (3)G, (6)C, (3)G
Row 149&150 (R) (3)G, (5)C, (2)G, (1)C, (2)G, (4)C, (7)G
Row 151&152 (R) (2)G, (3)C, (4)G, (6)C, (9)G
Row 153&154 (R) (7)G, (8)C, (6)G, (3)C
Row 155&156 (R) (5)G, (4)C, (8)G, (7)C
Row 157&158 (R) (3)G, (5)C, (3)G, (1)C, (3)G, (6)C, (3)G
Row 159&160 (R) (2)G, (17)C, (5)G
Row 161&162 (R) (1)G, (6)C, (1)G, (8)C, (8)G
Row 163&164 (R) (3)C, (5)G, (7)C, (6)G, (3)C
Row 165&166 (R) (7)G, (3)C, (8)G, (6)C
Row 167&168 (R) (7)G, (5)C, (3)G, (8)C, (1)G
Row 169&170 (R) (4)G, (17)C, (3)G
Row 171&172 (R) (3)G, (4)C, (2)G, (11)C, (3)G, (1)C
Row 173&174 (R) (5)C, (3)G, (8)C, (5)G, (3)C
Row 175&176 (R) (3)C, (4)G, (3)C, (2)G, (3)C, (5)G, (4)C
Row 177&178 (R) (6)C, (3)C, (2)G, (2)C, (2)G, (6)C, (3)G
Row 179&180 (R) (5)G, (3)C, (2)G, (9)C, (5)G
Row 181&182 (R) (4)G, (3)C, (2)G, (8)C, (4)G, (3)C
Row 183&184 (R) (2)G, (3)C, (4)G, (6)C, (4)G, (4)C, (1)G
Row 185&186 (R) (3)C, (5)G, (4)C, (3)G, (6)C, (3)G
Row 187&188 (R) (2)C, (5)G, (2)C, (2)G, (9)C, (4)G
Row 189&190 (R) (4)G, (4)C, (3)G, (6)C, (6)G, (1)C
Row 191&192 (R) (3)G, (3)C, (3)G, (6)C, (6)G, (3)C

Safari Nights Earrings
two-drop peyote

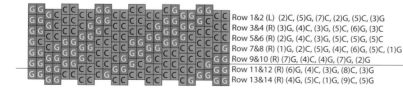

Row 1&2 (L) (2)C, (5)G, (7)C, (2)G, (5)C, (3)G
Row 3&4 (R) (3)G, (4)C, (3)G, (5)C, (6)G, (3)C
Row 5&6 (R) (2)G, (4)C, (3)G, (5)C, (5)G, (5)C
Row 7&8 (R) (1)G, (2)C, (5)G, (4)C, (6)G, (5)C, (1)G
Row 9&10 (R) (7)G, (4)C, (4)G, (7)C, (2)G
Row 11&12 (R) (6)G, (4)C, (3)G, (8)C, (3)G
Row 13&14 (R) (4)G, (5)C, (1)G, (9)C, (5)G

Stackable Zoo Bracelets

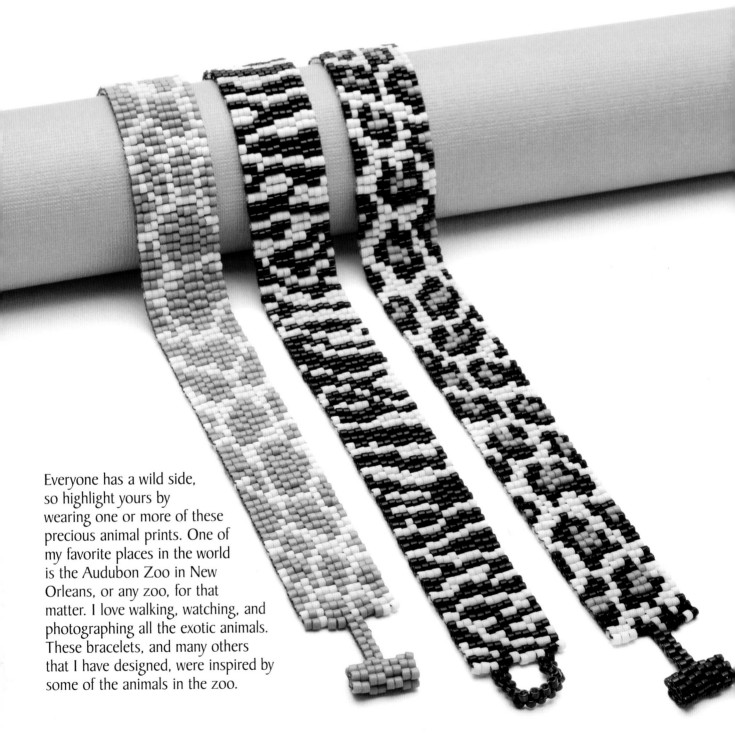

Everyone has a wild side, so highlight yours by wearing one or more of these precious animal prints. One of my favorite places in the world is the Audubon Zoo in New Orleans, or any zoo, for that matter. I love walking, watching, and photographing all the exotic animals. These bracelets, and many others that I have designed, were inspired by some of the animals in the zoo.

MATERIALS

- Fireline, 4-lb. or 6-lb. test
- Button(s) or closure (optional if making a toggle as shown here)
- 11° Delica beads in the following colors and quantities:

GIRAFFE (NATURAL)
- 3g (431) DB0352 matte cream (color A)
- 4g (721) DB0653 opaque pumpkin (color B)

ZEBRA (NATURAL)
- 4g (658) DB0310 matte black (color A)
- 3g (494) DB0352 matte cream (color B)

LEOPARD (NATURAL)
- 3g (467) DB0352 matte cream (color A)
- 3g (535) DB0310 matte black (color B)
- 1g (150) DB0653 opaque pumpkin (color C)

ALL THREE (NATURAL)
- 7g (1392) DB0352 matte cream
- 6g (1193) DB0310 matte black
- 5g (871) DB0653 opaque pumpkin

GIRAFFE (ALTERNATE)
- 3g (431) DB0356 matte lavender (color A)
- 4g (721) DB2140 dark orchid Duracoat opaque dyed (color B)

ZEBRA (ALTERNATE)
- 4g (658) DB2133 tiffany blue Duracoat opaque dyed (color A)
- 3g (494) DB0261 opaque luster news print white (color B)

LEOPARD (ALTERNATE)
- 3g (467) DB1457 opaque alabaster shell pink (color A)
- 3g (535) DB0761 matte opaque gray (color B)
- 1g (150) DB2118 mulberry pink Duracoat opaque dyed (color C)

MEASUREMENTS

½ in. wide and 6¾ in. long without the closure.

TOOLS

- Size 10 or 12 beading needle
- Thread cutters or scissors

Because the patterns are fairly random, they can be shortened by just stopping at the desired length.

Instructions

1 Refer to the *Giraffe*, *Zebra*, or *Leopard* three-drop pattern and word chart on pages 48 to 50. Follow the instructions for Fast Peyote (Techniques, p. 94) to create the peyote band. Add thread (Techniques, p. 97) as needed throughout the project.

Create the flat peyote loop

2 *The closure for this project consists of a flat peyote loop and a peyote toggle.* Reinforce the end of the bracelet (Techniques, p. 96, step 11). Exit at the location on the pattern marked by a black dot.

3 Follow the instructions for a flat peyote loop (Techniques, p. 98), using 12 rows of the desired color beads. Secure the other end of the loop at the location on the pattern marked with a black dot. Sew back through the loop and then weave into the piece. Use finishing knots to secure, then trim the thread and tuck into the piece.

Create the toggle tube and the toggle tail

4 Create the toggle by working eight or 12 columns (whichever you prefer) and six rows of two-drop peyote into a band. Zip up the band into a tube (Techniques, p. 103) and exit through the center of the tube.

5 Remove the stop bead and add thread (Techniques, p. 97) to the original tail at the opposite end of the piece. Weave into the piece, tucking the knot into a bead. Reinforce the end of the bracelet. Exit at the black dot marked on the pattern.

6 Follow the instructions to make a five-row toggle tail (Techniques, p. 103). Connect the toggle tube to the toggle tail (Techniques, p. 103). Weave back into the piece through several beads to form a strong base for the tail.

7 Weave into the end of the bracelet using finishing knots (Techniques, p. 97) to secure, then trim the thread, and tuck into the piece.

The more, the merrier

If you are making two or three bracelets to wear together, make the same length adjustment to all patterns and make the toggles all the same size so the finished bracelets lie nicely next to each other.

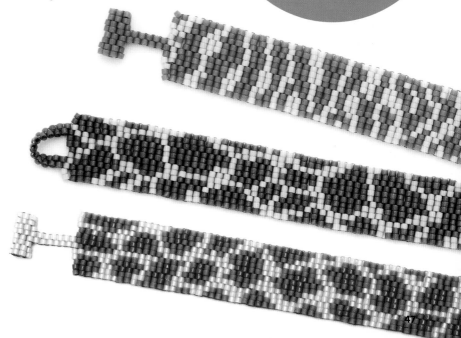

Giraffe
three-drop peyote

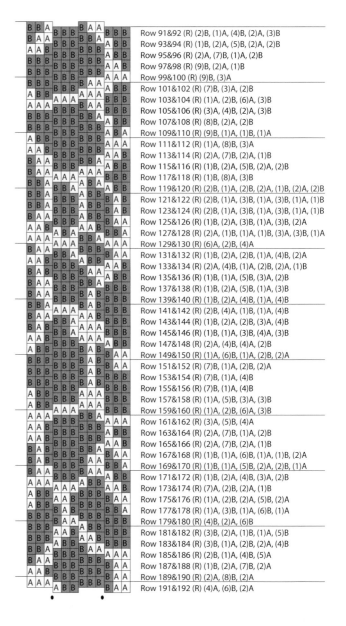

Row 1&2 (L) (2)B, (1)A, (3)B, (1)A, (3)B, (2)A
Row 3&4 (R) (3)A, (2)B, (1)A, (3)B, (1)A, (1)B, (1)A
Row 5&6 (R) (2)B, (4)A, (3)B, (2)A, (1)B
Row 7&8 (R) (2)B, (3)A, (1)B, (2)A, (1)B, (1)A, (2)B
Row 9&10 (R) (3)B, (1)A, (2)B, (4)A, (2)B
Row 11&12 (R) (3)B, (1)A, (3)B, (1)A, (1)B, (2)A, (1)B
Row 13&14 (R) (2)B, (1)A, (4)B, (1)A, (3)B, (1)A
Row 15&16 (R) (4)A, (3)B, (1)A, (3)B, (1)A
Row 17&18 (R) (1)B, (4)A, (1)B, (2)A, (4)B
Row 19&20 (R) (2)B, (5)A, (1)B, (2)A, (2)B
Row 21&22 (R) (1)B, (2)A, (1)B, (2)A, (4)B, (2)A
Row 23&24 (R) (2)A, (3)B, (2)A, (3)B, (2)A
Row 25&26 (R) (2)A, (4)B, (2)A, (1)B, (1)A, (2)B
Row 27&28 (R) (1)B, (1)A, (5)B, (2)A, (3)B
Row 29&30 (R) (1)B, (2)A, (5)B, (1)A, (3)B
Row 31&32 (R) (2)B, (1)A, (4)B, (1)A, (4)B
Row 33&34 (R) (2)B, (4)A, (1)B, (1)A, (4)B
Row 35&36 (R) (2)B, (1)A, (3)B, (3)A, (3)B
Row 37&38 (R) (1)B, (2)A, (4)B, (3)A, (2)B
Row 39&40 (R) (2)A, (5)B, (1)A, (2)B, (1)A, (1)B
Row 41&42 (R) (1)A, (6)B, (1)A, (2)B, (2)A
Row 43&44 (R) (1)A, (6)B, (1)A, (4)B
Row 45&46 (R) (1)A, (6)B, (1)A, (4)B
Row 47&48 (R) (2)A, (5)B, (2)A, (3)B
Row 49&50 (R) (2)A, (5)B, (2)A, (3)B
Row 51&52 (R) (2)B, (8)A, (2)B
Row 53&54 (R) (2)B, (3)A, (4)B, (3)A
Row 55&56 (R) (3)A, (6)B, (1)A, (2)B
Row 57&58 (R) (1)A, (1)B, (1)A, (6)B, (2)A, (1)B
Row 59&60 (R) (2)B, (1)A, (6)B, (1)A, (1)B, (1)A
Row 61&62 (R) (2)B, (2)A, (4)B, (2)A, (2)B
Row 63&64 (R) (2)B, (2)A, (3)B, (4)A, (1)B
Row 65&66 (R) (1)B, (11)A
Row 67&68 (R) (6)A, (4)B, (2)A
Row 69&70 (R) (1)A, (3)B, (1)A, (6)B, (1)A
Row 71&72 (R) (4)B, (2)A, (5)B, (1)A
Row 73&74 (R) (3)B, (3)A, (6)B
Row 75&76 (R) (3)B, (1)A, (2)B, (2)A, (4)B
Row 77&78 (R) (2)B, (1)A, (3)B, (5)A, (1)B
Row 79&80 (R) (1)B, (1)A, (8)B, (2)A
Row 81&82 (R) (2)A, (8)B, (2)A
Row 83&84 (R) (1)B, (2)A, (9)B
Row 85&86 (R) (2)B, (6)A, (4)B
Row 87&88 (R) (3)B, (5)A, (1)B, (2)A, (1)B
Row 89&90 (R) (3)B, (1)A, (3)B, (2)A, (1)B, (2)A

Row 91&92 (R) (2)B, (1)A, (4)B, (2)A, (3)B
Row 93&94 (R) (1)B, (2)A, (5)B, (2)A, (2)B
Row 95&96 (R) (2)A, (7)B, (1)A, (2)B
Row 97&98 (R) (9)B, (2)A, (1)B
Row 99&100 (R) (9)B, (3)A
Row 101&102 (R) (7)B, (3)A, (2)B
Row 103&104 (R) (1)A, (9)B, (2)A, (3)B
Row 105&106 (R) (3)A, (4)B, (2)A, (3)B
Row 107&108 (R) (8)B, (2)A, (2)B
Row 109&110 (R) (9)B, (1)A, (1)B, (1)A
Row 111&112 (R) (1)A, (8)B, (3)A
Row 113&114 (R) (2)A, (7)B, (2)A, (1)B
Row 115&116 (R) (1)B, (2)A, (5)B, (2)A, (2)B
Row 117&118 (R) (1)B, (8)A, (3)B
Row 119&120 (R) (2)B, (1)A, (2)B, (2)A, (1)B, (2)A, (2)B
Row 121&122 (R) (2)B, (1)A, (3)B, (1)A, (4)B, (2)A
Row 123&124 (R) (2)A, (1)B, (1)A, (3)B, (1)A, (3)B, (1)A, (1)B
Row 125&126 (R) (1)B, (2)A, (3)B, (1)A, (3)B, (2)A
Row 127&128 (R) (2)A, (1)B, (1)A, (1)B, (3)A, (3)B, (1)A
Row 129&130 (R) (6)A, (2)B, (4)A
Row 131&132 (R) (1)B, (2)A, (2)B, (1)A, (4)B, (2)A
Row 133&134 (R) (2)A, (4)B, (1)A, (2)B, (2)A, (1)B
Row 135&136 (R) (1)B, (1)A, (5)B, (3)A, (2)B
Row 137&138 (R) (1)B, (2)A, (5)B, (1)A, (3)B
Row 139&140 (R) (1)B, (2)A, (4)B, (1)A, (4)B
Row 141&142 (R) (2)B, (4)A, (1)B, (1)A, (4)B
Row 143&144 (R) (1)B, (2)A, (3)B, (3)A, (4)B
Row 145&146 (R) (1)B, (1)A, (3)B, (4)A, (3)B
Row 147&148 (R) (2)A, (4)B, (4)A, (2)B
Row 149&150 (R) (1)A, (6)B, (1)A, (2)B, (2)A
Row 151&152 (R) (7)B, (1)A, (2)B, (2)A
Row 153&154 (R) (7)B, (1)A, (4)B
Row 155&156 (R) (7)B, (1)A, (4)B
Row 157&158 (R) (1)A, (5)B, (3)A, (3)B
Row 159&160 (R) (1)A, (2)B, (6)A, (3)B
Row 161&162 (R) (3)A, (5)B, (4)A
Row 163&164 (R) (2)A, (7)B, (1)A, (2)B
Row 165&166 (R) (2)A, (7)B, (2)A, (1)B
Row 167&168 (R) (1)B, (1)A, (6)B, (1)A, (1)B, (2)A
Row 169&170 (R) (1)B, (1)A, (5)B, (2)A, (2)B, (1)A
Row 171&172 (R) (1)B, (2)A, (4)B, (3)A, (2)B
Row 173&174 (R) (7)A, (2)B, (2)A, (1)B
Row 175&176 (R) (1)A, (2)B, (2)A, (5)B, (2)A
Row 177&178 (R) (1)A, (3)B, (1)A, (6)B, (1)A
Row 179&180 (R) (4)B, (2)A, (6)B
Row 181&182 (R) (3)B, (2)A, (1)B, (1)A, (5)B
Row 183&184 (R) (3)B, (1)A, (2)B, (2)A, (4)B
Row 185&186 (R) (2)B, (1)A, (4)B, (5)A
Row 187&188 (R) (1)B, (2)A, (7)B, (2)A
Row 189&190 (R) (2)A, (8)B, (2)A
Row 191&192 (R) (4)A, (6)B, (2)A

Zebra
three-drop peyote

Row 1&2 (L) (2)A, (2)B, (2)A, (4)B, (2)A
Row 3&4 (R) (1)A, (3)B, (1)A, (4)B, (3)A
Row 5&6 (R) (3)B, (9)A
Row 7&8 (R) (1)B, (9)A, (2)B
Row 9&10 (R) (3)A, (3)B, (3)A, (3)B
Row 11&12 (R) (2)A, (8)B, (2)A
Row 13&14 (R) (1)A, (4)B, (7)A
Row 15&16 (R) (2)B, (10)A
Row 17&18 (R) (9)A, (3)B
Row 19&20 (R) (7)A, (4)B, (1)A
Row 21&22 (R) (9)B, (3)A
Row 23&24 (R) (12)A
Row 25&26 (R) (9)A, (3)B
Row 27&28 (R) (10)B, (2)A
Row 29&30 (R) (6)A, (3)B, (3)A
Row 31&32 (R) (9)A, (3)B
Row 33&34 (R) (9)B, (3)A
Row 35&36 (R) (6)A, (1)B, (2)A, (3)B
Row 37&38 (R) (8)A, (4)B
Row 39&40 (R) (6)B, (6)A
Row 41&42 (R) (11)B, (1)A
Row 43&44 (R) (11)A, (1)B
Row 45&46 (R) (9)A, (3)B
Row 47&48 (R) (3)A, (7)B, (2)A
Row 49&50 (R) (3)B, (8)A, (1)B
Row 51&52 (R) (5)A, (5)B, (2)A
Row 53&54 (R) (1)B, (2)A, (2)B, (1)A, (6)B
Row 55&56 (R) (6)B, (6)A
Row 57&58 (R) (3)B, (9)A
Row 59&60 (R) (3)A, (9)B
Row 61&62 (R) (6)B, (6)A
Row 63&64 (R) (4)A, (3)B, (2)A, (3)B
Row 65&66 (R) (1)A, (1)B, (4)A, (6)B
Row 67&68 (R) (2)A, (4)B, (4)A, (1)B, (1)A
Row 69&70 (R) (1)B, (8)A, (1)B, (2)A
Row 71&72 (R) (1)A, (3)B, (3)A, (2)B, (3)A
Row 73&74 (R) (3)A, (5)B, (1)A, (3)B
Row 75&76 (R) (2)B, (6)A, (2)B, (2)A
Row 77&78 (R) (5)A, (4)B, (1)A, (2)B
Row 79&80 (R) (8)B, (4)A

Row 81&82 (R) (3)B, (8)A, (1)B
Row 83&84 (R) (3)A, (8)B, (1)A
Row 85&86 (R) (9)B, (2)A, (1)B
Row 87&88 (R) (3)B, (6)A, (3)B
Row 89&90 (R) (8)A, (1)B, (3)A
Row 91&92 (R) (2)B, (1)A, (5)B, (4)A
Row 93&94 (R) (1)A, (5)B, (3)A, (1)B, (2)A
Row 95&96 (R) (3)B, (4)A, (2)B, (3)A
Row 97&98 (R) (3)A, (5)B, (4)A
Row 99&100 (R) (3)B, (8)A, (1)B
Row 101&102 (R) (9)A, (2)B, (1)A
Row 103&104 (R) (8)A, (1)B, (3)A
Row 105&106 (R) (8)B, (4)A
Row 107&108 (R) (1)B, (8)A, (2)B, (1)A
Row 109&110 (R) (4)B, (3)A, (2)B, (2)A, (1)B
Row 111&112 (R) (3)B, (2)A, (2)B, (4)A, (1)B
Row 113&114 (R) (2)B, (2)A, (1)B, (4)A, (2)B, (1)A
Row 115&116 (R) (3)A, (1)B, (2)A, (3)B, (3)A
Row 117&118 (R) (3)B, (8)A, (1)B
Row 119&120 (R) (3)A, (3)B, (3)A, (3)B
Row 121&122 (R) (9)B, (3)A
Row 123&124 (R) (3)B, (9)A
Row 125&126 (R) (1)B, (10)A, (1)B
Row 127&128 (R) (8)A, (4)B
Row 129&130 (R) (3)A, (6)B, (3)A
Row 131&132 (R) (6)B, (6)A
Row 133&134 (R) (1)A, (2)B, (6)A, (3)B
Row 135&136 (R) (7)A, (4)B, (1)A
Row 137&138 (R) (1)B, (2)A, (6)B, (3)A
Row 139&140 (R) (8)B, (3)A, (1)B
Row 141&142 (R) (9)A, (2)B, (1)A
Row 143&144 (R) (5)A, (4)B, (3)A
Row 145&146 (R) (5)B, (4)A, (1)B, (2)A
Row 147&148 (R) (5)A, (1)B, (3)A, (3)B
Row 149&150 (R) (6)A, (3)B, (3)A
Row 151&152 (R) (6)B, (6)A
Row 153&154 (R) (6)A, (6)B
Row 155&156 (R) (9)A, (1)B, (2)A
Row 157&158 (R) (3)A, (6)B, (3)A
Row 159&160 (R) (3)B, (3)A, (1)B, (2)A, (3)B
Row 161&162 (R) (3)A, (3)B, (6)A
Row 163&164 (R) (4)A, (6)B, (2)A
Row 165&166 (R) (4)B, (4)A, (4)B
Row 167&168 (R) (12)A
Row 169&170 (R) (3)A, (7)B, (2)A
Row 171&172 (R) (3)B, (7)A, (2)B
Row 173&174 (R) (1)A, (4)B, (4)A, (2)B, (1)A
Row 175&176 (R) (6)A, (4)B, (2)A
Row 177&178 (R) (5)B, (3)A, (1)B, (3)A
Row 179&180 (R) (2)A, (1)B, (3)A, (3)B, (2)A, (1)B
Row 181&182 (R) (1)B, (2)A, (4)B, (2)A, (3)B
Row 183&184 (R) (1)A, (2)B, (5)A, (1)B, (3)A
Row 185&186 (R) (4)B, (4)A, (3)B, (1)A, (3)B
Row 187&188 (R) (3)A, (3)B, (2)A, (1)B, (3)A
Row 189&190 (R) (3)B, (4)A, (1)B, (4)A
Row 191&192 (R) (3)A, (3)B, (5)A, (1)B

Leopard
three-drop peyote

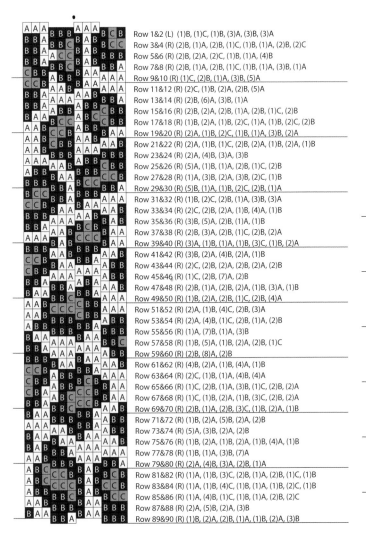

Row 1&2 (L) (1)B, (1)C, (1)B, (3)A, (3)B, (3)A
Row 3&4 (R) (2)B, (1)A, (2)B, (1)C, (1)B, (1)A, (2)B, (2)C
Row 5&6 (R) (2)B, (2)A, (2)C, (1)B, (1)A, (4)B
Row 7&8 (R) (2)B, (1)A, (2)B, (1)C, (1)B, (1)A, (3)B, (1)A
Row 9&10 (R) (1)C, (2)B, (1)A, (3)B, (5)A
Row 11&12 (R) (2)C, (1)B, (2)A, (2)B, (5)A
Row 13&14 (R) (2)B, (6)A, (3)B, (1)A
Row 15&16 (R) (2)B, (2)A, (2)B, (1)A, (2)B, (1)C, (2)B
Row 17&18 (R) (1)B, (2)A, (1)B, (2)C, (1)A, (1)B, (2)C, (2)B
Row 19&20 (R) (2)A, (1)B, (2)C, (1)B, (1)A, (3)B, (2)A
Row 21&22 (R) (2)A, (1)B, (1)C, (2)B, (2)A, (1)B, (2)A, (1)B
Row 23&24 (R) (2)A, (4)B, (3)A, (3)B
Row 25&26 (R) (5)A, (1)B, (1)A, (2)B, (1)C, (2)B
Row 27&28 (R) (1)A, (3)B, (2)A, (3)B, (2)C, (1)B
Row 29&30 (R) (5)B, (1)A, (1)B, (2)C, (2)B, (1)A
Row 31&32 (R) (1)B, (2)C, (2)B, (1)A, (3)B, (3)A
Row 33&34 (R) (2)C, (2)B, (2)A, (1)B, (4)A, (1)B
Row 35&36 (R) (3)B, (5)A, (2)B, (1)A, (1)B
Row 37&38 (R) (2)B, (3)A, (2)B, (1)C, (2)B, (2)A
Row 39&40 (R) (3)A, (1)B, (1)A, (1)B, (3)C, (1)B, (2)A
Row 41&42 (R) (3)B, (2)A, (4)B, (2)A, (1)B
Row 43&44 (R) (2)C, (2)B, (2)A, (2)B, (2)A, (2)B
Row 45&46 (R) (1)C, (2)B, (7)A, (2)B
Row 47&48 (R) (1)B, (1)A, (2)B, (2)A, (1)B, (3)A, (1)B
Row 49&50 (R) (1)B, (2)A, (2)B, (1)C, (2)B, (4)A
Row 51&52 (R) (2)A, (1)B, (4)C, (2)B, (3)A
Row 53&54 (R) (2)A, (4)B, (1)C, (2)B, (1)A, (2)B
Row 55&56 (R) (1)A, (7)B, (1)A, (3)B
Row 57&58 (R) (1)B, (5)A, (1)B, (2)A, (2)B, (1)C
Row 59&60 (R) (2)B, (8)A, (2)B
Row 61&62 (R) (4)B, (2)A, (1)B, (4)A, (1)B
Row 63&64 (R) (2)C, (1)B, (1)A, (4)B, (4)A
Row 65&66 (R) (1)C, (1)A, (3)B, (1)C, (2)B, (2)A
Row 67&68 (R) (1)C, (1)B, (2)A, (1)B, (3)C, (2)B, (2)A
Row 69&70 (R) (2)B, (1)A, (2)B, (3)C, (1)B, (2)A, (1)B
Row 71&72 (R) (1)B, (2)A, (5)B, (2)A, (2)B
Row 73&74 (R) (5)A, (3)B, (2)A, (2)B
Row 75&76 (R) (1)B, (2)A, (1)B, (2)A, (1)B, (4)A, (1)B
Row 77&78 (R) (1)B, (1)A, (3)B, (7)A
Row 79&80 (R) (2)A, (4)B, (3)A, (2)B, (1)A
Row 81&82 (R) (1)A, (1)B, (3)C, (2)B, (1)A, (2)B, (1)C, (1)B
Row 83&84 (R) (1)A, (1)B, (4)C, (1)B, (1)A, (1)B, (2)C, (1)B
Row 85&86 (R) (1)A, (4)B, (1)C, (1)B, (1)A, (2)B, (2)C
Row 87&88 (R) (2)A, (5)B, (2)A, (3)B
Row 89&90 (R) (1)B, (2)A, (2)B, (1)A, (1)B, (2)A, (3)B

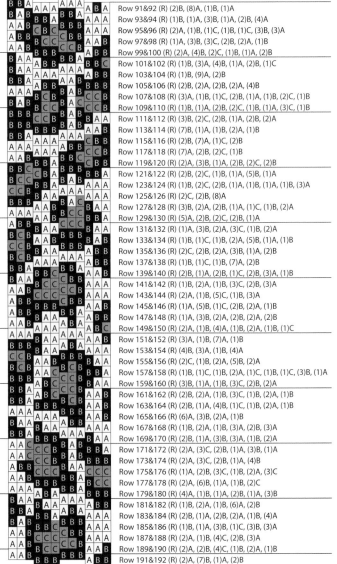

Row 91&92 (R) (2)B, (8)A, (1)B, (1)A
Row 93&94 (R) (1)B, (1)A, (3)B, (1)A, (2)B, (4)A
Row 95&96 (R) (2)A, (1)B, (1)C, (1)B, (1)C, (3)B, (3)A
Row 97&98 (R) (1)A, (3)B, (3)C, (2)B, (2)A, (1)B
Row 99&100 (R) (2)A, (4)B, (2)C, (1)B, (1)A, (2)B
Row 101&102 (R) (1)B, (3)A, (4)B, (1)A, (2)B, (1)C
Row 103&104 (R) (1)B, (9)A, (2)B
Row 105&106 (R) (2)B, (2)A, (2)B, (2)A, (4)B
Row 107&108 (R) (3)A, (1)B, (1)C, (2)B, (1)A, (1)B, (2)C, (1)B
Row 109&110 (R) (1)B, (1)A, (2)B, (2)C, (1)B, (1)A, (3)C, (1)B
Row 111&112 (R) (3)B, (2)C, (2)B, (1)A, (2)B, (2)A
Row 113&114 (R) (7)B, (1)A, (1)B, (2)A, (1)B
Row 115&116 (R) (7)B, (1)A, (1)C, (2)B
Row 117&118 (R) (7)A, (2)B, (2)C, (1)B
Row 119&120 (R) (2)A, (3)B, (1)A, (2)B, (2)C, (2)B
Row 121&122 (R) (2)B, (2)C, (1)B, (1)A, (5)B, (1)A
Row 123&124 (R) (1)C, (2)B, (1)A, (1)B, (1)A, (1)B, (3)A
Row 125&126 (R) (2)C, (2)B, (8)A
Row 127&128 (R) (3)B, (2)A, (2)B, (1)A, (1)C, (1)B, (2)A
Row 129&130 (R) (5)A, (2)B, (2)C, (2)B, (1)A
Row 131&132 (R) (1)A, (3)B, (2)A, (3)C, (1)B, (2)A
Row 133&134 (R) (1)B, (1)C, (1)B, (2)A, (5)B, (1)A, (1)B
Row 135&136 (R) (2)C, (2)B, (2)A, (3)B, (1)A, (2)B
Row 137&138 (R) (1)B, (1)C, (1)B, (7)A, (2)B
Row 139&140 (R) (2)B, (1)A, (2)B, (1)C, (2)B, (3)A, (1)B
Row 141&142 (R) (1)B, (2)A, (1)B, (2)C, (2)B, (3)A
Row 143&144 (R) (2)A, (1)B, (5)C, (1)B, (3)A
Row 145&146 (R) (1)A, (5)B, (1)C, (2)B, (2)A, (1)B
Row 147&148 (R) (1)A, (3)B, (2)A, (2)B, (2)A, (2)B
Row 149&150 (R) (2)A, (1)B, (4)A, (1)B, (2)A, (1)B, (1)C
Row 151&152 (R) (3)A, (1)B, (7)A, (1)B
Row 153&154 (R) (4)B, (3)A, (1)B, (4)A
Row 155&156 (R) (2)C, (1)B, (2)A, (5)B, (2)A
Row 157&158 (R) (1)B, (1)C, (1)B, (2)A, (1)C, (1)B, (1)C, (3)B, (1)A
Row 159&160 (R) (3)B, (1)A, (1)B, (3)C, (2)B, (2)A
Row 161&162 (R) (2)B, (2)A, (1)B, (3)C, (1)B, (2)A, (1)B
Row 163&164 (R) (2)B, (1)A, (4)B, (1)C, (1)B, (2)A, (1)B
Row 165&166 (R) (6)A, (3)B, (2)A, (1)B
Row 167&168 (R) (1)B, (2)A, (1)B, (3)A, (2)B, (3)A
Row 169&170 (R) (2)B, (1)A, (3)B, (3)A, (1)B, (2)A
Row 171&172 (R) (2)A, (3)C, (2)B, (1)A, (3)B, (1)A
Row 173&174 (R) (2)A, (3)C, (2)B, (1)A, (4)B
Row 175&176 (R) (1)A, (2)B, (3)C, (1)B, (2)A, (3)C
Row 177&178 (R) (2)A, (6)B, (1)A, (1)B, (2)C
Row 179&180 (R) (4)A, (1)B, (1)A, (2)B, (1)A, (3)B
Row 181&182 (R) (1)B, (2)A, (1)B, (6)A, (2)B
Row 183&184 (R) (2)B, (1)A, (2)B, (2)A, (1)B, (4)A
Row 185&186 (R) (1)B, (1)A, (3)B, (1)C, (3)B, (3)A
Row 187&188 (R) (2)A, (1)B, (4)C, (2)B, (3)A
Row 189&190 (R) (2)A, (2)B, (4)C, (1)B, (2)A, (1)B
Row 191&192 (R) (2)A, (7)B, (1)A, (2)B

Panda Snuggle

I recently saw the giant pandas at the San Diego zoo. Pandas are solitary creatures, but the mother devotes herself to her baby until it is ready to venture out on its own. Their beauty and serenity are depicted in this lovely pendant.

MATERIALS

- 11° Delica beads:
    - 2g (307) DB0010 black (color B)
    - 2g (335) DB0351 matte white (color W)
    - 1g (126) DB1226 matte transparent lime (color G)
- 1g 15° black rocailles or seed beads
- 1g 4mm black bugle beads
- 1g 3.4mm black Miyuki drop beads (magatamas)
- **14** 3mm peridot Swarovski bicones
- **1** 6x35mm Miyuki silver-plated two-strand slide end tube
- 24-gauge tarnish-resistant silver artistic wire
- 21-in. 2mm silver-plated fine cable beading chain
- 12x6mm silver-plated lobster claw clasp
- **2** 5mm jump rings
- Fireline, 4-lb. or 6-lb. test

TOOLS

- #10 or #12 beading needle
- Thread cutters or scissors
- Chainnose pliers

MEASUREMENTS

1¼ in. wide and 2¼ in. long without the fringe and 3½ in. long with the fringe.

Instructions

1 Refer to the *Panda Snuggle* two-drop pattern and word chart on page 53. Follow the instructions for Fast Peyote (Techniques, p. 94) to create the peyote band. Add thread (Techniques, p. 97) as needed throughout the project.

2 Reinforce the bottom of the pendant (Techniques, p. 96, step 11).

Add the fringe

3 Starting at point **a** marked on the bottom of the pattern, follow the instructions for adding V fringe (Techniques, p. 106). Follow the bead list below:

Column 1:   2 seed beads, 1 bugle bead, 1 seed bead, 1 bicone, 1 seed bead, 1 drop bead, 1 seed bead
Column 2:   4 seed beads, 1 bugle bead, 1 seed bead, 1 bicone, 1 seed bead, 1 drop bead, 1 seed bead
Column 3:   6 seed beads, 1 bugle bead, 1 seed bead, 1 bicone, 1 seed bead, 1 drop bead, 1 seed bead
Column 4:   8 seed beads, 1 bugle bead, 1 seed bead, 1 bicone, 1 seed bead, 1 drop bead, 1 seed bead
Column 5:   10 seed beads, 1 bugle bead, 1 seed bead, 1 bicone, 1 seed bead, 1 drop bead, 1 seed bead
Column 6:   13 seed beads, 1 bugle bead, 1 seed bead, 1 bicone, 1 seed bead, 1 drop bead, 1 seed bead
Column 7:   12 seed beads, 1 bugle bead, 1 seed bead, 1 bicone, 1 seed bead, 1 drop bead, 1 seed bead
Column 8:   10 seed beads, 1 bugle bead, 1 seed bead, 1 bicone, 1 seed bead, 1 drop bead, 1 seed bead
Column 9:   8 seed beads, 1 bugle bead, 1 seed bead, 1 bicone, 1 seed bead, 1 drop bead, 1 seed bead
Column 10: 6 seed beads, 1 bugle bead, 1 seed bead, 1 bicone, 1 seed bead, 1 drop bead, 1 seed bead
Column 11: 4 seed beads, 1 bugle bead, 1 seed bead, 1 bicone, 1 seed bead, 1 drop bead, 1 seed bead
Column 12: 2 seed beads, 1 bugle bead, 1 seed bead, 1 bicone, 1 seed bead, 1 drop bead, 1 seed bead

4 When the fringe is complete, sew back into the piece using finishing knots to secure (Techniques, p. 97), then trim the thread and weave into the piece.

Add the slide bar

5 Remove the stop bead and add thread to the original tail at the top of the piece. Pick up 24 color A beads and add the slide end tube following the instructions (Techniques, p. 108).

6. Add the chain. A simple chain or cord can be strung through the loops at either end of the bar. The bar loops can be opened and closed using chainnose pliers.

Panda Snuggle
two-drop peyote

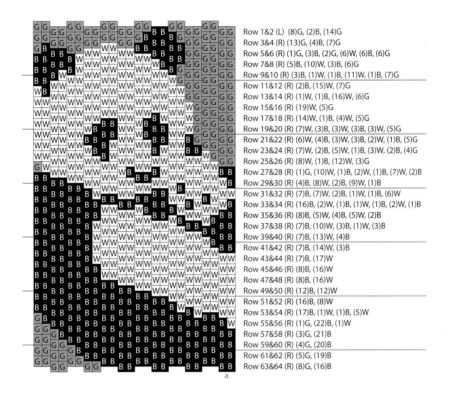

Row 1&2 (L) (8)G, (2)B, (14)G
Row 3&4 (R) (13)G, (4)B, (7)G
Row 5&6 (R) (1)G, (3)B, (2)G, (6)W, (6)B, (6)G
Row 7&8 (R) (5)B, (10)W, (3)B, (6)G
Row 9&10 (R) (3)B, (1)W, (1)B, (11)W, (1)B, (7)G
Row 11&12 (R) (2)B, (15)W, (7)G
Row 13&14 (R) (1)W, (1)B, (16)W, (6)G
Row 15&16 (R) (19)W, (5)G
Row 17&18 (R) (14)W, (1)B, (4)W, (5)G
Row 19&20 (R) (7)W, (3)B, (3)W, (3)B, (3)W, (5)G
Row 21&22 (R) (6)W, (4)B, (3)W, (3)B, (2)W, (1)B, (5)G
Row 23&24 (R) (7)W, (2)B, (5)W, (1)B, (3)W, (2)B, (4)G
Row 25&26 (R) (8)W, (1)B, (12)W, (3)G
Row 27&28 (R) (1)G, (10)W, (1)B, (2)W, (1)B, (7)W, (2)B
Row 29&30 (R) (4)B, (8)W, (2)B, (9)W, (1)B
Row 31&32 (R) (7)B, (7)W, (2)B, (1)W, (1)B, (6)W
Row 33&34 (R) (16)B, (2)W, (1)B, (1)W, (1)B, (2)W, (1)B
Row 35&36 (R) (8)B, (5)W, (4)B, (5)W, (2)B
Row 37&38 (R) (7)B, (10)W, (3)B, (1)W, (3)B
Row 39&40 (R) (7)B, (13)W, (4)B
Row 41&42 (R) (7)B, (14)W, (3)B
Row 43&44 (R) (7)B, (17)W
Row 45&46 (R) (8)B, (16)W
Row 47&48 (R) (8)B, (16)W
Row 49&50 (R) (12)B, (12)W
Row 51&52 (R) (16)B, (8)W
Row 53&54 (R) (17)B, (1)W, (1)B, (5)W
Row 55&56 (R) (1)G, (22)B, (1)W
Row 57&58 (R) (3)G, (21)B
Row 59&60 (R) (4)G, (20)B
Row 61&62 (R) (5)G, (19)B
Row 63&64 (R) (8)G, (16)B

a

Party!

There is always something to celebrate and if you get a little wild doing it, even better. These beautiful party streamers make a versatile, simple, and quick bracelet. Add the earrings and you've got a great pop of color for your next party or for an everyday outfit.

MATERIALS
- 11º Delica beads:
  4g (596) DB0035 metallic silver (color A)
  1g (165) DB0307 silver gray matte metallic (color B)
  1g (90) DB0306 dark gray matte metallic (color C)
  1g (136) DB0311 matte metallic olive green (color D)
  2g (165) DB1051 matte metallic bronze (color E)
- **1** 10mm silver square button
- **384** 3mm crystal venus Preciosa Czech crystal bicones
- 5g 15º silver-lined seed beads
- Fireline, 4-lb. or 6-lb. test

MATERIALS FOR ALTERNATE COLORS
- 11º Delica beads:
  4g (596) DB0310 matte black (color A)
  1g (165) DB0351 matte white (color B)
  1g (90) DB0756 matte opaque cobalt (color C)
  1g (136) DB0422 metallic magenta (color D)
  2g (165) DB0876 matte opaque chartreuse AB (color E)
- 19x5mm jet Swarovski elements crystal column

EARRING MATERIALS
- 11º Delica beads (in the colors and quantities from above)
  1g (161) (color A)
  1g (50) (color B)
  1g (54) (color C)
  1g (60) (color D)
  1g (58) (color E)
- **2** 28mm marquise open loop, 19-gauge Hill Tribes silver-plated brass earring wires

TOOLS
- #10 or #12 beading needle
- Thread cutters or scissors

MEASUREMENTS
½ in. wide without the fringe and 6¾ in. long before the closure is added.

Bracelet Instructions
1 Refer to the *Party!* three-drop pattern and word chart on pages 56 and 57. Follow the instructions for Fast Peyote (Techniques, p. 94) to create the peyote band. Add thread (Techniques, p. 97) as needed throughout the project.

Create a brick stitch loop
2 *The closure for this project consists of a brick stitch loop and a button.* Reinforce the end of the bracelet (Techniques, p. 96, step 11). Exit at the end of the pattern at the edge.

3 Follow the instructions to create the brick stitch loop (Techniques, p. 98) using two columns and 16 rows of color B Delicas. Secure the other end of the loop at the other edge of the bracelet.

4 Sew back through the loop. Weave into the piece and use finishing knots to secure (Techniques, p. 97). Exit the first edge bead and leave the thread hanging for the fringe.

5 Exit the first bracelet edge bead and leave the tail for fringe.

Note
The bold-colored option uses a flat peyote loop as part of the closure (Techniques, p. 98).

6 Remove the stop bead and add thread to the original tail at the opposite end of the piece. Weave into the piece, tucking the knot into a bead. Reinforce the end of the bracelet. Exit the pattern at the center.

Add the toggle tail and button
7 Pick up five color E beads, the button, and five Es. Sew back into the tail and use finishing knots to secure, then weave back into the piece, trim the thread, and tuck into the piece.

Fringed Version:
Add the trim
8 (If necessary, add thread to the tail left over from step 3.) Follow the instructions for anemone trim (Techniques, p. 104), using a 3mm bicone and a 15º seed bead.

9 When the trim is complete along both edges, weave back into the piece. Use finishing knots to secure, then trim the thread, and tuck into the piece.

Party! Earrings Instructions
1 Refer to the *Party! Earring* two-drop pattern and word chart on page 57. Follow the instructions for Fast Peyote (Techniques, p. 94) to create a small peyote square.

Create the loops for the earring wire
2 Exit the location at the end of the pattern at the edge. Pick up eight color A beads and enter the opposite side of the bead exited to create the loop. Sew back through the loop to reinforce. Weave back through the piece and exit at the edge one bead away from the end bead that holds the stop bead.

3 Remove the stop bead and thread the needle onto the original tail. Sew into the bead closest to the knot. Weave back into the piece using finishing knots to secure, then trim the thread, and weave into the piece.

4 Repeat steps 1–3 to create the second earring.

5 Hook an earring wire to each loop. Slightly twist open the loop of the wire with pliers, (Techniques, p. 109). Thread the open loop through the loop of the peyote tube earring. Gently close the loop.

Party!
three-drop peyote

Row 1&2 (L) (3)A, (1)D, (2)A, (2)E, (4)A
Row 3&4 (R) (4)A, (2)E, (2)A, (2)D, (2)A
Row 5&6 (R) (3)A, (2)E, (3)A, (2)D, (2)A
Row 7&8 (R) (1)B, (2)A, (2)E, (3)A, (2)D, (2)A
Row 9&10 (R) (2)B, (1)A, (2)E, (4)A, (1)D, (2)A
Row 11&12 (R) (3)B, (2)E, (4)A, (1)D, (2)A
Row 13&14 (R) (1)A, (1)B, (3)E, (4)A, (2)D, (1)A
Row 15&16 (R) (2)A, (2)E, (1)B, (4)A, (2)D, (1)A
Row 17&18 (R) (2)A, (2)E, (1)B, (4)A, (2)D, (1)A
Row 19&20 (R) (2)A, (2)E, (2)B, (3)A, (2)D, (1)A
Row 21&22 (R) (2)A, (2)E, (1)D, (1)B, (3)A, (2)D, (1)A
Row 23&24 (R) (1)C, (1)A, (3)E, (1)A, (1)B, (2)A, (2)D, (1)A
Row 25&26 (R) (1)C, (2)A, (2)E, (1)A, (2)B, (1)A, (2)D, (1)A
Row 27&28 (R) (2)C, (1)A, (2)E, (1)A, (2)B, (1)A, (1)D, (2)A
Row 29&30 (R) (2)C, (1)A, (2)E, (2)A, (2)B, (1)D, (2)A
Row 31&32 (R) (1)A, (1)C, (2)A, (1)E, (3)A, (2)B, (2)A
Row 33&34 (R) (1)A, (2)C, (1)A, (2)E, (2)A, (2)B, (2)A
Row 35&36 (R) (2)A, (2)C, (2)E, (2)A, (2)B, (2)A
Row 37&38 (R) (2)A, (2)C, (1)A, (1)E, (2)A, (1)D, (2)B, (1)A
Row 39&40 (R) (3)A, (1)C, (1)A, (2)E, (2)D, (2)B, (1)A
Row 41&42 (R) (3)A, (2)C, (1)A, (1)E, (2)D, (1)A, (2)B
Row 43&44 (R) (4)A, (1)C, (1)A, (1)E, (1)D, (2)A, (2)B
Row 45&46 (R) (4)A, (2)C, (2)E, (2)A, (2)B
Row 47&48 (R) (4)A, (2)C, (1)D, (1)E, (2)A, (2)B
Row 49&50 (R) (4)A, (2)C, (1)D, (2)E, (1)A, (2)B
Row 51&52 (R) (4)A, (1)D, (1)C, (1)A, (3)E, (1)A, (1)B
Row 53&54 (R) (4)A, (1)D, (1)C, (2)A, (2)E, (1)A, (1)B
Row 55&56 (R) (4)A, (1)D, (1)C, (2)A, (3)E, (1)B
Row 57&58 (R) (3)A, (2)D, (1)C, (3)A, (2)E, (1)B
Row 59&60 (R) (3)A, (2)D, (2)C, (2)A, (2)E, (1)B
Row 61&62 (R) (3)A, (1)D, (1)A, (2)C, (3)A, (1)E, (1)B
Row 63&64 (R) (2)A, (2)D, (1)A, (2)C, (3)A, (2)E
Row 65&66 (R) (2)A, (2)D, (1)A, (2)C, (3)A, (2)E
Row 67&68 (R) (2)A, (2)D, (1)A, (2)C, (3)A, (1)B, (1)E
Row 69&70 (R) (1)A, (2)D, (2)A, (2)C, (3)A, (1)B, (1)E
Row 71&72 (R) (1)A, (2)D, (2)A, (2)C, (3)A, (1)B, (1)E
Row 73&74 (R) (1)A, (2)D, (2)A, (2)C, (2)A, (3)B
Row 75&76 (R) (1)A, (2)D, (2)A, (2)C, (2)A, (3)B
Row 77&78 (R) (1)A, (1)D, (3)A, (1)C, (3)A, (2)B, (1)A
Row 79&80 (R) (2)D, (2)A, (2)C, (3)A, (2)B, (1)A
Row 81&82 (R) (2)D, (2)A, (2)C, (2)A, (2)B, (2)A
Row 83&84 (R) (2)D, (2)A, (2)C, (2)A, (2)B, (2)A
Row 85&86 (R) (2)D, (2)A, (2)C, (1)A, (2)B, (3)A
Row 87&88 (R) (2)D, (1)A, (2)C, (2)A, (2)B, (3)A
Row 89&90 (R) (2)D, (1)A, (2)C, (2)A, (2)B, (3)A
Row 91&92 (R) (2)D, (1)A, (2)C, (1)A, (2)B, (4)A
Row 93&94 (R) (3)D, (1)C, (1)A, (3)B, (4)A
Row 95&96 (R) (1)A, (1)D, (2)C, (1)A, (2)B, (4)A, (1)E
Row 97&98 (R) (1)A, (1)D, (2)C, (1)A, (2)B, (4)A, (1)E
Row 99&100 (R) (1)A, (2)C, (1)A, (3)B, (4)A, (1)E

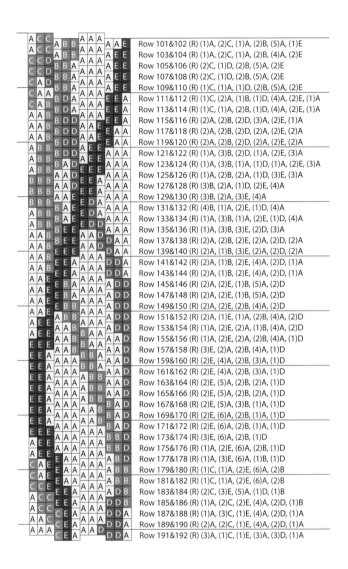

Row 101&102 (R) (1)A, (2)C, (1)A, (2)B, (5)A, (1)E
Row 103&104 (R) (1)A, (2)C, (1)A, (2)B, (4)A, (2)E
Row 105&106 (R) (2)C, (1)D, (2)B, (5)A, (2)E
Row 107&108 (R) (2)C, (1)D, (2)B, (5)A, (2)E
Row 109&110 (R) (1)C, (1)A, (1)D, (2)B, (5)A, (2)E
Row 111&112 (R) (1)C, (2)A, (1)B, (1)D, (4)A, (2)E, (1)A
Row 113&114 (R) (1)C, (1)A, (2)B, (1)D, (4)A, (2)E, (1)A
Row 115&116 (R) (2)A, (2)B, (2)D, (3)A, (2)E, (1)A
Row 117&118 (R) (2)A, (2)B, (2)D, (2)A, (2)E, (2)A
Row 119&120 (R) (2)A, (2)B, (2)D, (2)A, (2)E, (2)A
Row 121&122 (R) (1)A, (3)B, (2)D, (1)A, (2)E, (3)A
Row 123&124 (R) (1)A, (3)B, (1)A, (1)D, (1)A, (2)E, (3)A
Row 125&126 (R) (1)A, (2)B, (2)A, (1)D, (3)E, (3)A
Row 127&128 (R) (3)B, (2)A, (1)D, (2)E, (4)A
Row 129&130 (R) (3)B, (2)A, (3)E, (4)A
Row 131&132 (R) (4)B, (1)A, (2)E, (1)D, (4)A
Row 133&134 (R) (1)A, (3)B, (1)A, (2)E, (1)D, (4)A
Row 135&136 (R) (1)A, (3)B, (3)E, (2)D, (3)A
Row 137&138 (R) (2)A, (2)B, (2)E, (2)A, (2)D, (2)A
Row 139&140 (R) (2)A, (1)B, (3)E, (2)A, (2)D, (2)A
Row 141&142 (R) (2)A, (1)B, (2)E, (4)A, (2)D, (1)A
Row 143&144 (R) (2)A, (1)B, (2)E, (4)A, (2)D, (1)A
Row 145&146 (R) (2)A, (2)E, (1)B, (5)A, (2)D
Row 147&148 (R) (2)A, (2)E, (1)B, (5)A, (2)D
Row 149&150 (R) (2)A, (2)E, (2)B, (4)A, (2)D
Row 151&152 (R) (2)A, (1)E, (1)A, (2)B, (4)A, (2)D
Row 153&154 (R) (1)A, (2)E, (2)A, (1)B, (4)A, (2)D
Row 155&156 (R) (1)A, (2)E, (2)A, (2)B, (4)A, (1)D
Row 157&158 (R) (3)E, (2)A, (2)B, (4)A, (1)D
Row 159&160 (R) (2)E, (4)A, (2)B, (3)A, (1)D
Row 161&162 (R) (2)E, (4)A, (2)B, (3)A, (1)D
Row 163&164 (R) (2)E, (5)A, (2)B, (2)A, (1)D
Row 165&166 (R) (2)E, (5)A, (2)B, (2)A, (1)D
Row 167&168 (R) (2)E, (5)A, (3)B, (1)A, (1)D
Row 169&170 (R) (2)E, (6)A, (2)B, (1)A, (1)D
Row 171&172 (R) (2)E, (6)A, (2)B, (1)A, (1)D
Row 173&174 (R) (3)E, (6)A, (2)B, (1)D
Row 175&176 (R) (1)A, (2)E, (6)A, (2)B, (1)D
Row 177&178 (R) (1)A, (3)E, (6)A, (1)B, (1)D
Row 179&180 (R) (1)C, (1)A, (2)E, (6)A, (2)B
Row 181&182 (R) (1)C, (1)A, (2)E, (6)A, (2)B
Row 183&184 (R) (2)C, (3)E, (5)A, (1)D, (1)B
Row 185&186 (R) (1)A, (2)C, (2)E, (4)A, (2)D, (1)B
Row 187&188 (R) (1)A, (3)C, (1)E, (4)A, (2)D, (1)A
Row 189&190 (R) (2)A, (2)C, (1)E, (4)A, (2)D, (1)A
Row 191&192 (R) (3)A, (1)C, (1)E, (3)A, (3)D, (1)A

Party! earrings
two-drop peyote

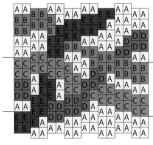

Row 1&2 (L) (4)A, (2)E, (6)A, (2)B, (2)A
Row 3&4 (R) (5)B, (1)A, (5)E, (5)A
Row 5&6 (R) (2)B, (2)A, (1)B, (5)E, (4)A, (2)D
Row 7&8 (R) (4)A, (2)E, (2)B, (5)A, (3)D
Row 9&10 (R) (2)A, (2)C, (2)E, (2)A, (4)B, (2)D, (2)A
Row 11&12 (R) (7)C, (2)A, (7)B
Row 13&14 (R) (2)C, (1)A, (1)E, (4)C, (1)A, (2)D, (1)A, (4)B
Row 15&16 (R) (2)D, (1)A, (2)E, (1)A, (2)C, (2)D, (2)C, (4)A
Row 17&18 (R) (2)D, (3)E, (1)A, (3)D, (7)C
Row 19&20 (R) (2)A, (2)E, (5)D, (3)A, (4)C
Row 21&22 (R) (3)E, (1)A, (2)D, (10)A
Row 23&24 (R) (2)E, (14)A

Southwest X's and O's

I spent some time in New Mexico after college. While there, I not only became fascinated by beaded art, but also fell in love with the southwestern prints and patterns that are so prevalent. This simple Southwest bracelet can be made in a variety of ways and with a varied number of colors, bead sizes, and styles.

MATERIALS
- 11° Toho beads:
  - 4g (400) brown Toho 46 (color A)
  - 3g (300) teal Toho 55 (color B)
  - 3g (260) galvanized silver Toho PF558 (color C)
- 16mm antique silver-plated pewter beaded zigzag button
- Fireline, 4-lb. or 6-lb. test

TOOLS
- #10 or #12 beading needle
- Thread cutters or scissors

MEASUREMENTS
½ in. wide by 6¾ in. long

Instructions

1 Refer to the *Southwest X's and O's* three-drop pattern and word chart on page 60. Follow the instructions for Fast Peyote (Techniques, p. 94) to create the peyote band. Add thread (Techniques, p. 97) as needed throughout the project.

Create brick stitch loop for the closure

2 *The closure for this project consists of a brick stitch loop and button.* Reinforce the end of the bracelet (Techniques, p. 96, step 11). Exit at the location at the end of the pattern at the edge of the bracelet.

3 Follow the instructions to create a brick stitch loop (Techniques, p. 98) using two columns and 12 rows of color B beads. Secure the other end of the loop at the other edge. Weave back into the piece.

4 Reinforce the end of the bracelet using finishing knots to secure (Techniques, p. 97), then trim the thread and tuck into the piece.

5 Remove the stop bead and add thread to the original tail at the opposite end of the piece. Weave into the piece, tucking the knot into a bead. Reinforce the end of the bracelet.

Add a toggle

6 Exit at the center and add a four-row and two column toggle (Techniques, p. 103) using color A beads. (Make length adjustments here.) Pick up three As, the button, and three As. Sew back through the beads, the button shank, and then through the tail to reinforce.

7 Weave into the piece using finishing knots to secure, then trim the thread, and tuck into the piece.

Southwest X's and O's
three-drop peyote

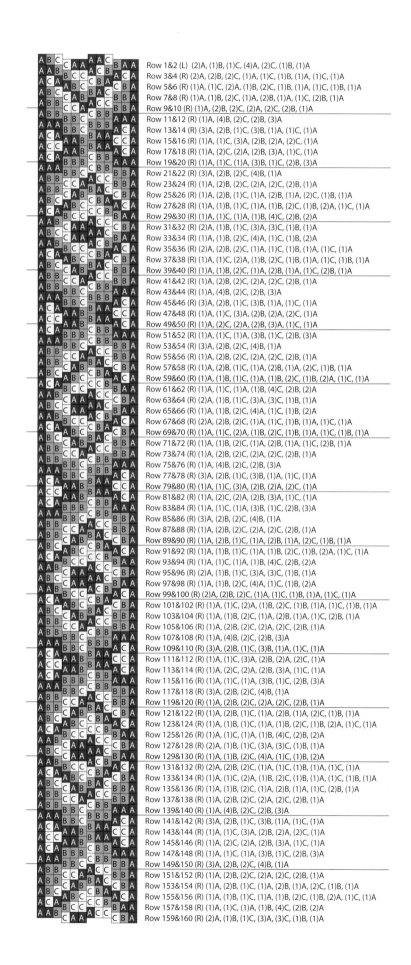

Row 1&2 (L) (2)A, (1)B, (1)C, (4)A, (2)C, (1)B, (1)A
Row 3&4 (R) (2)A, (2)B, (2)C, (1)A, (1)C, (1)B, (1)A, (1)C, (1)A
Row 5&6 (R) (1)A, (1)C, (2)A, (1)B, (2)C, (1)B, (1)A, (1)C, (1)B, (1)A
Row 7&8 (R) (1)A, (1)B, (2)C, (1)A, (2)B, (1)A, (1)C, (2)B, (1)A
Row 9&10 (R) (1)A, (2)B, (2)C, (2)A, (2)C, (2)B, (1)A
Row 11&12 (R) (1)A, (4)B, (2)C, (2)B, (3)A
Row 13&14 (R) (3)A, (2)B, (1)C, (3)B, (1)A, (1)C, (1)A
Row 15&16 (R) (1)A, (1)C, (3)A, (2)B, (2)A, (2)C, (1)A
Row 17&18 (R) (1)A, (2)C, (2)A, (2)B, (3)A, (1)C, (1)A
Row 19&20 (R) (1)A, (1)C, (1)A, (3)B, (1)C, (2)B, (3)A
Row 21&22 (R) (3)A, (2)B, (2)C, (4)B, (1)A
Row 23&24 (R) (1)A, (2)B, (2)C, (2)A, (2)C, (2)B, (1)A
Row 25&26 (R) (1)A, (2)B, (1)C, (1)A, (2)B, (1)A, (2)C, (1)B, (1)A
Row 27&28 (R) (1)A, (1)B, (1)C, (1)A, (1)B, (2)C, (1)B, (2)A, (1)C, (1)A
Row 29&30 (R) (1)A, (1)C, (1)A, (1)B, (4)C, (2)B, (2)A
Row 31&32 (R) (2)A, (1)B, (1)C, (3)A, (3)C, (1)B, (1)A
Row 33&34 (R) (1)A, (1)B, (2)C, (4)A, (1)C, (1)B, (2)A
Row 35&36 (R) (2)A, (2)B, (2)C, (1)A, (1)C, (1)B, (1)A, (1)C, (1)A
Row 37&38 (R) (1)A, (1)C, (2)A, (1)B, (2)C, (1)B, (1)A, (1)C, (1)B, (1)A
Row 39&40 (R) (1)A, (1)B, (2)C, (1)A, (2)B, (1)A, (1)C, (2)B, (1)A
Row 41&42 (R) (1)A, (2)B, (2)C, (2)A, (2)C, (2)B, (1)A
Row 43&44 (R) (1)A, (4)B, (2)C, (2)B, (3)A
Row 45&46 (R) (3)A, (2)B, (1)C, (3)B, (1)A, (1)C, (1)A
Row 47&48 (R) (1)A, (1)C, (3)A, (2)B, (2)A, (2)C, (1)A
Row 49&50 (R) (1)A, (2)C, (2)A, (2)B, (3)A, (1)C, (1)A
Row 51&52 (R) (1)A, (1)C, (1)A, (3)B, (1)C, (2)B, (3)A
Row 53&54 (R) (3)A, (2)B, (2)C, (4)B, (1)A
Row 55&56 (R) (1)A, (2)B, (2)C, (2)A, (2)C, (2)B, (1)A
Row 57&58 (R) (1)A, (2)B, (1)C, (1)A, (2)B, (1)A, (2)C, (1)B, (1)A
Row 59&60 (R) (1)A, (1)B, (1)C, (1)A, (1)B, (2)C, (1)B, (2)A, (1)C, (1)A
Row 61&62 (R) (1)A, (1)C, (1)A, (1)B, (4)C, (2)B, (2)A
Row 63&64 (R) (2)A, (1)B, (1)C, (3)A, (3)C, (1)B, (1)A
Row 65&66 (R) (1)A, (1)B, (2)C, (4)A, (1)C, (1)B, (2)A
Row 67&68 (R) (2)A, (2)B, (2)C, (1)A, (1)C, (1)B, (1)A, (1)C, (1)A
Row 69&70 (R) (1)A, (1)C, (2)A, (1)B, (2)C, (1)B, (1)A, (1)C, (1)B, (1)A
Row 71&72 (R) (1)A, (1)B, (2)C, (1)A, (2)B, (1)A, (1)C, (2)B, (1)A
Row 73&74 (R) (1)A, (2)B, (2)C, (2)A, (2)C, (2)B, (1)A
Row 75&76 (R) (1)A, (4)B, (2)C, (2)B, (3)A
Row 77&78 (R) (3)A, (2)B, (1)C, (3)B, (1)A, (1)C, (1)A
Row 79&80 (R) (1)A, (1)C, (3)A, (2)B, (2)A, (2)C, (1)A
Row 81&82 (R) (1)A, (2)C, (2)A, (2)B, (3)A, (1)C, (1)A
Row 83&84 (R) (1)A, (1)C, (1)A, (3)B, (1)C, (2)B, (3)A
Row 85&86 (R) (3)A, (2)B, (2)C, (4)B, (1)A
Row 87&88 (R) (1)A, (2)B, (2)C, (2)A, (2)C, (2)B, (1)A
Row 89&90 (R) (1)A, (2)B, (1)C, (1)A, (2)B, (1)A, (2)C, (1)B, (1)A
Row 91&92 (R) (1)A, (1)B, (1)C, (1)A, (1)B, (2)C, (1)B, (2)A, (1)C, (1)A
Row 93&94 (R) (1)A, (1)C, (1)A, (1)B, (4)C, (2)B, (2)A
Row 95&96 (R) (2)A, (1)B, (1)C, (3)A, (3)C, (1)B, (1)A
Row 97&98 (R) (1)A, (1)B, (2)C, (4)A, (1)C, (1)B, (2)A
Row 99&100 (R) (2)A, (2)B, (2)C, (1)A, (1)C, (1)B, (1)A, (1)C, (1)A
Row 101&102 (R) (1)A, (1)C, (2)A, (1)B, (2)C, (1)B, (1)A, (1)C, (1)B, (1)A
Row 103&104 (R) (1)A, (1)B, (2)C, (1)A, (2)B, (1)A, (1)C, (2)B, (1)A
Row 105&106 (R) (1)A, (2)B, (2)C, (2)A, (2)C, (2)B, (1)A
Row 107&108 (R) (1)A, (4)B, (2)C, (2)B, (3)A
Row 109&110 (R) (3)A, (2)B, (1)C, (3)B, (1)A, (1)C, (1)A
Row 111&112 (R) (1)A, (1)C, (3)A, (2)B, (2)A, (2)C, (1)A
Row 113&114 (R) (1)A, (2)C, (2)A, (2)B, (3)A, (1)C, (1)A
Row 115&116 (R) (1)A, (1)C, (1)A, (3)B, (1)C, (2)B, (3)A
Row 117&118 (R) (3)A, (2)B, (2)C, (4)B, (1)A
Row 119&120 (R) (1)A, (2)B, (2)C, (2)A, (2)C, (2)B, (1)A
Row 121&122 (R) (1)A, (2)B, (1)C, (1)A, (2)B, (1)A, (2)C, (1)B, (1)A
Row 123&124 (R) (1)A, (1)B, (1)C, (1)A, (1)B, (2)C, (1)B, (2)A, (1)C, (1)A
Row 125&126 (R) (1)A, (1)C, (1)A, (1)B, (4)C, (2)B, (2)A
Row 127&128 (R) (2)A, (1)B, (1)C, (3)A, (3)C, (1)B, (1)A
Row 129&130 (R) (1)A, (1)B, (2)C, (4)A, (1)C, (1)B, (2)A
Row 131&132 (R) (2)A, (2)B, (2)C, (1)A, (1)C, (1)B, (1)A, (1)C, (1)A
Row 133&134 (R) (1)A, (1)C, (2)A, (1)B, (2)C, (1)B, (1)A, (1)C, (1)B, (1)A
Row 135&136 (R) (1)A, (1)B, (2)C, (1)A, (2)B, (1)A, (1)C, (2)B, (1)A
Row 137&138 (R) (1)A, (2)B, (2)C, (2)A, (2)C, (2)B, (1)A
Row 139&140 (R) (1)A, (4)B, (2)C, (2)B, (3)A
Row 141&142 (R) (3)A, (2)B, (1)C, (3)B, (1)A, (1)C, (1)A
Row 143&144 (R) (1)A, (1)C, (3)A, (2)B, (2)A, (2)C, (1)A
Row 145&146 (R) (1)A, (2)C, (2)A, (2)B, (3)A, (1)C, (1)A
Row 147&148 (R) (1)A, (1)C, (1)A, (3)B, (1)C, (2)B, (3)A
Row 149&150 (R) (3)A, (2)B, (2)C, (4)B, (1)A
Row 151&152 (R) (1)A, (2)B, (2)C, (2)A, (2)C, (2)B, (1)A
Row 153&154 (R) (1)A, (2)B, (1)C, (1)A, (2)B, (1)A, (2)C, (1)B, (1)A
Row 155&156 (R) (1)A, (1)B, (1)C, (1)A, (1)B, (2)C, (1)B, (2)A, (1)C, (1)A
Row 157&158 (R) (1)A, (1)C, (1)A, (1)B, (4)C, (2)B, (2)A
Row 159&160 (R) (2)A, (1)B, (1)C, (3)A, (3)C, (1)B, (1)A

Tie Dye

Tie dye is always popular. Perhaps it is the abstract print and the blendy swirls of the colors that brings to mind college days. Tie dye prints are a whimsical and colorful addition to any outfit, and when done in subtle colors, can be worn for almost any occasion.

MATERIALS

- 11° Delica beads:
  - 3g (487) DB1515 matte opaque pink champagne (color C)
  - 4g (767) DB0376 matte metallic light grey blue (color B)
  - 3g (532) DB0114 transparent silver grey luster (color G)
  - 2g (308) DB0355 matte rose (color L)
  - 2g (306) DB0662 opaque dark mauve (colors M & D)

Note: The pattern is written using six colors, but colors M and D are combined in the materials list. One shade darker than M can be used for D if more detail is desired.

- 2 8mm light amethyst Swarovski bicones
- Fireline, 4-lb. or 6-lb. test

TOOLS

- #10 or #12 beading needle
- Thread cutters or scissors

MEASUREMENTS

1¼ in. wide and 7 in. long

To shorten, leave off as many rows on either end as necessary. To lengthen, make the toggle tail longer.

Instructions

1 Refer to the *Tie Dye* three-drop pattern and word chart on pages 62 and 63. Follow the instructions for Fast Peyote (Techniques, p. 94) to create the peyote band. Add thread (Techniques, p. 97) as needed throughout the project.

Create a flat peyote loop closure

2 *The closure for this project consists of a flat peyote loop and two 8mm Swarovski bicone beads.* Reinforce the end of the bracelet (Techniques, p. 96, step 11). Exit at the location on the pattern marked with a black dot.

3 Follow the instructions to create a flat peyote loop (Techniques, p. 98) using 15 rows of color C beads. Secure the other end of the loop at the next location marked by the next black dot. Sew back into the loop. Reinforce the base using finishing knots to secure (Techniques, p. 97).

4 Weave back into the piece using finishing knots to secure, then trim the thread, and tuck into the piece.

5 Remove the stop bead and add thread to the original tail at the opposite end of the piece. Weave into the piece, tucking the knot into a bead. Reinforce the end of the bracelet.

Add the toggle tail and bicone toggle

6 Exit at the black dot and follow the instruction to add the tail (Techniques, p. 103). Pick up nine color B beads, one bicone, one C, one bicone, and nine Bs. Weave back into the piece through several beads to form a strong base for the toggle.

7 Sew into the toggle through all of the beads, then into the end of the bracelet. To reinforce, use finishing knots to secure, then trim the thread, and tuck into the piece.

Tie Dye
three-drop peyote

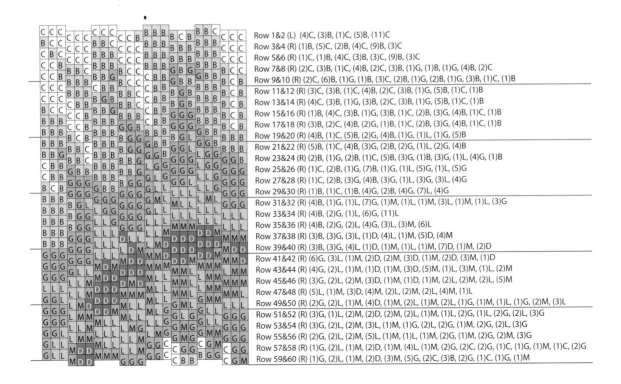

	Row 1&2 (L) (4)C, (3)B, (1)C, (5)B, (11)C
	Row 3&4 (R) (1)B, (5)C, (2)B, (4)C, (9)B, (3)C
	Row 5&6 (R) (1)C, (1)B, (4)C, (3)B, (3)C, (9)B, (3)C
	Row 7&8 (R) (2)C, (3)B, (1)C, (4)B, (2)C, (3)B, (1)G, (1)B, (1)G, (4)B, (2)C
	Row 9&10 (R) (2)C, (6)B, (1)G, (1)B, (3)C, (2)B, (1)G, (2)B, (1)G, (3)B, (1)C, (1)B
	Row 11&12 (R) (3)C, (3)B, (1)C, (4)B, (2)C, (3)B, (1)G, (5)B, (1)C, (1)B
	Row 13&14 (R) (4)C, (3)B, (1)G, (3)B, (2)C, (3)B, (1)G, (5)B, (1)C, (1)B
	Row 15&16 (R) (1)B, (4)C, (3)B, (1)G, (3)B, (1)C, (2)B, (3)G, (4)B, (1)C, (1)B
	Row 17&18 (R) (3)B, (2)C, (4)B, (2)G, (1)B, (1)C, (2)B, (3)G, (4)B, (1)C, (1)B
	Row 19&20 (R) (4)B, (1)C, (5)B, (2)G, (4)B, (1)G, (1)L, (1)G, (5)B
	Row 21&22 (R) (5)B, (1)C, (4)B, (3)G, (2)B, (2)G, (1)L, (2)G, (4)B
	Row 23&24 (R) (2)B, (1)G, (2)B, (1)C, (5)B, (3)G, (1)B, (3)G, (1)L, (4)G, (1)B
	Row 25&26 (R) (1)C, (2)B, (1)G, (7)B, (1)G, (1)L, (5)G, (1)L, (5)G
	Row 27&28 (R) (1)C, (2)B, (3)G, (4)B, (3)G, (1)L, (3)G, (3)L, (4)G
	Row 29&30 (R) (1)B, (1)C, (1)B, (4)G, (2)B, (4)G, (7)L, (4)G
	Row 31&32 (R) (4)B, (1)G, (1)L, (7)G, (1)M, (1)L, (1)M, (3)L, (1)M, (1)L, (3)G
	Row 33&34 (R) (4)B, (2)G, (1)L, (6)G, (11)L
	Row 35&36 (R) (4)B, (2)G, (2)L, (4)G, (3)L, (3)M, (6)L
	Row 37&38 (R) (3)B, (3)G, (3)L, (1)D, (4)L, (1)M, (5)D, (4)M
	Row 39&40 (R) (3)B, (3)G, (4)L, (1)D, (1)M, (1)L, (1)M, (7)D, (1)M, (2)D
	Row 41&42 (R) (6)G, (3)L, (1)M, (2)D, (2)M, (3)D, (1)M, (2)D, (3)M, (1)D
	Row 43&44 (R) (4)G, (2)L, (1)M, (1)D, (1)M, (3)D, (5)M, (1)L, (3)M, (1)L, (2)M
	Row 45&46 (R) (3)G, (2)L, (1)M, (2)D, (1)M, (1)D, (1)M, (2)L, (2)M, (2)L, (5)M
	Row 47&48 (R) (5)L, (1)M, (3)D, (4)M, (2)L, (2)M, (2)L, (4)M, (1)L
	Row 49&50 (R) (2)G, (2)L, (1)M, (4)D, (1)M, (2)L, (1)M, (2)L, (1)G, (1)M, (1)L, (1)G, (2)M, (3)L
	Row 51&52 (R) (3)G, (1)L, (2)M, (2)D, (2)M, (2)L, (1)M, (1)L, (2)G, (1)L, (2)G, (2)L, (3)G
	Row 53&54 (R) (3)G, (2)L, (2)M, (3)L, (1)M, (1)G, (2)L, (2)G, (1)M, (2)G, (2)L, (3)G
	Row 55&56 (R) (2)G, (2)L, (2)M, (5)L, (1)M, (1)L, (1)M, (2)G, (2)C, (2)G, (3)G
	Row 57&58 (R) (1)G, (2)L, (1)M, (2)D, (1)M, (4)L, (1)M, (2)G, (2)C, (2)G, (1)C, (1)G, (1)M, (1)C, (2)G
	Row 59&60 (R) (1)G, (2)L, (1)M, (2)D, (3)M, (5)G, (2)C, (3)B, (2)G, (1)C, (1)G, (1)M

	Row 61&62 (R) (3)L, (1)M, (2)D, (1)M, (2)L, (1)G, (2)C, (1)G, (9)B, (2)G
	Row 63&64 (R) (1)G, (3)L, (1)D, (5)M, (1)C, (4)B, (3)G, (5)B, (1)C
	Row 65&66 (R) (2)G, (3)L, (1)M, (3)L, (2)G, (2)B, (7)G, (3)B, (1)C
	Row 67&68 (R) (4)G, (1)L, (5)M, (1)G, (2)B, (4)G, (1)L, (2)G, (4)B
	Row 69&70 (R) (1)B, (3)G, (1)L, (3)D, (2)M, (2)G, (1)B, (2)G, (1)B, (5)G, (3)B
	Row 71&72 (R) (2)B, (2)G, (1)L, (1)M, (2)D, (1)M, (1)L, (3)G, (3)B, (2)G, (1)L, (3)G, (2)B
	Row 73&74 (R) (2)B, (2)G, (2)L, (3)M, (1)L, (2)M, (6)G, (1)L, (3)G, (2)B
	Row 75&76 (R) (2)B, (4)G, (3)L, (1)M, (2)D, (1)L, (2)G, (1)L, (1)G, (3)G, (3)B
	Row 77&78 (R) (2)B, (7)G, (3)L, (2)M, (3)L, (3)G, (3)B, (1)C
	Row 79&80 (R) (6)B, (3)G, (2)L, (2)G, (2)L, (5)G, (4)B
	Row 81&82 (R) (1)C, (6)B, (12)G, (4)B, (1)C
	Row 83&84 (R) (1)C, (3)B, (1)C, (3)B, (9)G, (3)B, (1)C, (2)B, (1)C
	Row 85&86 (R) (1)C, (2)B, (1)C, (4)B, (1)G, (4)B, (2)G, (6)B, (1)C, (1)B, (1)C
	Row 87&88 (R) (4)C, (18)B, (2)C
	Row 89&90 (R) (4)C, (2)B, (1)C, (4)B, (1)C, (3)B, (3)C, (1)B, (3)C, (2)G
	Row 91&92 (R) (4)C, (2)B, (2)C, (3)B, (1)C, (3)B, (1)C, (1)B, (7)C
	Row 93&94 (R) (4)C, (1)B, (3)C, (2)B, (1)C, (3)B, (1)C, (2)B, (7)C
	Row 95&96 (R) (3)C, (3)B, (1)C, (7)B, (1)C, (2)B, (1)C, (1)B, (5)C
	Row 97&98 (R) (3)C, (3)B, (1)C, (7)B, (1)C, (3)B, (3)C, (1)B, (2)C
	Row 99&100 (R) (1)C, (7)B, (1)G, (4)B, (1)G, (4)B, (2)C, (4)B
	Row 101&102 (R) (1)C, (4)B, (8)G, (3)B, (1)G, (6)B, (1)C, (4)B, (1)C
	Row 103&104 (R) (3)B, (3)G, (1)L, (2)G, (4)L, (2)B, (1)G, (7)B, (1)C
	Row 105&106 (R) (3)B, (1)G, (5)L, (2)M, (2)L, (1)L, (3)G, (1)B, (1)G, (5)B, (1)C
	Row 107&108 (R) (2)B, (1)G, (1)L, (2)G, (1)L, (1)M, (3)L, (1)M, (2)L, (2)G, (1)L, (1)G, (6)B
	Row 109&110 (R) (7)G, (1)D, (1)G, (1)B, (2)L, (1)D, (3)L, (1)G, (2)G, (3)B, (1)G, (6)B
	Row 111&112 (R) (2)G, (1)L, (1)G, (1)C, (2)B, (2)G, (1)B, (2)G, (1)B, (1)M, (3)L, (1)G, (1)B, (2)G, (3)B
	Row 113&114 (R) (1)G, (1)B, (2)L, (1)G, (6)B, (2)L, (3)M, (3)L, (1)G, (4)B
	Row 115&116 (R) (3)B, (3)G, (5)B, (1)C, (1)G, (1)L, (2)D, (1)M, (1)L, (2)G, (4)B
	Row 117&118 (R) (6)B, (1)G, (4)B, (3)G, (1)L, (2)D, (1)M, (1)L, (1)B, (1)G, (2)B
	Row 119&120 (R) (11)B, (1)G, (1)L, (1)M, (1)L, (1)M, (1)D, (1)M, (1)L, (3)G, (2)B
	Row 121&122 (R) (10)B, (1)C, (1)B, (1)G, (2)L, (1)M, (1)L, (2)M, (1)L, (3)G, (1)B
	Row 123&124 (R) (10)B, (1)G, (1)C, (1)B, (1)G, (1)L, (2)M, (3)L, (1)G, (1)L, (2)G
	Row 125&126 (R) (5)B, (1)C, (2)B, (5)G, (2)L, (2)D, (2)M, (1)L, (1)M, (2)G, (1)B
	Row 127&128 (R) (2)G, (1)B, (3)G, (1)B, (3)G, (1)L, (3)G, (1)L, (3)D, (1)M, (2)L, (3)B
	Row 129&130 (R) (1)G, (1)C, (1)B, (2)G, (1)B, (1)C, (1)G, (1)L, (2)G, (4)L, (3)D, (1)M, (1)L, (1)G, (1)B, (2)C
	Row 131&132 (R) (1)L, (1)C, (1)B, (4)G, (1)C, (2)L, (1)G, (1)L, (1)M, (2)L, (2)D, (2)M, (1)L, (1)G, (2)B, (1)C
	Row 133&134 (R) (1)L, (1)C, (3)G, (1)L, (2)G, (5)L, (1)M, (1)D, (3)M, (2)L, (2)G, (2)B
	Row 135&136 (R) (3)L, (1)G, (2)L, (2)G, (1)L, (1)D, (6)M, (1)L, (1)M, (1)L, (5)G
	Row 137&138 (R) (5)L, (1)M, (3)L, (4)D, (1)M, (2)L, (1)M, (2)L, (3)G, (2)B
	Row 139&140 (R) (2)M, (3)L, (3)M, (5)D, (2)M, (4)L, (1)M, (1)L, (3)B
	Row 141&142 (R) (1)M, (1)L, (8)M, (2)D, (3)M, (1)L, (6)G, (2)B
	Row 143&144 (R) (4)M, (3)D, (2)M, (1)L, (3)D, (1)M, (3)G, (6)B
	Row 145&146 (R) (2)M, (6)D, (1)M, (1)L, (2)M, (1)L, (1)M, (2)G, (7)B
	Row 147&148 (R) (1)M, (6)D, (3)M, (5)L, (1)G, (8)B
	Row 149&150 (R) (9)M, (2)L, (3)G, (1)M, (1)L, (1)G, (3)B, (1)C, (3)B
	Row 151&152 (R) (2)L, (2)M, (3)L, (1)M, (1)L, (3)G, (1)B, (2)G, (1)L, (1)G, (4)B, (2)C, (1)B
	Row 153&154 (R) (1)G, (2)L, (1)M, (5)L, (2)G, (3)B, (4)G, (4)B, (2)C
	Row 155&156 (R) (2)G, (2)L, (3)G, (2)L, (8)B, (1)G, (4)B, (2)C
	Row 157&158 (R) (3)G, (1)L, (1)G, (1)B, (2)G, (1)M, (1)G, (3)B, (1)C, (4)B, (1)G, (4)B, (1)C
	Row 159&160 (R) (2)B, (3)G, (2)B, (1)G, (1)L, (1)G, (4)B, (1)C, (4)B, (1)G, (3)B, (1)C
	Row 161&162 (R) (2)B, (3)G, (4)B, (2)G, (3)B, (3)C, (4)B, (2)C, (1)B
	Row 163&164 (R) (3)B, (2)G, (5)B, (1)G, (4)B, (3)C, (3)B, (3)C
	Row 165&166 (R) (4)B, (1)G, (1)B, (1)C, (4)B, (1)G, (4)B, (3)C, (2)B, (3)C
	Row 167&168 (R) (1)C, (3)B, (1)G, (1)B, (2)C, (4)B, (1)G, (3)B, (4)C, (1)B, (3)C
	Row 169&170 (R) (1)B, (1)C, (5)B, (3)C, (3)B, (1)G, (3)B, (3)C, (1)B, (3)C
	Row 171&172 (R) (2)B, (1)C, (5)B, (3)C, (7)B, (3)C, (1)B, (2)C
	Row 173&174 (R) (3)B, (1)C, (4)B, (4)C, (3)B, (2)C, (1)B, (2)C, (1)G, (1)C, (1)B, (1)C
	Row 175&176 (R) (3)B, (2)C, (4)B, (4)C, (2)B, (3)C, (1)B, (5)C
	Row 177&178 (R) (4)B, (1)C, (2)B, (1)C, (1)B, (5)C, (2)B, (2)C, (1)B, (5)C
	Row 179&180 (R) (1)C, (3)B, (2)C, (1)B, (1)C, (2)B, (6)C, (1)B, (2)C, (1)B, (4)C
	Row 181&182 (R) (1)C, (3)B, (2)C, (1)B, (4)C, (1)G, (8)C, (1)B, (3)C
	Row 183&184 (R) (2)C, (2)B, (7)C, (1)G, (12)C
	Row 185&186 (R) (1)G, (1)C, (1)B, (8)C, (2)G, (11)C
	Row 187&188 (R) (1)G, (11)C, (11)C
	Row 189&190 (R) (2)G, (4)C, (1)G, (5)C, (1)G, (11)C
	Row 191&192 (R) (2)G, (10)C, (1)G, (2)C, (1)G, (7)C, (1)G
	Row 193&194 (R) (3)G, (12)C, (2)G, (4)C, (3)G
	Row 195&196 (R) (2)G, (1)C, (1)G, (11)C, (1)G, (5)C, (3)G
	Row 197&198 (R) (2)G, (2)C, (1)G, (1)C, (1)G, (7)C, (2)G, (4)C, (3)G
	Row 199&200 (R) (2)C, (4)G, (5)C, (1)G, (3)C, (6)G, (1)M, (2)G

Deco Fans

This simple, elegant, but bold bracelet can be made a few different ways for a variety of looks. It is thin enough to make several and wear them together. They are quick to make and fun to wear or share.

MATERIALS
- 11º Delica beads:
  2g (344) DB0335 matte metallic silver (color A)
  1g (191) DB0662 opaque dark mauve (color B)
  2g (209) DB0377 matte metallic dark grey blue (color C)
- Fireline, 4-lb. or 6-lb. test

MATERIALS FOR ALTERNATE TOHO BRACELET
- 11º Toho beads:
  4g (315) black Toho 49 (color A)
  2g (175) red Toho 45 (color B)
  2g (190) galvanized silver Toho PF558 (color C)
- 10mm round black Czech crystal

TOOLS
- #10 or #12 beading needle
- Thread cutters or scissors

MEASUREMENTS
Delicas: ½ in. wide and 6½ in. long
Toho beads: ½ in. wide and 7¾ in. long
(Toho beads are larger.)

To shorten, stop the pattern at your desired length.

Instructions

1 Refer to the *Deco Fans* two-drop pattern and word chart on page 66. Follow the instructions for Fast Peyote (Techniques, p. 94) to create the peyote band. Add thread (Techniques, p. 97) as needed throughout the project.

Create the loop for the closure

2 *The closure for this project consists of a brick stitch loop and a peyote toggle.* Exit the end of the pattern at the edge of the bracelet.

3 Follow the instructions for the brick stitch loop (Techniques, p. 98), using two columns and 12 rows of color B bead. Secure the other end of the loop at the opposite edge of the bracelet.

4 Weave back through the loop. Reinforce the base using finishing knots to secure (Techniques, p. 97), then trim the thread and weave into the piece.

5 Remove the stop bead and add thread to the original tail at the opposite end of the piece. Weave into the piece, tucking the knot into a bead. Reinforce the end of the bracelet.

Add a toggle tail and peyote tube

6 *Delica version:* Exit at the center of the piece and follow instructions to add a two-drop tail that is three rows long (Techniques, p. 103).

7 On a new, 3-ft. length of Fireline, create a two-drop peyote toggle that is 6 rows long and 8 columns wide using color A beads or a mix of colors. Zip up the six-row band to create a peyote tube (Techniques, p. 103).

8 Add the peyote tube to the tail (Techniques, p. 103). Sew back into the tail to reinforce. Weave into the piece using finishing knots to secure, then trim the thread, and tuck into the piece.

Add toggle tail and Czech crystal

9 *Toho version:* Exit at the center and pick up two As, a Czech crystal, and a color B bead. Sew back into the crystal and the two As, then weave back into the tail and reinforce. Weave back into the piece using finishing knots to secure, then trim the thread, and tuck into the piece.

Deco Fans
two-drop peyote

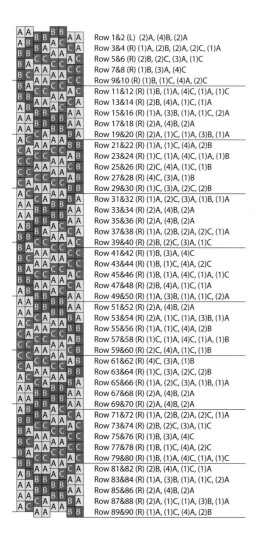

Row 1&2 (L) (2)A, (4)B, (2)A
Row 3&4 (R) (1)A, (2)B, (2)A, (2)C, (1)A
Row 5&6 (R) (2)B, (2)C, (3)A, (1)C
Row 7&8 (R) (1)B, (3)A, (4)C
Row 9&10 (R) (1)B, (1)C, (4)A, (2)C
Row 11&12 (R) (1)B, (1)A, (4)C, (1)A, (1)C
Row 13&14 (R) (2)B, (4)A, (1)C, (1)A
Row 15&16 (R) (1)A, (3)B, (1)A, (1)C, (2)A
Row 17&18 (R) (2)A, (4)B, (2)A
Row 19&20 (R) (2)A, (1)C, (1)A, (3)B, (1)A
Row 21&22 (R) (1)A, (1)C, (4)A, (2)B
Row 23&24 (R) (1)C, (1)A, (4)C, (1)A, (1)B
Row 25&26 (R) (2)C, (4)A, (1)C, (1)B
Row 27&28 (R) (4)C, (3)A, (1)B
Row 29&30 (R) (1)C, (3)A, (2)C, (2)B
Row 31&32 (R) (1)A, (2)C, (3)A, (1)B, (1)A
Row 33&34 (R) (2)A, (4)B, (2)A
Row 35&36 (R) (2)A, (4)B, (2)A
Row 37&38 (R) (1)A, (2)B, (2)A, (2)C, (1)A
Row 39&40 (R) (2)B, (2)C, (3)A, (1)C
Row 41&42 (R) (1)B, (3)A, (4)C
Row 43&44 (R) (1)B, (1)C, (4)A, (2)C
Row 45&46 (R) (1)B, (1)A, (4)C, (1)A, (1)C
Row 47&48 (R) (2)B, (4)A, (1)C, (1)A
Row 49&50 (R) (1)A, (3)B, (1)A, (1)C, (2)A
Row 51&52 (R) (2)A, (4)B, (2)A
Row 53&54 (R) (2)A, (1)C, (1)A, (3)B, (1)A
Row 55&56 (R) (1)A, (1)C, (4)A, (2)B
Row 57&58 (R) (1)C, (1)A, (4)C, (1)A, (1)B
Row 59&60 (R) (2)C, (4)A, (1)C, (1)B
Row 61&62 (R) (4)C, (3)A, (1)B
Row 63&64 (R) (1)C, (3)A, (2)C, (2)B
Row 65&66 (R) (1)A, (2)C, (3)A, (1)B, (1)A
Row 67&68 (R) (2)A, (4)B, (2)A
Row 69&70 (R) (2)A, (4)B, (2)A
Row 71&72 (R) (1)A, (2)B, (2)A, (2)C, (1)A
Row 73&74 (R) (2)B, (2)C, (3)A, (1)C
Row 75&76 (R) (1)B, (3)A, (4)C
Row 77&78 (R) (1)B, (1)C, (4)A, (2)C
Row 79&80 (R) (1)B, (1)A, (4)C, (1)A, (1)C
Row 81&82 (R) (2)B, (4)A, (1)C, (1)A
Row 83&84 (R) (1)A, (3)B, (1)A, (1)C, (2)A
Row 85&86 (R) (2)A, (4)B, (2)A
Row 87&88 (R) (2)A, (1)C, (1)A, (3)B, (1)A
Row 89&90 (R) (1)A, (1)C, (4)A, (2)B

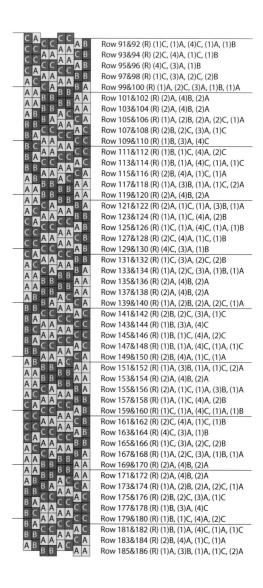

Row 91&92 (R) (1)C, (1)A, (4)C, (1)A, (1)B
Row 93&94 (R) (2)C, (4)A, (1)C, (1)B
Row 95&96 (R) (4)C, (3)A, (1)B
Row 97&98 (R) (1)C, (3)A, (2)C, (2)B
Row 99&100 (R) (1)A, (2)C, (3)A, (1)B, (1)A
Row 101&102 (R) (2)A, (4)B, (2)A
Row 103&104 (R) (2)A, (4)B, (2)A
Row 105&106 (R) (1)A, (2)B, (2)A, (2)C, (1)A
Row 107&108 (R) (2)B, (2)C, (3)A, (1)C
Row 109&110 (R) (1)B, (3)A, (4)C
Row 111&112 (R) (1)B, (1)C, (4)A, (2)C
Row 113&114 (R) (1)B, (1)A, (4)C, (1)A, (1)C
Row 115&116 (R) (2)B, (4)A, (1)C, (1)A
Row 117&118 (R) (1)A, (3)B, (1)A, (1)C, (2)A
Row 119&120 (R) (2)A, (4)B, (2)A
Row 121&122 (R) (2)A, (1)C, (1)A, (3)B, (1)A
Row 123&124 (R) (1)A, (1)C, (4)A, (2)B
Row 125&126 (R) (1)C, (1)A, (4)C, (1)A, (1)B
Row 127&128 (R) (2)C, (4)A, (1)C, (1)B
Row 129&130 (R) (4)C, (3)A, (1)B
Row 131&132 (R) (1)C, (3)A, (2)C, (2)B
Row 133&134 (R) (1)A, (2)C, (3)A, (1)B, (1)A
Row 135&136 (R) (2)A, (4)B, (2)A
Row 137&138 (R) (2)A, (4)B, (2)A
Row 139&140 (R) (1)A, (2)B, (2)A, (2)C, (1)A
Row 141&142 (R) (2)B, (2)C, (3)A, (1)C
Row 143&144 (R) (1)B, (3)A, (4)C
Row 145&146 (R) (1)B, (1)C, (4)A, (2)C
Row 147&148 (R) (1)B, (1)A, (4)C, (1)A, (1)C
Row 149&150 (R) (2)B, (4)A, (1)C, (1)A
Row 151&152 (R) (1)A, (3)B, (1)A, (1)C, (2)A
Row 153&154 (R) (2)A, (4)B, (2)A
Row 155&156 (R) (2)A, (1)C, (1)A, (3)B, (1)A
Row 157&158 (R) (1)A, (1)C, (4)A, (2)B
Row 159&160 (R) (1)C, (1)A, (4)C, (1)A, (1)B
Row 161&162 (R) (2)C, (4)A, (1)C, (1)B
Row 163&164 (R) (4)C, (3)A, (1)B
Row 165&166 (R) (1)C, (3)A, (2)C, (2)B
Row 167&168 (R) (1)A, (2)C, (3)A, (1)B, (1)A
Row 169&170 (R) (2)A, (4)B, (2)A
Row 171&172 (R) (2)A, (4)B, (2)A
Row 173&174 (R) (1)A, (2)B, (2)A, (2)C, (1)A
Row 175&176 (R) (2)B, (2)C, (3)A, (1)C
Row 177&178 (R) (1)B, (3)A, (4)C
Row 179&180 (R) (1)B, (1)C, (4)A, (2)C
Row 181&182 (R) (1)B, (1)A, (4)C, (1)A, (1)C
Row 183&184 (R) (2)B, (4)A, (1)C, (1)A
Row 185&186 (R) (1)A, (3)B, (1)A, (1)C, (2)A

Stained Glass

Stained glass is a beautiful classic that can be found in many places, such as churches and museums. The art of stained glass has a long and rich history.

MATERIALS

- 11º Delica beads:
  - 3g (564) DB0310 jet black matte (color K)
  - 3g (463) DB1269 matte transparent ocean blue (color B)
  - 2g (300) DB1270 matte transparent azure (color D)
  - 3g (401) DB1266 matte transparent lime (color G)
- **12** 6mm black Swarovski crystals (for beaded bead) OR 18mm bead or button
- **62** 3mm Czech glass round beads
- 1g 15º black round seed beads
- Fireline, 4-lb. or 6-lb. test

TOOLS

- #10 or #12 beading needle
- Thread cutters or scissors

MEASUREMENTS

1 in. wide and 6¾ in. long

To shorten, remove rows from either end of the pattern.

Stained Glass
three-drop peyote

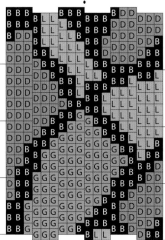

Row 1&2 (L)	(5)D, (7)B, (2)L, (4)B
Row 3&4 (R)	(4)B, (3)L, (5)B, (6)D
Row 5&6 (R)	(1)B, (2)D, (1)B, (4)L, (3)B, (6)D, (1)B
Row 7&8 (R)	(3)D, (2)B, (4)L, (2)B, (5)D, (2)B
Row 9&10 (R)	(4)D, (2)B, (4)L, (2)B, (3)D, (3)B
Row 11&12 (R)	(5)D, (2)B, (4)L, (6)B, (1)L
Row 13&14 (R)	(6)D, (2)B, (1)L, (5)B, (4)L
Row 15&16 (R)	(6)D, (2)B, (1)L, (2)B, (7)L
Row 17&18 (R)	(7)D, (4)B, (7)L
Row 19&20 (R)	(5)D, (3)B, (2)G, (2)B, (6)L
Row 21&22 (R)	(4)D, (3)B, (4)G, (2)B, (5)L
Row 23&24 (R)	(3)D, (2)B, (7)G, (2)B, (3)L, (1)B
Row 25&26 (R)	(2)D, (2)B, (9)G, (2)B, (1)L, (2)B
Row 27&28 (R)	(2)D, (2)B, (10)G, (3)B, (1)D
Row 29&30 (R)	(1)D, (2)B, (10)G, (3)B, (2)D
Row 31&32 (R)	(1)D, (2)B, (9)G, (3)B, (3)D
Row 33&34 (R)	(1)D, (2)B, (8)G, (3)B, (4)D
Row 35&36 (R)	(2)B, (8)G, (3)B, (5)D
Row 37&38 (R)	(2)B, (7)G, (4)B, (4)D, (1)B
Row 39&40 (R)	(2)B, (6)G, (2)B, (2)L, (2)B, (2)D, (2)B

Instructions

1 Refer to the *Stained Glass* three-drop pattern and word chart on page 68 and 69. Follow the instructions for Fast Peyote (Techniques, p. 94) to create the peyote band. Add thread (Techniques, p. 97) as needed throughout the project.

Create a flat peyote loop

2 *The closure for this project consists of a flat peyote loop and a beaded bead made with Swarovski bicones.* Reinforce the end of the bracelet (Techniques, p. 96, step 11). Exit at the location on the pattern marked with a black dot.

3 Pick up 39 beads and weave back into the bracelet at the location on the pattern marked with the next black dot. Sew back through the loop, weave into the piece, and exit at the original black dot.

Create a three-bead picot trim for the loop

4 Follow the instructions for picot trim (Techniques, p. 104). Weave through the first bead in the loop. Pick up three beads, skip two beads on the loop, and then sew into the next bead on the loop. Repeat until the loop is completed.

5 Weave back into the piece using finishing knots to secure (Techniques, p. 97), trim the thread, and weave the tail into the piece.

6 Remove the stop bead and add thread to the original tail at the opposite end of the piece. Weave into the piece, tucking the knot into a bead. Reinforce the end of the bracelet. Exit at the black dot marked at the center of the pattern.

7 Add a peyote toggle tail (Techniques, p. 103), making it three rows long. Leave the Fireline hanging.

Create a right-angle weave beaded bead

8 Follow instructions (Techniques, p. 108). To make sure the bead is tight, secure with finishing knots in various locations. Exit the bead and connect it to the toggle tail by weaving through the last beads of the tail.

9 Sew back through the toggle tail, into the piece, and then through several beads to form a strong base for the bead.

Add the trim

10 Exit the piece at the end, along the bracelet edge. Follow the instructions for picot trim (Techniques, p. 104) using a 15º bead on either side of a 3mm Czech bead.

11 When the trim is complete along both edges, weave back into the piece using finishing knots to secure, then trim the thread, and tuck into the piece.

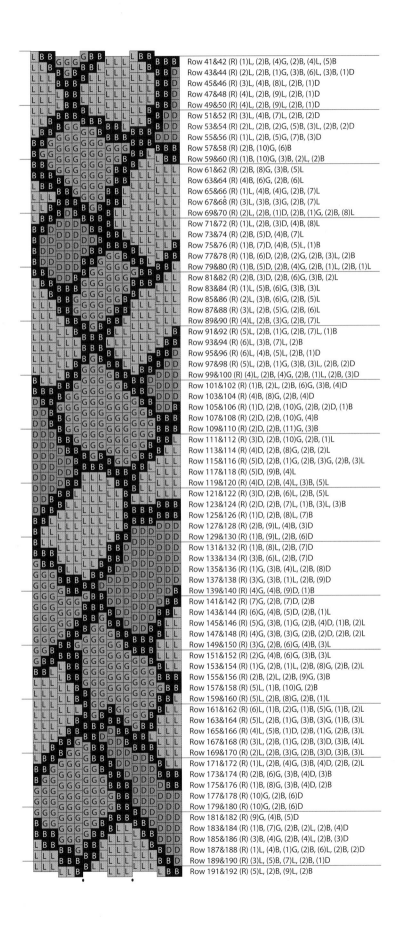

Row 41&42 (R) (1)L, (2)B, (4)G, (2)B, (4)L, (5)B
Row 43&44 (R) (2)L, (2)B, (1)G, (3)B, (6)L, (3)B, (1)D
Row 45&46 (R) (3)L, (4)B, (8)L, (2)B, (1)D
Row 47&48 (R) (4)L, (2)B, (9)L, (2)B, (1)D
Row 49&50 (R) (4)L, (2)B, (9)L, (2)B, (1)D
Row 51&52 (R) (3)L, (4)B, (7)L, (2)B, (2)D
Row 53&54 (R) (2)L, (2)B, (2)G, (5)B, (3)L, (2)B, (2)D
Row 55&56 (R) (1)L, (2)B, (5)G, (7)B, (3)D
Row 57&58 (R) (2)B, (10)G, (6)B
Row 59&60 (R) (1)B, (10)G, (3)B, (2)L, (2)B
Row 61&62 (R) (2)B, (8)G, (3)B, (5)L
Row 63&64 (R) (4)B, (6)G, (2)B, (6)L
Row 65&66 (R) (1)L, (4)B, (4)G, (2)B, (7)L
Row 67&68 (R) (3)L, (3)B, (3)G, (2)B, (7)L
Row 69&70 (R) (2)L, (2)B, (1)D, (2)B, (1)G, (2)B, (8)L
Row 71&72 (R) (1)L, (2)B, (3)D, (4)B, (8)L
Row 73&74 (R) (2)B, (5)D, (4)B, (7)L
Row 75&76 (R) (1)B, (7)D, (4)B, (5)L, (1)B
Row 77&78 (R) (1)B, (6)D, (2)B, (2)G, (2)B, (3)L, (2)B
Row 79&80 (R) (1)B, (5)D, (2)B, (4)G, (2)B, (1)L, (2)B, (1)L
Row 81&82 (R) (2)B, (3)D, (2)B, (6)G, (3)B, (2)L
Row 83&84 (R) (1)L, (5)B, (6)G, (3)B, (3)L
Row 85&86 (R) (2)L, (3)B, (6)G, (2)B, (5)L
Row 87&88 (R) (3)L, (2)B, (5)G, (2)B, (6)L
Row 89&90 (R) (4)L, (2)B, (3)G, (2)B, (7)L
Row 91&92 (R) (5)L, (2)B, (1)G, (2)B, (7)L, (1)B
Row 93&94 (R) (6)L, (3)B, (7)L, (2)B
Row 95&96 (R) (6)L, (4)B, (5)L, (2)B, (1)D
Row 97&98 (R) (5)L, (2)B, (1)G, (3)B, (3)L, (2)B, (2)D
Row 99&100 (R) (4)L, (2)B, (4)G, (2)B, (1)L, (2)B, (3)D
Row 101&102 (R) (1)B, (2)L, (2)B, (6)G, (3)B, (4)D
Row 103&104 (R) (4)B, (8)G, (2)B, (4)D
Row 105&106 (R) (1)D, (2)B, (10)G, (2)B, (2)D, (1)B
Row 107&108 (R) (2)D, (2)B, (10)G, (4)B
Row 109&110 (R) (2)D, (2)B, (11)G, (3)B
Row 111&112 (R) (3)D, (2)B, (10)G, (2)B, (1)L
Row 113&114 (R) (4)D, (2)B, (8)G, (2)B, (2)L
Row 115&116 (R) (5)D, (2)B, (1)G, (2)B, (3)G, (2)B, (3)L
Row 117&118 (R) (5)D, (9)B, (4)L
Row 119&120 (R) (4)D, (2)B, (4)L, (3)B, (5)L
Row 121&122 (R) (3)D, (2)B, (6)L, (2)B, (5)L
Row 123&124 (R) (2)D, (2)B, (7)L, (1)B, (3)L, (3)B
Row 125&126 (R) (1)D, (2)B, (8)L, (7)B
Row 127&128 (R) (2)B, (9)L, (4)B, (3)D
Row 129&130 (R) (1)B, (9)L, (2)B, (6)D
Row 131&132 (R) (1)B, (8)L, (2)B, (7)D
Row 133&134 (R) (3)B, (6)L, (2)B, (7)D
Row 135&136 (R) (1)G, (3)B, (4)L, (2)B, (8)D
Row 137&138 (R) (3)G, (3)B, (1)L, (2)B, (9)D
Row 139&140 (R) (4)G, (4)B, (9)D, (1)B
Row 141&142 (R) (7)G, (2)B, (7)D, (2)B
Row 143&144 (R) (6)G, (4)B, (5)D, (2)B, (1)L
Row 145&146 (R) (5)G, (3)B, (1)G, (2)B, (4)D, (1)B, (2)L
Row 147&148 (R) (4)G, (3)B, (3)G, (2)B, (2)D, (2)B, (2)L
Row 149&150 (R) (3)G, (2)B, (6)G, (4)B, (3)L
Row 151&152 (R) (2)G, (4)B, (6)G, (3)B, (3)L
Row 153&154 (R) (1)G, (2)B, (1)L, (2)B, (8)G, (2)B, (2)L
Row 155&156 (R) (2)B, (2)L, (2)B, (9)G, (3)B
Row 157&158 (R) (5)L, (1)B, (10)G, (2)B
Row 159&160 (R) (5)L, (2)B, (8)G, (2)B, (1)L
Row 161&162 (R) (6)L, (1)B, (2)G, (1)B, (5)G, (1)B, (2)L
Row 163&164 (R) (5)L, (2)B, (1)G, (3)B, (3)G, (1)B, (3)L
Row 165&166 (R) (4)L, (5)B, (1)D, (2)B, (1)G, (2)B, (3)L
Row 167&168 (R) (3)L, (2)B, (1)G, (2)B, (3)D, (3)B, (4)L
Row 169&170 (R) (2)L, (2)B, (3)G, (2)B, (3)D, (3)B, (3)L
Row 171&172 (R) (1)L, (2)B, (4)G, (3)B, (4)D, (2)B, (2)L
Row 173&174 (R) (2)B, (6)G, (3)B, (4)D, (3)B
Row 175&176 (R) (1)B, (8)G, (3)B, (4)D, (2)B
Row 177&178 (R) (10)G, (2)B, (6)D
Row 179&180 (R) (10)G, (2)B, (6)D
Row 181&182 (R) (9)G, (4)B, (5)D
Row 183&184 (R) (1)B, (7)G, (2)B, (2)L, (2)B, (4)D
Row 185&186 (R) (3)B, (4)G, (2)B, (4)L, (2)B, (3)D
Row 187&188 (R) (1)L, (4)B, (1)G, (2)B, (6)L, (2)B, (2)D
Row 189&190 (R) (3)L, (5)B, (7)L, (2)B, (1)D
Row 191&192 (R) (5)L, (2)B, (9)L, (2)B

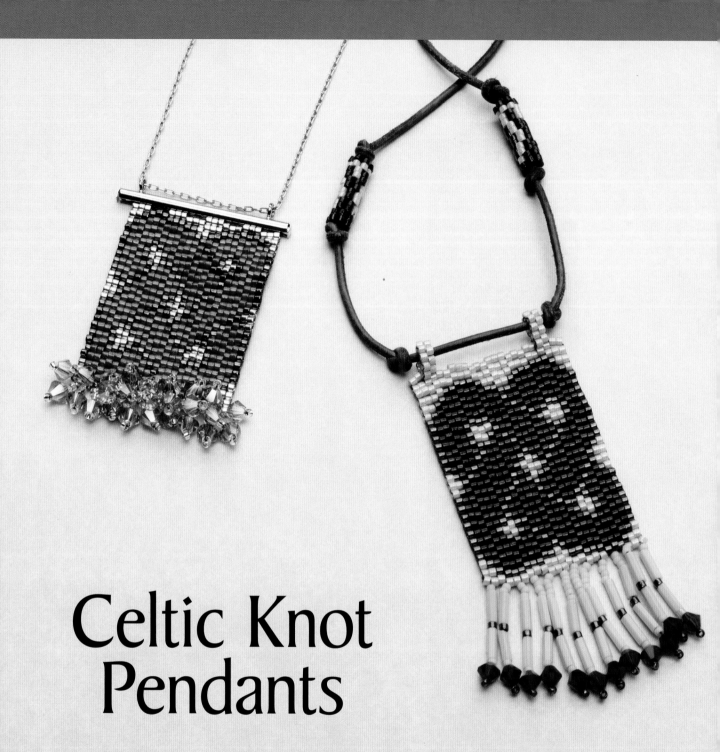

Celtic Knot Pendants

The Celtic knot or endless knot is a familiar pattern that dates back centuries. The neverending, interwoven design of Celtic knots symbolizes the cycle of life. This simple version, which can be seen as two hearts entwined, is similar to a Solomon's knot and is thought to be a symbol of love or the connection between man and God.

Instructions

1 Refer to the *Celtic Knot* three-drop pattern and word chart on page 72. Follow the instructions for Fast Peyote (Techniques, p. 94) to create the peyote band. Add thread (Techniques, p. 97) as needed throughout the project.

Follow the bead list below:

Column 1: 1 A bead, 1 bugle bead, 1 C bead, 1 bugle bead, 1 A bead, 1 bicone, 1 seed bead
Column 2: 2 A beads, 1 bugle bead, 1 C bead, 1 bugle bead, 1 A bead, 1 bicone, 1 seed bead
Column 3: 3 A beads, 1 bugle bead, 1 C bead, 1 bugle bead, 1 A bead, 1 bicone, 1 seed bead
Column 4: 4 A beads, 1 bugle bead, 1 C bead, 1 bugle bead, 1 A bead, 1 bicone, 1 seed bead
Column 5: 5 A beads, 1 bugle bead, 1 C bead, 1 bugle bead, 1 A bead, 1 bicone, 1 seed bead
Column 6: 6 A beads, 1 bugle bead, 1 C bead, 1 bugle bead, 1 A bead, 1 bicone, 1 seed bead
Column 7: 6 A beads, 1 bugle bead, 1 C bead, 1 bugle bead, 1 A bead, 1 bicone, 1 seed bead
Column 8: 5 A beads, 1 bugle bead, 1 C bead, 1 bugle bead, 1 A bead, 1 bicone, 1 seed bead
Column 9: 4 A beads, 1 bugle bead, 1 C bead, 1 bugle bead, 1 A bead, 1 bicone, 1 seed bead
Column 10: 3 A beads, 1 bugle bead, 1 C bead, 1 bugle bead, 1 A bead, 1 bicone, 1 seed bead
Column 11: 2 A beads, 1 bugle bead, 1 C bead, 1 bugle bead, 1 A bead, 1 bicone, 1 seed bead
Column 12: 1 A bead, 1 bugle bead, 1 C bead, 1 bugle bead, 1 A bead, 1 bicone, 1 seed bead

4 When the fringe is complete, sew back into the piece using finishing knots to secure (Techniques, p. 97), then trim the thread and weave into the piece.

5 Remove the stop bead and add thread to the original tail at the top of the piece. Weave into the piece and reinforce along the end.

Pink option:

Starting at the edge, follow the instructions for adding tufted fringe (Techniques, p. 107) using nine bicones with a seed bead for each of the three rows of fringe.

Finish the top

Green option:

6(a) Exit the piece at the black dot marked at the top of the pattern. *Add a flat peyote loop (Techniques, p. 98) that is two beads wide and eight rows long. Secure the loop at its base and create a folded over loop for the cord. Use finishing knots to secure the loop to the piece (Techniques, p. 97). Weave through the piece and exit the next black dot marked at the top of the pattern.

2 Reinforce the bottom of the pendant (Techniques, p. 96, step 11).

Add the fringe

Green option:

3 Starting at point **a** marked on the bottom of the pattern, follow the instructions for adding pendant fringe (Techniques, p. 106) or tufted fringe (Techniques, p. 107).

6(b) Repeat from * to add the second loop.

6(c) Weave back into the piece and through the base of the loop for strength. Use finishing knots to secure, then trim the thread and tuck the tail into a neighboring bead.

Pink option:

Pick up 24 color A beads and add the slide end tube following the instructions (Techniques, p. 108).

Add the cord and embellish

7 A simple chain or cord can be strung through the peyote loops or through the loops of a slide end tube. The bar loops can be opened and closed using chainnose pliers.

8 If desired, follow the instructions to create two peyote tubes that are 12 beads wide and six rows long (Techniques, p. 103). Follow the pattern instructions on page 72. Zip up the peyote beads (Techniques, p. 103). Knot and trim the thread.

MATERIALS

GREEN OPTION (ON CORD)
- 11º Delica beads:
  1g (156) DB0732 opaque cream (color A)
  1g (155) DB0461 metallic copper (color B)
  2g (361) DB0663 forest green opaque (color C)
- 1g 15º green rocailles or seed beads
- 1g 4mm cream-colored bugle beads
- **12** 4mm palace green opal Swarovski bicones
- Fireline, 4-lb. or 6-lb. test

CORD MATERIALS
- 24 in. 2mm leather cord
- 12x6mm silver-plated lobster clasp
- **2** 5mm jump rings
- **2** fold-over cord ends with loops
- Loc Tite glue

PINK OPTION (ON CHAIN)
- 11º Delica beads:
  1g (156) DB0035 galvanized silver (color A)
  1g (155) DB1002 metallic rainbow dark copper (color B)
  2 g (361) DB1016 metallic rainbow berry (color C)
- 1g 15º silver-lined clear rocailles or seed beads
- **27** 4mm light Colorado topaz AB2X Swarovski bicones
- Fireline, 4-lb. or 6-lb. test Cord Materials

CORD MATERIALS
- 12x6mm silver-plated lobster clasp
- **2** 5mm jump rings
- 6x35mm Miyuki silver-plated slide end tube
- 24 in. 2mm silver-plated fine cable beading chain

TOOLS
- #10 or #12 beading needle
- Thread cutters or scissors

MEASUREMENTS
1¼ in. wide and 2 in. long without the fringe; 2¾ in. long with the green option fringe.

9 String the loops of the pendant on the cord and knot the cord on the outside of the loops. *Measure about 1 in. and make a new knot in the cord. String the peyote bead and knot the cord on the side of it.

10 Repeat from * on the other side.

11 Finish the cord ends (Techniques, p. 109). Add a jump ring (Techniques, p. 109) on one side and the clasp on the other side.

Celtic Knot Pendants
three-drop peyote

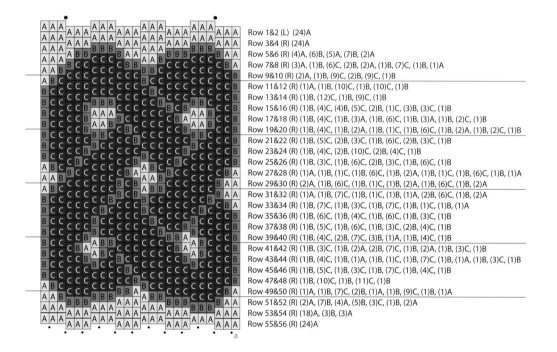

Row 1&2 (L) (24)A
Row 3&4 (R) (24)A
Row 5&6 (R) (4)A, (6)B, (5)A, (7)B, (2)A
Row 7&8 (R) (3)A, (1)B, (6)C, (2)B, (2)A, (1)B, (7)C, (1)B, (1)A
Row 9&10 (R) (2)A, (1)B, (9)C, (2)B, (9)C, (1)B
Row 11&12 (R) (1)A, (1)B, (10)C, (1)B, (10)C, (1)B
Row 13&14 (R) (1)B, (12)C, (1)B, (9)C, (1)B
Row 15&16 (R) (1)B, (4)C, (4)B, (5)C, (2)B, (1)C, (3)B, (3)C, (1)B
Row 17&18 (R) (1)B, (4)C, (1)B, (3)A, (1)B, (6)C, (1)B, (3)A, (1)B, (2)C, (1)B
Row 19&20 (R) (1)B, (4)C, (1)B, (2)A, (1)B, (1)C, (1)B, (6)C, (1)B, (2)A, (1)B, (2)C, (1)B
Row 21&22 (R) (1)B, (5)C, (2)B, (3)C, (1)B, (6)C, (2)B, (3)C, (1)B
Row 23&24 (R) (1)B, (4)C, (2)B, (10)C, (2)B, (4)C, (1)B
Row 25&26 (R) (1)B, (3)C, (1)B, (6)C, (2)B, (3)C, (1)B, (6)C, (1)B
Row 27&28 (R) (1)A, (1)B, (1)C, (1)B, (6)C, (1)B, (2)A, (1)B, (1)C, (1)B, (6)C, (1)B, (1)A
Row 29&30 (R) (2)A, (1)B, (6)C, (1)B, (1)C, (1)B, (2)A, (1)B, (6)C, (1)B, (2)A
Row 31&32 (R) (1)A, (1)B, (7)C, (1)B, (1)C, (1)B, (1)A, (2)B, (6)C, (1)B, (2)A
Row 33&34 (R) (1)B, (7)C, (1)B, (3)C, (1)B, (7)C, (1)B, (1)C, (1)B, (1)A
Row 35&36 (R) (1)B, (6)C, (1)B, (4)C, (1)B, (6)C, (1)B, (3)C, (1)B
Row 37&38 (R) (1)B, (5)C, (1)B, (6)C, (1)B, (3)C, (2)B, (4)C, (1)B
Row 39&40 (R) (1)B, (4)C, (2)B, (7)C, (3)B, (1)A, (1)B, (4)C, (1)B
Row 41&42 (R) (1)B, (3)C, (1)B, (2)A, (2)B, (7)C, (1)B, (2)A, (1)B, (3)C, (1)B
Row 43&44 (R) (1)B, (4)C, (1)B, (1)A, (1)B, (1)C, (1)B, (7)C, (1)B, (1)A, (1)B, (3)C, (1)B
Row 45&46 (R) (1)B, (5)C, (1)B, (3)C, (1)B, (7)C, (1)B, (4)C, (1)B
Row 47&48 (R) (1)B, (10)C, (1)B, (11)C, (1)B
Row 49&50 (R) (1)A, (1)B, (7)C, (2)B, (1)A, (1)B, (9)C, (1)B, (1)A
Row 51&52 (R) (2)A, (7)B, (4)A, (5)B, (3)C, (1)B, (2)A
Row 53&54 (R) (18)A, (3)B, (3)A
Row 55&56 (R) (24)A

a

Celtic Tube Bead
two-drop peyote

Row 1&2 (L) (1)C, (3)A, (6)C, (1)A, (1)C
Row 3&4 (R) (2)C, (6)A, (2)C, (1)A, (1)C
Row 5&6 (R) (1)C, (1)A, (6)B, (3)A, (1)C
Row 7&8 (R) (1)C, (3)B, (2)C, (4)B, (1)A, (1)C
Row 9&10 (R) (1)C, (3)A, (2)B, (5)A, (1)C
Row 11&12 (R) (4)C, (2)A, (4)C, (1)A, (1)C

Harmony

Musical notation has been used
for centuries, and the symbols
used to guide musicians in their
art are elegant and beautiful. The
Harmony bracelet uses these symbols
to pay tribute to musicians and to the
art of music that is a big part of life for
me and my family.

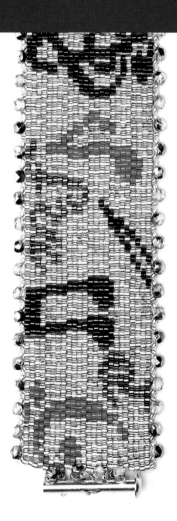

MATERIALS
- 11º Delica beads:
  - 10g (1819) DB0035 metallic silver (color A)
  - 1g (157) DB0010 black (color B)
  - 1g (166) DB0791 opaque red (color R)
  - 1g (138) DB0610 silver-lined violet (color V)
  - 1g (120) DB0458 galvanized dark green (color G)
- 1g 15º round silver seed beads
- **80** 4mm crystal vitrail fire-polished round Czech beads (about 2 8-in. strands)
- Four-strand silver tube bar clasp
- Fireline, 4-lb. or 6-lb. test

TOOLS
- #10 or #12 beading needle
- Thread cutters or scissors

MEASUREMENTS
1¼ in. wide and 7 in. long

To lengthen or shorten, add or remove rows at either end.

Instructions

1 Refer to the *Harmony* four-drop pattern and word chart on pages 75 and 76. Follow the instructions for Fast Peyote (Techniques, p. 94) to create the peyote band. Add thread (Techniques, p. 97) as needed throughout the project.

Add the trim

2 Exit the piece at the end of the bracelet, along the edge. Follow the instructions for picot trim (Techniques, p. 104), using a 15º seed bead on either side of a 4mm crystal bead.

3 When the trim is complete along both edges, weave into the piece using finishing knots to secure (Techniques, p. 97).

Add the slide bar

4 Exit the piece at one of the black dots (closest to the edge) on the end just exited. If the black dot is on an "up bead," sew through one of the loops of the slide bar and add a crystal and a seed bead (otherwise add a color A bead, a crystal, and a seed bead). Sew back through crystal. Weave back into the piece, and then exit at the next black dot.

5 Repeat step 4 until all four loops of the slide bar are secured with a bead, a crystal, and a seed bead. Flip the piece over and repeat on the other side of the bracelet.

6 Remove the stop bead and add thread to the original tail at the opposite end of the piece. Secure the other part of the slide bar as in step 4. (Make sure the slide will close properly before attaching the opposite part of the slide.) Weave into the piece, tucking the knot into a bead. Reinforce the end of the bracelet.

7 When both sides of the clasp are secure, weave into the piece, trim the thread, and tuck into the piece.

Harmony
four-drop peyote

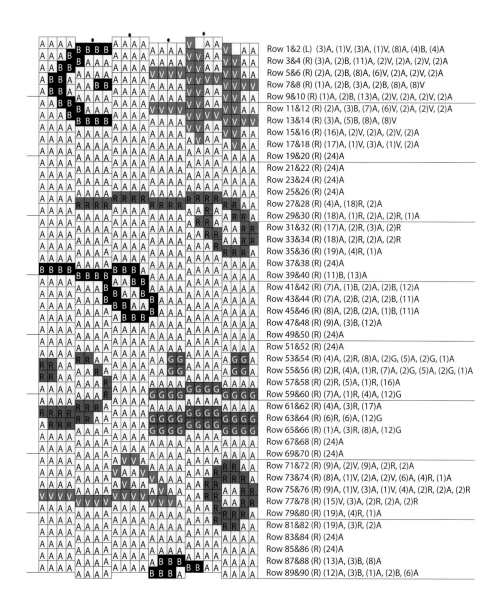

Row 1&2 (L) (3)A, (1)V, (3)A, (1)V, (8)A, (4)B, (4)A
Row 3&4 (R) (3)A, (2)B, (11)A, (2)V, (2)A, (2)V, (2)A
Row 5&6 (R) (2)A, (2)B, (8)A, (6)V, (2)A, (2)V, (2)A
Row 7&8 (R) (1)A, (2)B, (3)A, (2)B, (8)A, (8)V
Row 9&10 (R) (1)A, (2)B, (13)A, (2)V, (2)A, (2)V, (2)A
Row 11&12 (R) (2)A, (3)B, (7)A, (6)V, (2)A, (2)V, (2)A
Row 13&14 (R) (3)A, (5)B, (8)A, (8)V
Row 15&16 (R) (16)A, (2)V, (2)A, (2)V, (2)A
Row 17&18 (R) (17)A, (1)V, (3)A, (1)V, (2)A
Row 19&20 (R) (24)A
Row 21&22 (R) (24)A
Row 23&24 (R) (24)A
Row 25&26 (R) (24)A
Row 27&28 (R) (4)A, (18)R, (2)A
Row 29&30 (R) (18)A, (1)R, (2)A, (2)R, (1)A
Row 31&32 (R) (17)A, (2)R, (3)A, (2)R
Row 33&34 (R) (18)A, (2)R, (2)A, (2)R
Row 35&36 (R) (19)A, (4)R, (1)A
Row 37&38 (R) (24)A
Row 39&40 (R) (11)B, (13)A
Row 41&42 (R) (7)A, (1)B, (2)A, (2)B, (12)A
Row 43&44 (R) (7)A, (2)B, (2)A, (2)B, (11)A
Row 45&46 (R) (8)A, (2)B, (2)A, (1)B, (11)A
Row 47&48 (R) (9)A, (3)B, (12)A
Row 49&50 (R) (24)A
Row 51&52 (R) (24)A
Row 53&54 (R) (4)A, (2)R, (8)A, (2)G, (5)A, (2)G, (1)A
Row 55&56 (R) (2)R, (4)A, (1)R, (7)A, (2)G, (5)A, (2)G, (1)A
Row 57&58 (R) (2)R, (5)A, (1)R, (16)A
Row 59&60 (R) (7)A, (1)R, (4)A, (12)G
Row 61&62 (R) (4)A, (3)R, (17)A
Row 63&64 (R) (6)R, (6)A, (12)G
Row 65&66 (R) (1)A, (3)R, (8)A, (12)G
Row 67&68 (R) (24)A
Row 69&70 (R) (24)A
Row 71&72 (R) (9)A, (2)V, (9)A, (2)R, (2)A
Row 73&74 (R) (8)A, (1)V, (2)A, (2)V, (6)A, (4)R, (1)A
Row 75&76 (R) (9)A, (1)V, (3)A, (1)V, (4)A, (2)R, (2)A, (2)R
Row 77&78 (R) (15)V, (3)A, (2)R, (2)A, (2)R
Row 79&80 (R) (19)A, (4)R, (1)A
Row 81&82 (R) (19)A, (3)R, (2)A
Row 83&84 (R) (24)A
Row 85&86 (R) (24)A
Row 87&88 (R) (13)A, (3)B, (8)A
Row 89&90 (R) (12)A, (3)B, (1)A, (2)B, (6)A

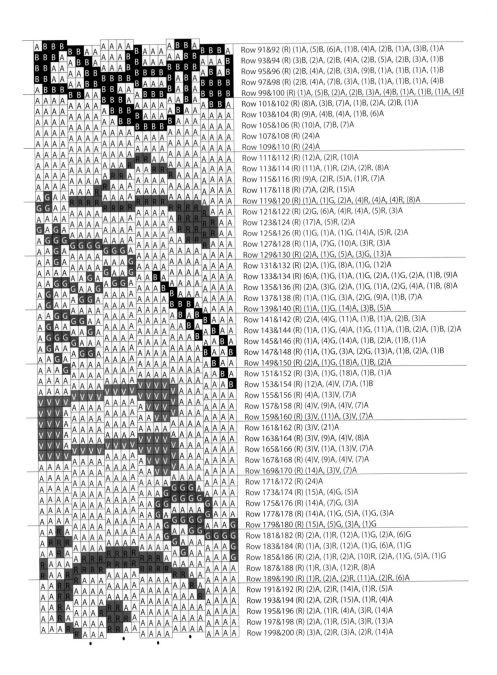

Row 91&92 (R) (1)A, (5)B, (6)A, (1)B, (4)A, (2)B, (1)A, (3)B, (1)A
Row 93&94 (R) (3)B, (2)A, (2)B, (4)A, (2)B, (5)A, (2)B, (3)A, (1)B
Row 95&96 (R) (2)B, (4)A, (2)B, (3)A, (9)B, (1)A, (1)B, (1)A, (1)B
Row 97&98 (R) (2)B, (4)A, (7)B, (3)A, (1)B, (1)A, (1)B, (1)A, (4)B
Row 99&100 (R) (1)A, (5)B, (2)A, (2)B, (3)A, (4)B, (1)A, (1)B, (1)A, (4)B
Row 101&102 (R) (8)A, (3)B, (7)A, (1)B, (2)A, (2)B, (1)A
Row 103&104 (R) (9)A, (4)B, (4)A, (1)B, (6)A
Row 105&106 (R) (10)A, (7)B, (7)A
Row 107&108 (R) (24)A
Row 109&110 (R) (24)A
Row 111&112 (R) (12)A, (2)R, (10)A
Row 113&114 (R) (11)A, (1)R, (2)A, (2)R, (8)A
Row 115&116 (R) (9)A, (2)R, (5)A, (1)R, (7)A
Row 117&118 (R) (7)A, (2)R, (15)A
Row 119&120 (R) (1)A, (1)G, (2)A, (4)R, (4)A, (4)R, (8)A
Row 121&122 (R) (2)G, (6)A, (4)R, (4)A, (5)R, (3)A
Row 123&124 (R) (17)A, (5)R, (2)A
Row 125&126 (R) (1)G, (1)A, (1)G, (14)A, (5)R, (2)A
Row 127&128 (R) (1)A, (7)G, (10)A, (3)R, (3)A
Row 129&130 (R) (2)A, (1)G, (5)A, (3)G, (13)A
Row 131&132 (R) (2)A, (1)G, (8)A, (1)G, (12)A
Row 133&134 (R) (6)A, (1)G, (1)A, (1)G, (2)A, (1)G, (2)A, (1)B, (9)A
Row 135&136 (R) (2)A, (3)G, (2)A, (1)G, (1)A, (2)G, (4)A, (1)B, (8)A
Row 137&138 (R) (1)A, (1)G, (3)A, (2)G, (9)A, (1)B, (7)A
Row 139&140 (R) (1)A, (1)G, (14)A, (3)B, (5)A
Row 141&142 (R) (2)A, (4)G, (11)A, (1)B, (1)A, (2)B, (3)A
Row 143&144 (R) (1)A, (1)G, (4)A, (1)G, (11)A, (1)B, (2)A, (1)B, (2)A
Row 145&146 (R) (1)A, (4)G, (14)A, (1)B, (2)A, (1)B, (1)A
Row 147&148 (R) (1)A, (1)G, (3)A, (2)G, (13)A, (1)B, (2)A, (1)B
Row 149&150 (R) (2)A, (1)G, (18)A, (1)B, (2)A
Row 151&152 (R) (3)A, (1)G, (18)A, (1)B, (1)A
Row 153&154 (R) (12)A, (4)V, (7)A, (1)B
Row 155&156 (R) (4)A, (13)V, (7)A
Row 157&158 (R) (4)V, (9)A, (4)V, (7)A
Row 159&160 (R) (3)V, (11)A, (3)V, (7)A
Row 161&162 (R) (3)V, (21)A
Row 163&164 (R) (3)V, (9)A, (4)V, (8)A
Row 165&166 (R) (3)V, (1)A, (13)V, (7)A
Row 167&168 (R) (4)V, (9)A, (4)V, (7)A
Row 169&170 (R) (14)A, (3)V, (7)A
Row 171&172 (R) (24)A
Row 173&174 (R) (15)A, (4)G, (5)A
Row 175&176 (R) (14)A, (7)G, (3)A
Row 177&178 (R) (14)A, (1)G, (5)A, (1)G, (3)A
Row 179&180 (R) (15)A, (5)G, (3)A, (1)G
Row 181&182 (R) (2)A, (1)R, (12)A, (1)G, (2)A, (6)G
Row 183&184 (R) (1)A, (3)R, (12)A, (1)G, (6)A, (1)G
Row 185&186 (R) (2)A, (1)R, (2)A, (10)R, (2)A, (1)G, (5)A, (1)G
Row 187&188 (R) (1)R, (3)A, (12)R, (8)A
Row 189&190 (R) (1)R, (2)A, (2)R, (11)A, (2)R, (6)A
Row 191&192 (R) (2)A, (2)R, (14)A, (1)R, (5)A
Row 193&194 (R) (2)A, (2)R, (15)A, (1)R, (4)A
Row 195&196 (R) (2)A, (1)R, (4)A, (3)R, (14)A
Row 197&198 (R) (2)A, (1)R, (5)A, (3)R, (13)A
Row 199&200 (R) (3)A, (2)R, (3)A, (2)R, (14)A

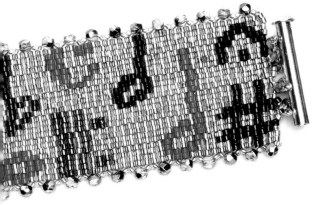

Geared Up

Steampunk (items with gears and related themes) is very popular. I found these Jim Holtz mini gears at my local hobby store. Their smooth edges and perfect size made a wonderful embellishment and toggle for this marvelously modern Geared Up bracelet.

Instructions

1 Refer to the *Geared Up* four-drop pattern and word chart on pages 79 and 80. Follow the instructions for Fast Peyote (Techniques, p. 94) to create the peyote band. Add thread (Techniques, p. 97) as needed throughout the project.

Create a flat peyote loop

2 *The closure for this project consists of a flat peyote loop and a gear toggle.* Reinforce the end of the bracelet (Techniques, p. 96, step 11). Exit at the location on the pattern marked with a black dot.

3 Follow the instructions to create the flat loop (Techniques, p. 98) using 22 rows of color A beads. Secure the other end of the loop at the opposite location marked on the pattern with a black dot.

4 Weave back into the piece using finishing knots to secure (Techniques, p. 97), trim the thread and tuck into the piece.

5 Remove the stop bead and add thread to the original tail at the opposite end of the piece. Weave into the piece, tucking the knot into a bead. Reinforce the end of the bracelet.

Add the toggle tail

6 Exit at the center of the pattern and add a two-drop tail that is 12 rows long (Techniques, p. 103). (Make length adjustments here.) Leave the Fireline tail hanging.

Make the toggle

7 On a 18-in. length of thread, sew through a round 11º bead and knot with a surgeon's knot (Techniques, p. 97). This bead will be the anchor for the toggle.

8 Pick up a large bronze gear and a medium copper gear. Sew through a round 11º bead (for the anchor on the other side), then sew back through the gears and the first anchor bead; pull tight. Repeat this path using finishing knots to secure, then trim the thread and weave into the piece.

Add the gear toggle to the toggle tail

9 Thread the toggle tail through the needle. Sew through the gap in the gears and secure the end of the tail to the base of the toggle tail. Weave into the piece using finishing knots to secure, then trim the thread and weave into the piece.

Add gear embellishments to the peyote band

10 Place a new, 3-ft. length of Fireline near the yellow dots marked on the pattern, closest to the toggle. Select which side to add the embellishments, making sure to always add them to the same side.

11 Pick up one large copper gear, sew through an anchor bead, and then weave back into the piece where the Fireline exited. Weave back into the piece and through several beads at the base of the embellishment to add strength.

12 Weave into the piece, exit at the next yellow dot, and repeat step 11 with the following embellishments until complete: small silver gear, medium bronze gear, large silver gear, small bronze gear, medium silver gear, and small silver gear.

13 When all embellishments have been added, weave into the piece using finishing knots to secure, then trim the thread, and weave back into the piece.

Geared Up
four-drop peyote

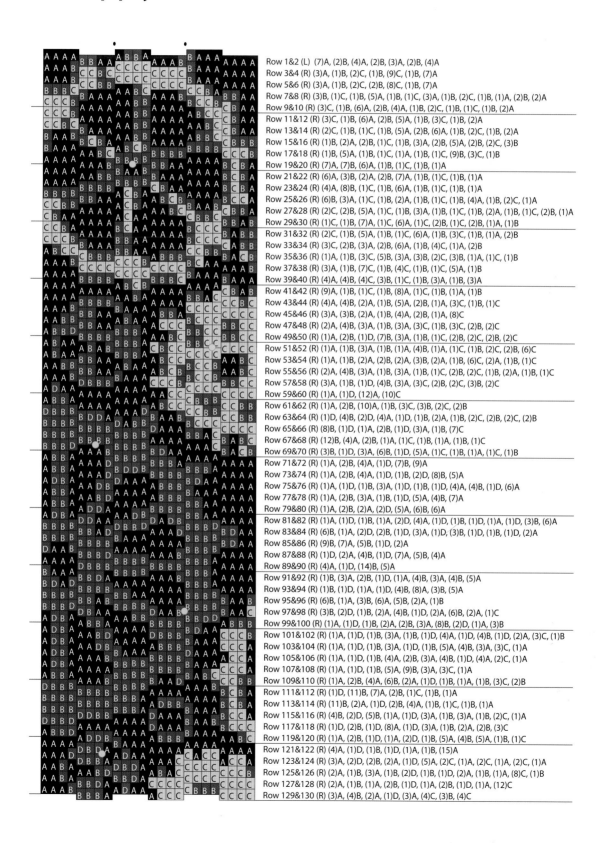

Row 1&2 (L) (7)A, (2)B, (4)A, (2)B, (3)A, (2)B, (4)A
Row 3&4 (R) (3)A, (1)B, (2)C, (1)B, (9)C, (1)B, (7)A
Row 5&6 (R) (3)A, (1)B, (2)C, (2)B, (8)C, (1)B, (7)A
Row 7&8 (R) (3)B, (1)C, (1)B, (5)A, (1)B, (1)C, (3)A, (1)B, (2)C, (1)B, (1)A, (2)B, (2)A
Row 9&10 (R) (3)C, (1)B, (6)A, (2)B, (4)A, (1)B, (2)C, (1)B, (1)C, (1)B, (2)A
Row 11&12 (R) (3)C, (1)B, (6)A, (2)B, (5)A, (1)B, (3)C, (1)B, (2)A
Row 13&14 (R) (2)C, (1)B, (1)C, (1)B, (5)A, (2)B, (6)A, (1)B, (2)C, (1)B, (2)A
Row 15&16 (R) (1)B, (2)A, (2)B, (1)C, (1)B, (3)A, (2)B, (5)A, (2)B, (2)C, (3)B
Row 17&18 (R) (1)B, (5)A, (1)B, (1)C, (1)A, (1)B, (1)C, (9)B, (3)C, (1)B
Row 19&20 (R) (7)A, (7)B, (6)A, (1)B, (1)C, (1)B, (1)A
Row 21&22 (R) (6)A, (3)B, (2)A, (2)B, (7)A, (1)B, (1)C, (1)B, (1)A
Row 23&24 (R) (4)A, (8)B, (1)C, (1)B, (6)A, (1)B, (1)C, (1)B, (1)A
Row 25&26 (R) (6)B, (3)A, (1)C, (1)B, (2)A, (1)B, (1)C, (1)B, (4)A, (1)B, (2)C, (1)A
Row 27&28 (R) (2)C, (2)B, (5)A, (1)C, (1)B, (3)A, (1)B, (1)C, (1)B, (2)A, (1)B, (1)C, (2)B, (1)A
Row 29&30 (R) (1)C, (1)B, (7)A, (1)C, (6)A, (1)C, (2)B, (1)C, (2)B, (1)A, (1)B
Row 31&32 (R) (2)C, (1)B, (5)A, (1)B, (1)C, (6)A, (1)B, (3)C, (1)B, (1)A, (2)B
Row 33&34 (R) (3)C, (2)B, (3)A, (2)B, (6)A, (1)B, (4)C, (1)A, (2)B
Row 35&36 (R) (1)A, (1)B, (3)C, (5)B, (3)A, (3)B, (2)C, (3)B, (1)A, (1)C, (1)B
Row 37&38 (R) (3)A, (1)B, (7)C, (1)B, (4)C, (1)B, (1)C, (5)A, (1)B
Row 39&40 (R) (4)A, (4)B, (4)C, (3)B, (1)C, (1)B, (3)A, (1)B, (3)A
Row 41&42 (R) (9)A, (1)B, (1)C, (1)B, (8)A, (1)C, (1)B, (1)A, (1)B
Row 43&44 (R) (4)A, (4)B, (2)A, (1)B, (5)A, (2)B, (1)A, (3)C, (1)B, (1)C
Row 45&46 (R) (3)A, (3)B, (2)A, (1)B, (4)A, (2)B, (1)A, (8)C
Row 47&48 (R) (2)A, (4)B, (3)A, (1)B, (3)A, (3)C, (1)B, (3)C, (2)B, (2)C
Row 49&50 (R) (1)A, (2)B, (1)D, (7)B, (3)A, (1)B, (1)C, (2)B, (2)C, (2)B, (2)C
Row 51&52 (R) (1)A, (1)B, (3)A, (1)B, (1)A, (4)B, (1)A, (1)C, (1)B, (2)C, (2)B, (6)C
Row 53&54 (R) (1)A, (1)B, (2)A, (2)B, (2)A, (3)B, (2)A, (1)B, (6)C, (2)A, (1)B, (1)C
Row 55&56 (R) (2)A, (4)B, (3)A, (1)B, (3)A, (1)B, (1)C, (2)B, (2)C, (1)B, (2)A, (1)B, (1)C
Row 57&58 (R) (3)A, (1)B, (1)D, (4)B, (3)A, (3)C, (2)B, (2)C, (3)B, (2)C
Row 59&60 (R) (1)A, (1)D, (12)A, (10)C
Row 61&62 (R) (1)A, (2)B, (10)A, (1)B, (3)C, (3)B, (2)C, (2)B
Row 63&64 (R) (1)D, (4)B, (2)D, (4)A, (1)D, (1)B, (2)A, (1)B, (2)C, (2)B, (2)C, (2)B
Row 65&66 (R) (8)B, (1)D, (1)A, (2)B, (1)D, (3)A, (1)B, (7)C
Row 67&68 (R) (12)B, (4)A, (2)B, (1)A, (1)C, (1)B, (1)A, (1)B, (1)C
Row 69&70 (R) (3)B, (1)D, (3)A, (6)B, (1)D, (5)A, (1)C, (1)B, (1)A, (1)C, (1)B
Row 71&72 (R) (1)A, (2)B, (4)A, (1)D, (7)B, (9)A
Row 73&74 (R) (1)A, (2)B, (4)A, (1)D, (1)B, (2)D, (8)B, (5)A
Row 75&76 (R) (1)A, (1)D, (1)B, (3)A, (1)D, (1)B, (1)D, (4)A, (4)B, (1)D, (6)A
Row 77&78 (R) (1)A, (2)B, (3)A, (1)B, (1)D, (5)A, (4)B, (7)A
Row 79&80 (R) (1)A, (2)B, (2)A, (2)D, (5)A, (6)B, (6)A
Row 81&82 (R) (1)A, (1)D, (1)B, (1)D, (2)A, (4)D, (1)D, (1)B, (1)D, (1)A, (1)D, (3)B, (6)A
Row 83&84 (R) (6)B, (1)A, (2)D, (2)B, (1)D, (3)A, (1)D, (3)B, (1)D, (1)B, (1)D, (2)A
Row 85&86 (R) (9)B, (7)A, (5)B, (1)D, (2)A
Row 87&88 (R) (1)D, (2)A, (4)B, (1)D, (7)A, (5)B, (4)A
Row 89&90 (R) (4)A, (1)D, (14)B, (5)A
Row 91&92 (R) (1)B, (3)A, (2)B, (1)D, (1)A, (4)B, (3)A, (4)B, (5)A
Row 93&94 (R) (1)B, (1)D, (1)A, (1)D, (4)B, (8)A, (3)B, (5)A
Row 95&96 (R) (6)B, (1)A, (3)B, (6)A, (5)B, (2)A, (1)B
Row 97&98 (R) (3)B, (2)D, (1)B, (2)A, (4)B, (1)D, (2)A, (6)B, (2)A, (1)C
Row 99&100 (R) (1)A, (1)D, (1)B, (2)A, (2)B, (3)A, (8)B, (2)D, (1)A, (3)B
Row 101&102 (R) (1)A, (1)D, (1)B, (3)A, (1)B, (1)D, (4)A, (1)D, (4)B, (1)D, (2)D, (2)A, (3)C, (1)B
Row 103&104 (R) (1)A, (1)D, (1)B, (3)A, (1)B, (1)D, (3)A, (4)B, (3)A, (3)C, (1)A
Row 105&106 (R) (1)A, (1)D, (1)B, (4)A, (2)B, (3)A, (4)B, (1)D, (4)A, (2)C, (1)A
Row 107&108 (R) (1)A, (1)D, (1)B, (5)A, (9)B, (3)A, (3)C, (1)A
Row 109&110 (R) (1)A, (2)B, (4)A, (6)B, (2)A, (1)D, (1)B, (1)A, (1)B, (3)C, (2)B
Row 111&112 (R) (1)D, (11)B, (7)A, (2)B, (1)C, (1)B, (1)A
Row 113&114 (R) (11)B, (2)A, (1)D, (5)B, (2)A, (1)B, (1)C, (1)B, (1)A
Row 115&116 (R) (4)B, (2)D, (5)B, (1)A, (1)D, (3)A, (1)B, (3)A, (1)B, (2)C, (1)A
Row 117&118 (R) (1)D, (2)B, (1)D, (8)A, (1)D, (3)A, (1)B, (2)A, (2)B, (3)C
Row 119&120 (R) (1)A, (2)B, (1)D, (1)A, (2)D, (1)B, (5)A, (4)B, (5)A, (1)B, (1)C
Row 121&122 (R) (4)A, (1)D, (1)B, (1)D, (1)A, (1)B, (15)A
Row 123&124 (R) (3)A, (2)D, (2)B, (2)A, (1)D, (5)A, (2)C, (1)A, (2)C, (1)A, (2)C, (1)A
Row 125&126 (R) (3)A, (3)B, (1)D, (3)A, (1)B, (2)D, (1)B, (1)D, (2)A, (1)B, (1)A, (8)C, (1)B
Row 127&128 (R) (2)A, (1)B, (1)A, (2)B, (1)D, (1)A, (1)D, (1)A, (12)C
Row 129&130 (R) (3)A, (4)B, (2)A, (1)D, (3)A, (4)C, (3)B, (4)C

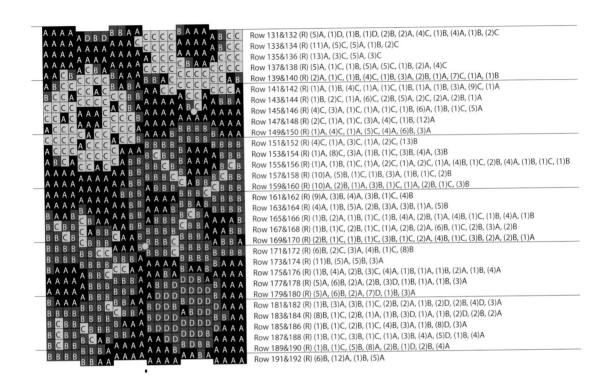

Row 131&132 (R) (5)A, (1)D, (1)B, (1)D, (2)B, (2)A, (4)C, (1)B, (4)A, (1)B, (2)C
Row 133&134 (R) (11)A, (5)C, (5)A, (1)B, (2)C
Row 135&136 (R) (13)A, (3)C, (5)A, (3)C
Row 137&138 (R) (5)A, (1)C, (1)B, (5)A, (5)C, (1)B, (2)A, (4)C
Row 139&140 (R) (2)A, (1)C, (1)B, (4)C, (1)B, (3)A, (2)B, (1)A, (7)C, (1)A, (1)B
Row 141&142 (R) (1)A, (1)B, (4)C, (1)A, (1)C, (1)B, (1)A, (1)B, (3)A, (9)C, (1)A
Row 143&144 (R) (1)B, (2)C, (1)A, (6)C, (2)B, (5)A, (2)C, (2)A, (2)B, (1)A
Row 145&146 (R) (4)C, (3)A, (1)C, (1)A, (1)C, (1)B, (6)A, (1)B, (1)C, (5)A
Row 147&148 (R) (2)C, (1)A, (1)C, (3)A, (4)C, (1)B, (12)A
Row 149&150 (R) (1)A, (4)C, (1)A, (5)C, (4)A, (6)B, (3)A
Row 151&152 (R) (4)C, (1)A, (3)C, (1)A, (2)C, (13)B
Row 153&154 (R) (1)A, (8)C, (3)A, (1)B, (1)C, (3)B, (4)A, (3)B
Row 155&156 (R) (1)A, (1)B, (1)C, (1)A, (2)C, (1)A, (2)C, (1)A, (4)B, (1)C, (2)B, (4)A, (1)B, (1)C, (1)B
Row 157&158 (R) (10)A, (5)B, (1)C, (1)B, (3)A, (1)B, (1)C, (2)B
Row 159&160 (R) (10)A, (2)B, (1)A, (3)B, (1)C, (1)A, (2)B, (1)C, (3)B
Row 161&162 (R) (9)A, (3)B, (4)A, (3)B, (1)C, (4)B
Row 163&164 (R) (4)A, (1)B, (5)A, (2)B, (3)A, (3)B, (1)A, (5)B
Row 165&166 (R) (1)B, (2)A, (1)B, (1)C, (1)B, (4)A, (2)B, (1)A, (4)B, (1)C, (1)B, (4)A, (1)B
Row 167&168 (R) (1)B, (1)C, (2)B, (1)C, (1)A, (2)B, (2)A, (6)B, (1)C, (2)B, (3)A, (2)B
Row 169&170 (R) (2)B, (1)C, (1)B, (1)C, (3)B, (1)C, (2)A, (4)B, (1)C, (3)B, (2)A, (2)B, (1)A
Row 171&172 (R) (6)B, (2)C, (3)A, (4)B, (1)C, (8)B
Row 173&174 (R) (11)B, (5)A, (5)B, (3)A
Row 175&176 (R) (1)B, (4)A, (2)B, (3)C, (4)A, (1)B, (1)A, (1)B, (2)A, (1)B, (4)A
Row 177&178 (R) (5)A, (6)B, (2)A, (2)B, (3)D, (1)B, (1)A, (1)B, (3)A
Row 179&180 (R) (5)A, (6)B, (2)A, (7)D, (1)B, (3)A
Row 181&182 (R) (1)B, (3)A, (3)B, (1)C, (2)B, (2)A, (1)B, (2)D, (2)B, (4)D, (3)A
Row 183&184 (R) (8)B, (1)C, (2)B, (1)A, (1)B, (3)D, (1)A, (1)B, (2)D, (2)B, (2)A
Row 185&186 (R) (1)B, (1)C, (2)B, (1)C, (4)B, (3)A, (1)B, (8)D, (3)A
Row 187&188 (R) (1)B, (1)C, (3)B, (1)C, (1)A, (3)B, (4)A, (5)D, (1)B, (4)A
Row 189&190 (R) (1)B, (1)C, (5)B, (8)A, (2)B, (1)D, (2)B, (4)A
Row 191&192 (R) (6)B, (12)A, (1)B, (5)A

Words to Live By

The world we live in is full of distractions. Keep in mind that the ultimate success is happiness. This bracelet is a reminder of what is truly important.

MATERIALS

- 11º Delica beads:
    8g (1527) DB0630 silver-lined light taupe alabaster (color A)
    3g (408) DB0660 opaque lavender (color B)
    2g (369) DB0609 silver-lined dark purple (color C)
- 22x6mm Swarovski elements crystal column
- 4mm Swarovski crystal bicone
- Fireline, 4-lb. or 6-lb. test

TOOLS

- #10 or #12 beading needle
- Thread cutters or scissors

MEASUREMENTS

1¼ in. wide and 6¾ in. long

To shorten, simply leave off one or two rows at either end. To lengthen, add rows of the background color or adjust the toggle tail for the desired drape.

Instructions

1 Refer to the *Words to Live By* three-drop pattern and word chart on pages 82 and 83. Follow the instructions for Fast Peyote (Techniques, p. 94) to create the peyote band. Add thread (Techniques, p. 97) as needed throughout the project.

Create a flat peyote loop

2 *The closure for this project consists of a flat peyote loop and a crystal bar toggle.* Reinforce the end of the bracelet (Techniques, p. 96, step 11). Exit at the location on the pattern marked by two black dots.

3 Follow the instructions to create the flat peyote loop (Techniques, p. 98) using 14 rows of color A beads. Secure the other end of the loop at the second location marked on the pattern with a black dot.

4 Weave back into the piece using finishing knots to secure (Techniques, p. 97), trim the thread and tuck into the piece.

Add the toggle tail and toggle

5 Remove the stop bead and add thread to the original tail at the opposite end of the piece. Weave into the piece, tucking the knot into a bead. Reinforce the end of the bracelet. Exit at the center of the pattern and add a two-drop tail (Techniques, p. 103) that is two rows long. (Make length adjustments here.)

6 Pick up the Swarovski column bead, the bicone, and a color C bead. Then sew back into the bicone, the column bead, and the tail.

7 Weave into the piece using finishing knots to secure, then trim the thread and weave into the piece.

Words to Live By
three-drop peyote

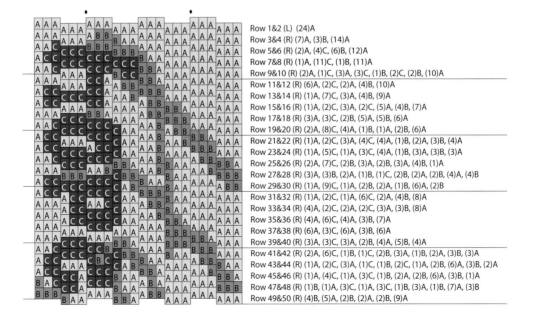

Row 1&2 (L) (24)A
Row 3&4 (R) (7)A, (3)B, (14)A
Row 5&6 (R) (2)A, (4)C, (6)B, (12)A
Row 7&8 (R) (1)A, (11)C, (1)B, (11)A
Row 9&10 (R) (2)A, (1)C, (3)A, (3)C, (1)B, (2)C, (2)B, (10)A
Row 11&12 (R) (6)A, (2)C, (2)A, (4)B, (10)A
Row 13&14 (R) (1)A, (7)C, (3)A, (4)B, (9)A
Row 15&16 (R) (1)A, (2)C, (3)A, (2)C, (5)A, (4)B, (7)A
Row 17&18 (R) (3)A, (3)C, (2)B, (5)A, (5)B, (6)A
Row 19&20 (R) (2)A, (8)C, (4)A, (1)B, (1)A, (2)B, (6)A
Row 21&22 (R) (1)A, (2)C, (3)A, (4)C, (4)A, (1)B, (2)A, (3)B, (4)A
Row 23&24 (R) (1)A, (5)C, (1)A, (3)C, (4)A, (1)B, (3)A, (3)B, (3)A
Row 25&26 (R) (2)A, (7)C, (2)B, (3)A, (2)B, (3)A, (4)B, (1)A
Row 27&28 (R) (3)A, (3)B, (2)A, (1)B, (1)C, (2)B, (2)A, (2)B, (4)A, (4)B
Row 29&30 (R) (1)A, (9)C, (1)A, (2)B, (2)A, (1)B, (6)A, (2)B
Row 31&32 (R) (1)A, (2)C, (1)A, (6)C, (2)A, (4)B, (8)A
Row 33&34 (R) (4)A, (2)C, (2)A, (2)C, (3)A, (3)B, (8)A
Row 35&36 (R) (4)A, (6)C, (4)A, (3)B, (7)A
Row 37&38 (R) (6)A, (3)C, (6)A, (3)B, (6)A
Row 39&40 (R) (3)A, (3)C, (3)A, (2)B, (4)A, (5)B, (4)A
Row 41&42 (R) (2)A, (6)C, (1)B, (1)C, (2)B, (3)A, (1)B, (2)A, (3)B, (3)A
Row 43&44 (R) (1)A, (2)C, (3)A, (1)C, (1)B, (2)C, (1)A, (2)B, (6)A, (3)B, (2)A
Row 45&46 (R) (1)A, (4)C, (1)A, (3)C, (1)B, (2)A, (2)B, (6)A, (3)B, (1)A
Row 47&48 (R) (1)B, (1)A, (3)C, (1)A, (3)C, (1)B, (3)A, (1)B, (7)A, (3)B
Row 49&50 (R) (4)B, (5)A, (2)B, (2)A, (2)B, (9)A

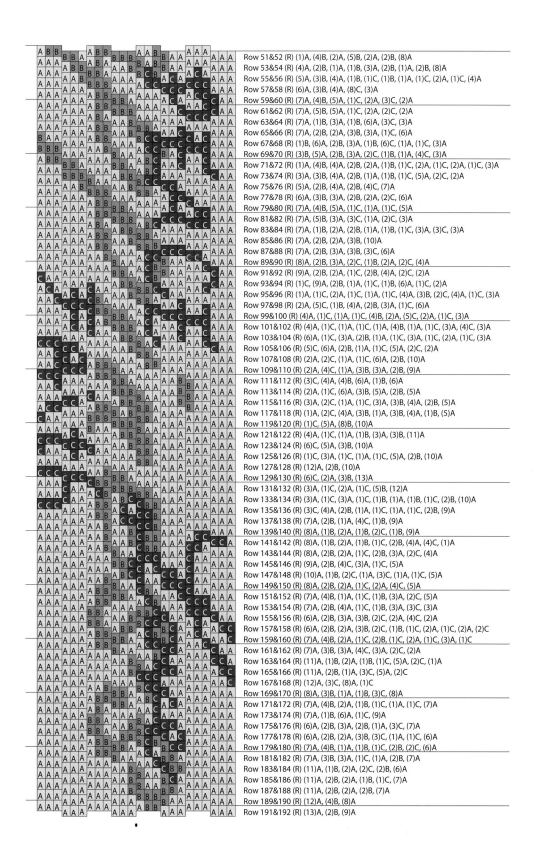

Row 51&52 (R) (1)A, (4)B, (2)A, (5)B, (2)A, (2)B, (8)A
Row 53&54 (R) (4)A, (2)B, (1)A, (1)B, (3)A, (2)B, (1)A, (2)B, (8)A
Row 55&56 (R) (5)A, (3)B, (4)A, (1)B, (1)C, (1)B, (1)A, (1)C, (2)A, (1)C, (4)A
Row 57&58 (R) (6)A, (3)B, (4)A, (8)C, (3)A
Row 59&60 (R) (7)A, (4)B, (5)A, (1)C, (2)A, (3)C, (2)A
Row 61&62 (R) (7)A, (5)B, (5)A, (1)C, (2)A, (2)C, (2)A
Row 63&64 (R) (7)A, (1)B, (3)A, (1)B, (6)A, (3)C, (3)A
Row 65&66 (R) (7)A, (2)B, (2)A, (3)B, (3)A, (1)C, (6)A
Row 67&68 (R) (1)B, (6)A, (2)B, (3)A, (1)B, (6)C, (1)A, (1)C, (3)A
Row 69&70 (R) (3)B, (5)A, (2)B, (3)A, (2)C, (1)B, (1)A, (4)C, (3)A
Row 71&72 (R) (1)A, (4)B, (4)A, (2)B, (2)A, (1)B, (1)C, (2)A, (1)C, (2)A, (1)C, (3)A
Row 73&74 (R) (3)A, (3)B, (4)A, (2)B, (1)A, (1)B, (1)C, (5)A, (2)C, (2)A
Row 75&76 (R) (5)A, (2)B, (4)A, (2)B, (4)C, (7)A
Row 77&78 (R) (6)A, (3)B, (3)A, (2)B, (2)A, (2)C, (6)A
Row 79&80 (R) (7)A, (4)B, (5)A, (1)C, (1)A, (1)C, (5)A
Row 81&82 (R) (7)A, (5)B, (3)A, (3)C, (1)A, (2)C, (3)A
Row 83&84 (R) (7)A, (1)B, (2)A, (2)B, (1)A, (1)B, (1)C, (3)A, (3)C, (3)A
Row 85&86 (R) (7)A, (2)B, (2)A, (3)B, (10)A
Row 87&88 (R) (7)A, (2)B, (3)A, (3)B, (3)C, (6)A
Row 89&90 (R) (8)A, (2)B, (3)A, (2)C, (1)B, (2)A, (2)C, (4)A
Row 91&92 (R) (9)A, (2)B, (2)A, (1)C, (2)B, (4)A, (2)C, (2)A
Row 93&94 (R) (1)C, (9)A, (2)B, (1)A, (1)C, (1)B, (6)A, (1)C, (2)A
Row 95&96 (R) (1)A, (1)C, (2)A, (1)C, (1)A, (1)C, (4)A, (3)B, (2)C, (4)A, (1)C, (3)A
Row 97&98 (R) (2)A, (5)C, (1)B, (4)A, (2)B, (3)A, (1)C, (6)A
Row 99&100 (R) (4)A, (1)C, (1)A, (1)C, (4)B, (2)A, (5)C, (2)A, (1)C, (3)A
Row 101&102 (R) (4)A, (1)C, (1)A, (1)C, (1)A, (4)B, (1)A, (1)C, (3)A, (4)C, (3)A
Row 103&104 (R) (6)A, (1)C, (3)A, (2)B, (1)A, (1)C, (3)A, (1)C, (2)A, (1)C, (3)A
Row 105&106 (R) (5)C, (6)A, (2)B, (1)A, (1)C, (5)A, (2)C, (2)A
Row 107&108 (R) (2)A, (2)C, (1)A, (1)C, (6)A, (2)B, (10)A
Row 109&110 (R) (2)A, (4)C, (1)A, (3)B, (3)A, (2)B, (9)A
Row 111&112 (R) (3)C, (4)A, (4)B, (6)A, (1)B, (6)A
Row 113&114 (R) (2)A, (1)C, (6)A, (3)B, (5)A, (2)B, (5)A
Row 115&116 (R) (3)A, (2)C, (1)A, (1)C, (3)A, (3)B, (4)A, (2)B, (5)A
Row 117&118 (R) (1)A, (2)C, (4)A, (3)B, (1)A, (3)B, (4)A, (1)B, (5)A
Row 119&120 (R) (1)C, (5)A, (8)B, (10)A
Row 121&122 (R) (4)A, (1)C, (1)A, (1)B, (3)A, (3)B, (11)A
Row 123&124 (R) (6)C, (5)A, (3)B, (10)A
Row 125&126 (R) (1)C, (3)A, (1)C, (1)A, (1)C, (5)A, (2)B, (10)A
Row 127&128 (R) (12)A, (2)B, (10)A
Row 129&130 (R) (6)C, (2)A, (3)B, (13)A
Row 131&132 (R) (3)A, (1)C, (2)A, (1)C, (5)B, (12)A
Row 133&134 (R) (3)A, (1)C, (3)A, (1)C, (1)B, (1)A, (1)B, (1)C, (2)B, (10)A
Row 135&136 (R) (3)C, (4)A, (2)B, (1)A, (1)C, (1)A, (1)C, (2)B, (9)A
Row 137&138 (R) (7)A, (2)B, (1)A, (4)C, (1)B, (9)A
Row 139&140 (R) (8)A, (1)B, (2)A, (1)B, (2)C, (1)B, (9)A
Row 141&142 (R) (8)A, (1)B, (2)A, (1)B, (1)C, (2)B, (4)A, (4)C, (1)A
Row 143&144 (R) (8)A, (2)B, (2)A, (1)C, (2)B, (3)A, (2)C, (4)A
Row 145&146 (R) (9)A, (2)B, (4)C, (3)A, (1)C, (5)A
Row 147&148 (R) (10)A, (1)B, (2)C, (1)A, (3)C, (1)A, (1)C, (5)A
Row 149&150 (R) (8)A, (2)B, (2)A, (1)C, (2)A, (4)C, (5)A
Row 151&152 (R) (7)A, (4)B, (1)A, (1)C, (1)B, (3)A, (2)C, (5)A
Row 153&154 (R) (7)A, (2)B, (4)A, (1)C, (1)B, (3)A, (3)C, (3)A
Row 155&156 (R) (6)A, (2)B, (3)A, (3)B, (2)C, (2)A, (4)C, (2)A
Row 157&158 (R) (6)A, (2)B, (2)A, (3)B, (2)C, (1)B, (1)C, (2)A, (1)C, (2)A, (2)C
Row 159&160 (R) (7)A, (4)B, (2)A, (1)C, (2)B, (1)C, (2)A, (1)C, (3)A, (1)C
Row 161&162 (R) (7)A, (3)B, (3)A, (4)C, (3)A, (2)C, (2)A
Row 163&164 (R) (11)A, (1)B, (2)A, (1)B, (1)C, (5)A, (2)C, (1)A
Row 165&166 (R) (11)A, (2)B, (1)A, (3)C, (5)A, (2)C
Row 167&168 (R) (12)A, (3)C, (8)A, (1)C
Row 169&170 (R) (8)A, (3)B, (1)A, (1)B, (3)C, (8)A
Row 171&172 (R) (7)A, (4)B, (2)A, (1)B, (1)C, (1)A, (1)C, (7)A
Row 173&174 (R) (7)A, (1)B, (6)A, (1)C, (9)A
Row 175&176 (R) (6)A, (2)B, (3)A, (2)B, (1)A, (3)C, (7)A
Row 177&178 (R) (6)A, (2)B, (2)A, (3)B, (3)C, (1)A, (1)C, (6)A
Row 179&180 (R) (7)A, (4)B, (1)A, (1)B, (1)C, (2)C, (6)A
Row 181&182 (R) (7)A, (3)B, (3)A, (1)C, (1)A, (2)B, (7)A
Row 183&184 (R) (11)A, (1)B, (2)A, (2)C, (2)B, (6)A
Row 185&186 (R) (11)A, (2)B, (2)A, (1)B, (1)C, (7)A
Row 187&188 (R) (11)A, (2)B, (2)A, (2)B, (7)A
Row 189&190 (R) (12)A, (4)B, (8)A
Row 191&192 (R) (13)A, (2)B, (9)A

New York Skyline

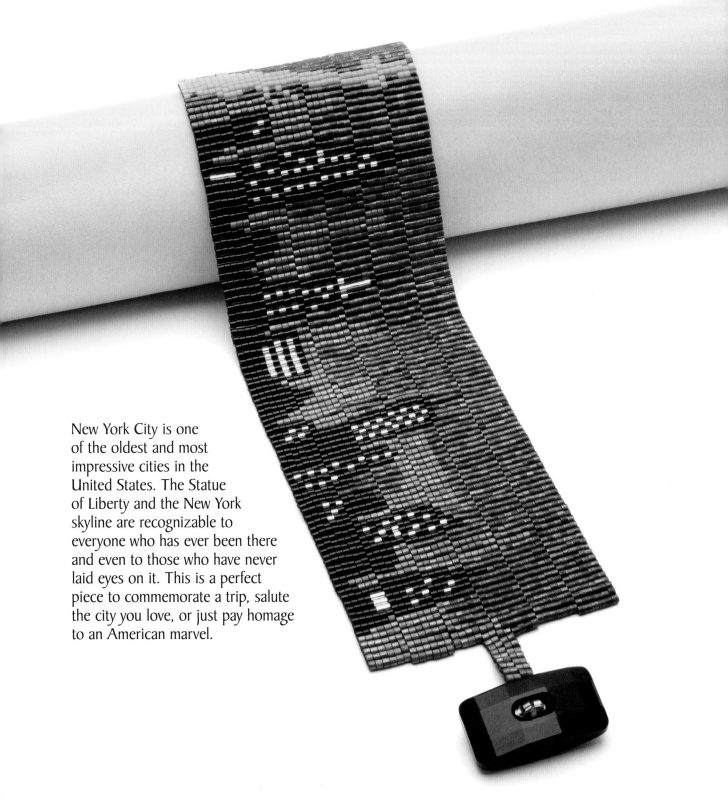

New York City is one of the oldest and most impressive cities in the United States. The Statue of Liberty and the New York skyline are recognizable to everyone who has ever been there and even to those who have never laid eyes on it. This is a perfect piece to commemorate a trip, salute the city you love, or just pay homage to an American marvel.

MATERIALS

- 15º Delica beads:
  - 5g (1739) DBS0301 matte blue grey (color A)
  - 3g (946) DBS0010 black (color B)
  - 2g (593) DBS0307 silver-grey matte metallic (color C)
  - 1g (149) DBS0374 matte metallic seafoam green (color D)
  - 1g (101) DBS0042 gold-lined crystal (color G)
- 21mm x 11mm black Swarovski rectangular button
- Fireline, 4-lb. test

TOOLS

- #10 or #12 beading needle
- Thread cutters or scissors

MEASUREMENTS

1½ in. wide and 6½ in. long

NOTE

Using 15º beads gives the design a different, more sophisticated look than the 11º beads. Remember when buying beads for this project that because the 15ºs are smaller, there are more per gram. (See the Appendix for specific amounts per gram for the Delica size.)

To lengthen this bracelet, adjust the toggle tail for the desired drape.

Instructions

1 Refer to the *New York Skyline* six-drop pattern and word chart on pages 85 and 86. Follow the instructions for Fast Peyote (Techniques, p. 94) to create the peyote band. Add thread (Techniques, p. 97) as needed throughout the project.

Create a toggle tail and a simple round loop

2 *The closure for this project consists of a simple round loop and a rectangular crystal button.* Reinforce the end of the bracelet (Techniques, p. 96, step 11). Exit at the center of the pattern. Create a two-drop tail that is four rows long using color A beads (Techniques, p. 103).

3 At the end of the tail, add a simple round loop (Techniques, p. 99), using 32 As. Weave back through the end of the piece and sew back through the loop. Weave back into the piece using finishing knots to secure (Techniques, p. 97). Trim the thread and tuck into the piece.

4 Remove the stop bead and add thread to the original tail at the opposite end of the piece. Weave into the piece, tucking the knot into a bead. Reinforce the end of the bracelet. Exit at the center.

5 Using A beads, add a two-drop tail that is 14 rows long. (Make length adjustments here.) Weave into the piece and then sew back through the tail.

6 Weave back into the piece and exit at the center of the tail. Pick up four As, four color G beads, the crystal button, and four As. Sew back into the tail and then back through the beads and the button.

7 Weave back into the piece using finishing knots to secure, then trim the thread, and tuck into the piece.

New York Skyline
six-drop peyote

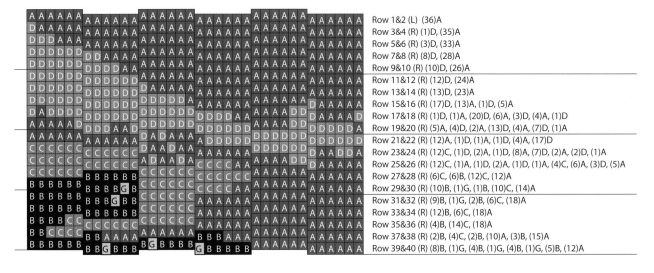

Row 1&2 (L)	(36)A
Row 3&4 (R)	(1)D, (35)A
Row 5&6 (R)	(3)D, (33)A
Row 7&8 (R)	(8)D, (28)A
Row 9&10 (R)	(10)D, (26)A
Row 11&12 (R)	(12)D, (24)A
Row 13&14 (R)	(13)D, (23)A
Row 15&16 (R)	(17)D, (13)A, (1)D, (5)A
Row 17&18 (R)	(1)D, (1)A, (20)D, (6)A, (3)D, (4)A, (1)D
Row 19&20 (R)	(5)A, (4)D, (2)A, (13)D, (4)A, (7)D, (1)A
Row 21&22 (R)	(12)A, (1)D, (1)A, (1)D, (4)A, (17)D
Row 23&24 (R)	(12)C, (1)D, (2)A, (1)D, (8)A, (7)D, (2)A, (2)D, (1)A
Row 25&26 (R)	(12)C, (1)A, (1)D, (2)A, (1)D, (1)A, (4)C, (6)A, (3)D, (5)A
Row 27&28 (R)	(6)C, (6)B, (12)C, (12)A
Row 29&30 (R)	(10)B, (1)G, (1)B, (10)C, (14)A
Row 31&32 (R)	(9)B, (1)G, (2)B, (6)C, (18)A
Row 33&34 (R)	(12)B, (6)C, (18)A
Row 35&36 (R)	(4)B, (14)C, (18)A
Row 37&38 (R)	(2)B, (4)C, (2)B, (10)A, (3)B, (15)A
Row 39&40 (R)	(8)B, (1)G, (4)B, (1)G, (4)B, (1)G, (5)B, (12)A

Row 41&42 (R) (1)B, (4)G, (5)B, (1)G, (4)B, (1)G, (2)B, (1)G, (1)B, (1)G, (1)B, (1)G, (4)B, (9)A

Row 43&44 (R) (7)B, (1)G, (4)B, (1)G, (1)B, (1)G, (1)B, (1)G, (8)B, (1)G, (10)B

Row 45&46 (R) (9)B, (1)G, (8)B, (1)G, (1)B, (1)G, (1)B, (1)G, (1)B, (1)G, (3)B, (6)A

Row 47&48 (R) (7)B, (1)G, (2)B, (1)G, (1)B, (1)G, (1)B, (1)G, (1)B, (1)G, (11)B, (8)A

Row 49&50 (R) (21)B, (15)A

Row 51&52 (R) (6)B, (6)C, (24)A

Row 53&54 (R) (3)B, (10)C, (23)A

Row 55&56 (R) (5)B, (1)C, (3)B, (9)C, (18)A

Row 57&58 (R) (10)B, (8)C, (7)A, (2)C, (9)A

Row 59&60 (R) (10)B, (19)C, (7)A

Row 61&62 (R) (9)B, (9)C, (7)A, (2)C, (9)A

Row 63&64 (R) (6)B, (11)C, (19)A

Row 65&66 (R) (5)B, (1)C, (1)B, (9)C, (20)A

Row 67&68 (R) (7)B, (7)C, (22)A

Row 69&70 (R) (12)B, (2)C, (4)A, (1)B, (17)A

Row 71&72 (R) (6)B, (1)G, (1)B, (1)G, (1)B, (1)G, (7)B, (1)G, (3)B, (14)A

Row 73&74 (R) (12)B, (1)G, (1)B, (1)G, (1)B, (1)G, (1)B, (5)G, (6)B, (7)A

Row 75&76 (R) (6)B, (1)G, (1)B, (1)G, (1)B, (1)G, (4)B, (1)G, (2)B, (1)G, (3)B, (14)A

Row 77&78 (R) (13)B, (1)G, (5)B, (17)A

Row 79&80 (R) (6)B, (5)C, (25)A

Row 81&82 (R) (5)B, (1)C, (4)B, (1)C, (25)A

Row 83&84 (R) (6)B, (1)G, (1)B, (1)G, (1)B, (11)C, (15)A

Row 85&86 (R) (4)B, (1)G, (1)B, (1)G, (1)B, (1)G, (1)B, (12)C, (14)A

Row 87&88 (R) (4)B, (1)G, (1)B, (1)G, (1)B, (1)G, (1)B, (13)C, (13)A

Row 89&90 (R) (4)B, (1)G, (1)B, (1)G, (1)B, (1)G, (1)B, (2)C, (24)A

Row 91&92 (R) (4)B, (1)G, (1)B, (1)G, (1)B, (1)G, (1)B, (2)C, (24)A

Row 93&94 (R) (4)B, (1)G, (1)B, (1)G, (1)B, (1)G, (1)B, (4)C, (22)A

Row 95&96 (R) (10)B, (4)C, (22)A

Row 97&98 (R) (5)B, (7)C, (24)A

Row 99&100 (R) (7)B, (6)C, (23)A

Row 101&102 (R) (9)B, (3)C, (24)A

Row 103&104 (R) (9)B, (8)C, (19)A

Row 105&106 (R) (7)B, (11)C, (18)A

Row 107&108 (R) (6)B, (11)C, (19)A

Row 109&110 (R) (4)B, (14)C, (18)A

Row 111&112 (R) (2)B, (8)C, (26)A

Row 113&114 (R) (7)B, (7)C, (22)A

Row 115&116 (R) (3)B, (1)G, (1)B, (1)G, (1)B, (7)C, (4)A, (6)B, (12)A

Row 117&118 (R) (2)B, (1)G, (1)B, (1)G, (20)B, (11)A

Row 119&120 (R) (25)B, (11)A

Row 121&122 (R) (25)B, (11)A

Row 123&124 (R) (25)B, (11)A

Row 125&126 (R) (18)B, (18)A

Row 127&128 (R) (12)B, (10)C, (14)A

Row 129&130 (R) (11)B, (1)G, (4)B, (6)C, (14)A

Row 131&132 (R) (13)B, (1)G, (1)B, (1)G, (1)B, (5)C, (14)A

Row 133&134 (R) (16)B, (6)C, (14)A

Row 135&136 (R) (9)B, (6)A, (7)C, (14)A

Row 137&138 (R) (9)B, (7)A, (6)C, (14)A

Row 139&140 (R) (6)B, (10)A, (6)C, (14)A

Row 141&142 (R) (11)B, (5)A, (6)C, (14)A

Row 143&144 (R) (3)B, (1)G, (1)B, (1)G, (5)B, (4)A, (7)C, (14)A

Row 145&146 (R) (4)B, (1)G, (7)B, (10)C, (14)A

Row 147&148 (R) (3)B, (1)G, (8)B, (10)C, (14)A

Row 149&150 (R) (7)B, (15)C, (14)A

Row 151&152 (R) (17)B, (5)C, (14)A

Row 153&154 (R) (7)B, (1)G, (2)B, (1)G, (1)B, (1)G, (1)B, (1)G, (4)B, (17)A

Row 155&156 (R) (9)B, (1)G, (1)B, (1)G, (4)B, (1)G, (1)B, (17)A

Row 157&158 (R) (8)B, (1)G, (2)B, (1)G, (2)B, (1)G, (3)B, (1)G, (1)B, (16)A

Row 159&160 (R) (13)B, (1)G, (2)B, (1)G, (4)B, (15)A

Row 161&162 (R) (10)B, (2)C, (6)B, (18)A

Row 163&164 (R) (10)B, (3)C, (23)A

Row 165&166 (R) (10)B, (14)C, (12)A

Row 167&168 (R) (9)B, (16)C, (11)A

Row 169&170 (R) (2)B, (27)C, (7)A

Row 171&172 (R) (3)B, (3)C, (6)B, (6)C, (6)A, (1)C, (11)A

Row 173&174 (R) (16)B, (20)A

Row 175&176 (R) (4)B, (2)G, (3)B, (1)G, (2)B, (1)G, (8)B, (15)A

Row 177&178 (R) (4)B, (2)G, (5)B, (1)G, (3)B, (1)G, (2)B, (18)A

Row 179&180 (R) (4)B, (2)G, (3)B, (1)G, (4)B, (1)G, (3)B, (18)A

Row 181&182 (R) (16)B, (20)A

Row 183&184 (R) (5)B, (9)C, (22)A

Row 185&186 (R) (2)B, (11)C, (23)A

Row 187&188 (R) (15)C, (21)A

Row 189&190 (R) (14)C, (22)A

Row 191&192 (R) (14)C, (4)A, (1)C, (17)A

Row 193&194 (R) (19)C, (17)A

Row 195&196 (R) (20)C, (16)A

Holiday Swirls

These simple, lovely swirls can be done in any color combination to make a versatile piece that shows your holiday spirit. Use grinchy green, red, and white for Christmas; purple, black, and orange for Halloween; or, choose the colors of your favorite sports team—the possibilities are endless. Top it off with an appropriate button.

MATERIALS

- 11º Delica beads:
  7g (1212) DB0351 white (color A)
  4g (645) DB0723 opaque red (color B)
  3g (447) DB0733 opaque lime green (color C)
- **20** 3mm Siam Swarovski bicones
- **41** 3mm opal Swarovski bicones
- 19x5mm crystal silver shade Swarovski crystal column bead
- Fireline, 4-lb. or 6-lb. test

TOOLS

- #10 or #12 beading needle
- Thread cutters or scissors

MEASUREMENTS

1¼ in. wide and 6¾ in. long

To shorten this pattern, leave off as many rows as necessary; to lengthen, the toggle tail can be made longer.

Instructions

1 Refer to the *Holiday Swirls* three-drop pattern and word chart on pages 88 and 89. Follow the instructions for Fast Peyote (Techniques, p. 94) to create the peyote band. Add thread (Techniques, p. 97) as needed throughout the project.

Create a flat peyote loop

2 *The closure for this project consists of a flat peyote loop and a crystal column bead (button).* Reinforce the end of the bracelet (Techniques, p. 96, step 11). Exit at the location on the pattern marked by a black dot.

Note

If using a different size bead (or button), make adjustments to the loop as needed.

3 Follow the instructions to create the flat loop (Techniques, p. 98) using 21 rows of color B beads or a mix of beads. Secure the other end of the loop at the second location marked on the pattern with a black dot.

4 Weave back into the piece using finishing knots to secure (Techniques, p. 97). Trim the thread and tuck into the piece.

5 Remove the stop bead and add thread to the original tail at the opposite end of the piece. Weave into the piece, tucking the knot into a bead. Reinforce the end of the bracelet. Exit at the location on the pattern marked by a black dot.

Create a peyote tail and connect the column bead

6 Follow instructions to make a peyote tail (Techniques, p. 103) two beads wide and five beads long. Pick up the column bead, a bicone, and a color A bead, and sew back into the bicone, column bead, and the tail.

7 Weave back into the piece and reinforce the base using finishing knots to secure. Then trim the thread and tuck into the piece.

Holiday Swirls
three-drop peyote

Row 1&2 (L) (4)A, (6)C, (3)A, (2)B, (9)A
Row 3&4 (R) (9)A, (1)B, (3)A, (2)C, (3)A, (4)C, (2)A
Row 5&6 (R) (1)B, (6)A, (3)B, (2)A, (2)C, (6)A, (3)C, (1)A
Row 7&8 (R) (2)B, (3)A, (4)B, (2)A, (2)C, (3)A, (2)B, (4)A, (2)C
Row 9&10 (R) (8)B, (2)A, (2)C, (3)A, (5)B, (3)A, (1)C
Row 11&12 (R) (1)A, (6)B, (3)A, (1)C, (3)A, (7)B, (3)A
Row 13&14 (R) (2)A, (3)B, (4)A, (2)C, (2)A, (3)B, (2)A, (5)B, (1)A
Row 15&16 (R) (9)A, (1)C, (2)A, (3)B, (5)A, (4)B
Row 17&18 (R) (1)C, (7)A, (2)C, (2)A, (3)B, (7)A, (2)B
Row 19&20 (R) (2)C, (5)A, (2)C, (2)A, (3)B, (9)A, (1)B
Row 21&22 (R) (1)A, (7)C, (2)A, (4)B, (2)A, (6)C, (2)A
Row 23&24 (R) (2)A, (5)C, (2)A, (4)B, (2)A, (2)C, (5)A, (1)C, (1)A
Row 25&26 (R) (1)B, (8)A, (2)B, (4)A, (1)C, (7)A, (1)C
Row 27&28 (R) (2)B, (6)A, (3)B, (3)A, (1)C, (9)A
Row 29&30 (R) (1)A, (9)B, (3)A, (2)C, (6)A, (2)B, (1)A
Row 31&32 (R) (2)A, (7)B, (4)A, (1)C, (4)A, (6)B
Row 33&34 (R) (1)C, (10)A, (3)C, (3)A, (7)B
Row 35&36 (R) (2)C, (7)A, (4)C, (3)A, (5)B, (3)A
Row 37&38 (R) (1)A, (10)C, (4)A, (4)B, (5)A
Row 39&40 (R) (2)A, (8)C, (4)A, (4)B, (4)A, (2)C

Row 41&42 (R) (1)B, (5)A, (3)C, (5)A, (3)B, (4)A, (3)C
Row 43&44 (R) (2)B, (11)A, (3)B, (5)A, (2)C, (1)A
Row 45&46 (R) (4)B, (5)A, (6)B, (5)A, (2)C, (2)A
Row 47&48 (R) (14)B, (5)A, (2)C, (3)A
Row 49&50 (R) (2)A, (11)B, (4)A, (3)C, (4)A
Row 51&52 (R) (6)A, (3)B, (7)A, (3)C, (5)A
Row 53&54 (R) (15)A, (2)C, (5)A, (2)B
Row 55&56 (R) (1)C, (12)A, (3)C, (5)A, (3)B
Row 57&58 (R) (2)C, (7)A, (6)C, (5)A, (4)B
Row 59&60 (R) (14)C, (5)A, (5)B
Row 61&62 (R) (11)C, (6)A, (4)B, (3)A
Row 63&64 (R) (9)C, (7)A, (3)B, (5)A
Row 65&66 (R) (3)C, (12)A, (2)B, (7)A
Row 67&68 (R) (14)A, (2)B, (5)A, (3)C
Row 69&70 (R) (13)A, (2)B, (5)A, (4)C
Row 71&72 (R) (1)B, (10)A, (4)B, (4)A, (2)C, (3)A
Row 73&74 (R) (6)B, (3)A, (5)B, (3)A, (3)C, (4)A
Row 75&76 (R) (13)B, (3)A, (3)C, (5)A
Row 77&78 (R) (11)B, (5)A, (2)C, (3)A, (3)B
Row 79&80 (R) (10)B, (5)A, (2)C, (4)A, (3)B
Row 81&82 (R) (9)B, (6)A, (2)C, (3)A, (4)B
Row 83&84 (R) (1)A, (7)B, (6)A, (2)C, (3)A, (5)B
Row 85&86 (R) (13)A, (2)C, (3)A, (6)B
Row 87&88 (R) (13)A, (2)C, (2)A, (7)B
Row 89&90 (R) (1)C, (10)A, (3)C, (2)A, (8)B
Row 91&92 (R) (2)C, (8)A, (4)C, (2)A, (8)B
Row 93&94 (R) (4)C, (5)A, (4)C, (2)A, (9)B
Row 95&96 (R) (1)A, (11)C, (2)A, (3)B, (4)A, (3)B
Row 97&98 (R) (2)A, (8)C, (3)A, (2)B, (7)A, (2)B
Row 99&100 (R) (4)A, (5)C, (2)A, (3)B, (2)A, (2)C, (5)A, (1)B
Row 101&102 (R) (1)B, (8)A, (4)B, (2)A, (5)C, (4)A
Row 103&104 (R) (2)B, (6)A, (3)B, (3)A, (2)C, (2)A, (3)C, (3)A
Row 105&106 (R) (4)B, (3)A, (3)B, (3)A, (2)C, (5)A, (3)C, (1)A
Row 107&108 (R) (9)B, (2)A, (3)C, (2)A, (2)B, (4)A, (2)C
Row 109&110 (R) (8)B, (3)A, (2)C, (2)A, (5)B, (3)A, (1)C
Row 111&112 (R) (1)A, (7)B, (2)A, (2)C, (2)A, (7)B, (3)A
Row 113&114 (R) (2)A, (5)B, (2)A, (2)C, (2)A, (3)B, (2)A, (5)B, (1)A
Row 115&116 (R) (9)A, (1)C, (2)A, (3)B, (5)A, (4)B
Row 117&118 (R) (1)C, (7)A, (2)C, (2)A, (3)B, (7)A, (2)B
Row 119&120 (R) (2)C, (6)A, (1)C, (2)A, (3)B, (9)A, (1)B
Row 121&122 (R) (1)A, (8)C, (1)A, (4)B, (2)A, (6)C, (2)A
Row 123&124 (R) (2)A, (6)C, (1)A, (4)B, (2)A, (2)C, (5)A, (1)C, (1)A
Row 125&126 (R) (1)B, (8)A, (2)B, (4)A, (1)C, (7)A, (1)C
Row 127&128 (R) (2)B, (6)A, (3)B, (3)A, (1)C, (9)A
Row 129&130 (R) (1)A, (9)B, (3)A, (2)C, (6)A, (2)B, (1)A
Row 131&132 (R) (2)A, (7)B, (4)A, (1)C, (4)A, (6)B
Row 133&134 (R) (1)C, (10)A, (3)C, (3)A, (7)B
Row 135&136 (R) (2)C, (7)A, (4)C, (3)A, (5)B, (3)A
Row 137&138 (R) (1)A, (10)C, (4)A, (4)B, (4)A, (1)C
Row 139&140 (R) (2)A, (8)C, (4)A, (4)B, (4)A, (2)C
Row 141&142 (R) (1)B, (5)A, (3)C, (5)A, (3)B, (4)A, (3)C
Row 143&144 (R) (2)B, (11)A, (3)B, (4)A, (3)C, (1)A
Row 145&146 (R) (4)B, (5)A, (6)B, (4)A, (3)C, (2)A
Row 147&148 (R) (14)B, (4)A, (3)C, (3)A
Row 149&150 (R) (2)A, (11)B, (4)A, (3)C, (4)A
Row 151&152 (R) (6)A, (3)B, (7)A, (3)C, (5)A
Row 153&154 (R) (15)A, (3)C, (4)A, (2)B
Row 155&156 (R) (1)C, (12)A, (4)C, (4)A, (3)B
Row 157&158 (R) (2)C, (7)A, (6)C, (4)A, (4)B
Row 159&160 (R) (15)C, (4)A, (5)B
Row 161&162 (R) (13)C, (4)A, (4)B, (3)A
Row 163&164 (R) (10)C, (6)A, (3)B, (5)A
Row 165&166 (R) (9)C, (6)A, (2)B, (7)A
Row 167&168 (R) (14)A, (2)B, (5)A, (3)C
Row 169&170 (R) (13)A, (2)B, (5)A, (4)C
Row 171&172 (R) (1)B, (10)A, (4)B, (4)A, (2)C, (3)A
Row 173&174 (R) (6)B, (3)A, (5)B, (3)A, (3)C, (1)B
Row 175&176 (R) (13)B, (3)A, (3)C, (2)A, (3)B
Row 177&178 (R) (11)B, (5)A, (2)C, (2)A, (3)B, (1)A
Row 179&180 (R) (10)B, (5)A, (2)C, (3)A, (2)B, (2)A
Row 181&182 (R) (9)B, (6)A, (2)C, (2)A, (2)B, (3)A
Row 183&184 (R) (8)B, (6)A, (2)C, (3)A, (2)B, (3)A
Row 185&186 (R) (13)A, (2)C, (3)A, (3)B, (3)A
Row 187&188 (R) (13)A, (2)C, (2)A, (3)B, (4)A
Row 189&190 (R) (1)C, (10)A, (3)C, (2)A, (3)B, (5)A
Row 191&192 (R) (2)C, (8)A, (4)C, (2)A, (3)B, (5)A

Math Geek

Math is a powerful language that has the power to describe and explain much of our natural world. The symbols of math can be beautiful, especially when woven in lovely glass and metallic beads!

MATERIALS

- 11º Delica:
    2g (216) DB1847f galvanized blue denim (color A)
    9g (1691) DB0035 metallic silver (color B)
    2g (274) DB0135 metallic midnight purple (color C)
    1g (123) DB0306 dark grey matte metallic (color D)
- **80** 3mm crystal vitral fire polished round Czech beads
- 1g 15º silver-lined rocaille seed beads
- 14mm shadow Swarovski rivoli button
- Fireline, 4-lb. or 6-lb. test

TOOLS

- #10 or #12 beading needles
- Thread cutters or scissors

MEASUREMENTS

1¼ in. wide and 6½ in. long

To shorten this abstract pattern, leave off as many rows as necessary; to lengthen, the toggle tail can be made longer.

Instructions

1 Refer to the *Math Geek* four-drop pattern and word chart on pages 91 and 92. Follow the instructions for Fast Peyote (Techniques, p. 94) to create the peyote band. Add thread (Techniques, p. 97) as needed throughout the project.

Create a flat peyote loop

2 *The closure for this project consists of a flat peyote loop and a Swarovski rivoli button.* Reinforce the end of the bracelet (Techniques, p. 96, step 11). Exit at the location on the pattern marked by a black dot.

3 Follow the instructions to create the flat loop (Techniques, p. 98) using 19 rows of color B beads. Secure the other end of the loop at the second location marked on the pattern with a black dot.

4 Weave back into the piece using finishing knots to secure (Techniques, p. 97). Trim the thread and tuck into the piece.

5 Remove the stop bead and add thread to the original tail at the opposite end of the piece. Weave into the piece, tucking the

knot into a bead. Reinforce the end of the bracelet. Exit at the location on the pattern marked by a black dot.

Create a toggle tail and a button

6 Follow instructions to make a toggle tail (Techniques, p. 103) two columns wide and four beads long using Bs.

7 Pick up five Bs, the button, and five Bs. Sew back through the seed beads, the button, and into the tail.

8 Reinforce the tail and weave into the piece, using finishing knots to secure.

Add the trim

9 Exit the piece at the end, along the edge. Add picot trim (Techniques, p. 104) using a 15º seed bead on either side of a 3mm Czech bead.

10 When the trim is complete along both sides, weave through the piece, using finishing knots to secure, then trim the thread, and weave into the piece.

Math Geek
four-drop peyote

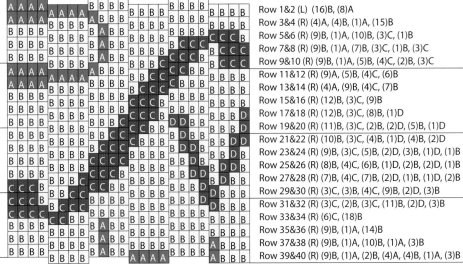

| Row 1&2 (L) (16)B, (8)A |
| Row 3&4 (R) (4)A, (4)B, (1)A, (15)B |
| Row 5&6 (R) (9)B, (1)A, (10)B, (3)C, (1)B |
| Row 7&8 (R) (9)B, (1)A, (7)B, (3)C, (1)B, (3)C |
| Row 9&10 (R) (9)B, (1)A, (5)B, (4)C, (2)B, (3)C |
| Row 11&12 (R) (9)A, (5)B, (4)C, (6)B |
| Row 13&14 (R) (4)A, (9)B, (4)C, (7)B |
| Row 15&16 (R) (12)B, (3)C, (9)B |
| Row 17&18 (R) (12)B, (3)C, (8)B, (1)D |
| Row 19&20 (R) (11)B, (3)C, (2)B, (2)D, (5)B, (1)D |
| Row 21&22 (R) (10)B, (3)C, (4)B, (1)D, (4)B, (2)D |
| Row 23&24 (R) (9)B, (3)C, (5)B, (2)D, (3)B, (1)D, (1)B |
| Row 25&26 (R) (8)B, (4)C, (6)B, (1)D, (2)B, (2)D, (1)B |
| Row 27&28 (R) (7)B, (4)C, (7)B, (2)D, (1)B, (1)D, (2)B |
| Row 29&30 (R) (3)C, (3)B, (4)C, (9)B, (2)D, (3)B |
| Row 31&32 (R) (3)C, (2)B, (3)C, (11)B, (2)D, (3)B |
| Row 33&34 (R) (6)C, (18)B |
| Row 35&36 (R) (9)B, (1)A, (14)B |
| Row 37&38 (R) (9)B, (1)A, (10)B, (1)A, (3)B |
| Row 39&40 (R) (9)B, (1)A, (2)B, (4)A, (4)B, (1)A, (3)B |

Row 41&42 (R) (9)B, (13)A, (2)B
Row 43&44 (R) (2)B, (2)D, (5)B, (1)A, (14)B
Row 45&46 (R) (2)B, (2)D, (5)B, (1)A, (14)B
Row 47&48 (R) (2)B, (2)D, (5)B, (1)A, (2)B, (1)C, (11)B
Row 49&50 (R) (8)D, (4)B, (2)C, (10)B

Row 51&52 (R) (8)D, (4)B, (4)C, (8)B
Row 53&54 (R) (2)B, (2)D, (8)B, (2)C, (2)B, (1)C, (6)B, (1)C
Row 55&56 (R) (2)B, (2)D, (8)B, (2)C, (3)B, (1)C, (4)B, (2)C
Row 57&58 (R) (2)B, (2)D, (8)B, (2)C, (4)B, (5)C, (1)B
Row 59&60 (R) (1)A, (11)B, (2)C, (6)B, (2)C, (2)B

Row 61&62 (R) (2)A, (10)B, (3)C, (9)B
Row 63&64 (R) (4)A, (9)B, (3)C, (8)B
Row 65&66 (R) (2)A, (2)B, (2)A, (12)B, (2)D, (4)B
Row 67&68 (R) (2)A, (4)B, (2)A, (10)B, (3)D, (3)B
Row 69&70 (R) (2)A, (2)B, (5)A, (8)B, (4)D, (3)B

Row 71&72 (R) (4)A, (4)B, (2)A, (6)B, (2)D, (2)B, (2)D, (2)B
Row 73&74 (R) (2)A, (13)B, (2)D, (4)B, (1)D, (2)B
Row 75&76 (R) (2)A, (12)B, (2)D, (5)B, (2)D, (1)B
Row 77&78 (R) (24)B
Row 79&80 (R) (4)B, (4)C, (16)B

Row 81&82 (R) (3)B, (3)C, (10)B, (5)C, (3)B
Row 83&84 (R) (2)B, (3)C, (13)B, (3)C, (3)B
Row 85&86 (R) (2)B, (4)C, (12)B, (3)C, (3)B
Row 87&88 (R) (3)B, (5)C, (4)B, (4)C, (2)B, (4)C, (2)B
Row 89&90 (R) (8)B, (14)C, (2)B

Row 91&92 (R) (18)B, (4)C, (2)B
Row 93&94 (R) (18)B, (4)C, (2)B
Row 95&96 (R) (18)B, (4)C, (2)B
Row 97&98 (R) (18)B, (4)C, (2)B
Row 99&100 (R) (4)B, (17)C, (3)B

Row 101&102 (R) (3)B, (18)C, (3)B
Row 103&104 (R) (2)B, (19)C, (3)B
Row 105&106 (R) (2)B, (2)C, (14)B, (3)C, (3)B
Row 107&108 (R) (2)B, (2)C, (14)B, (3)C, (3)B
Row 109&110 (R) (2)B, (3)C, (13)B, (4)C, (2)B

Row 111&112 (R) (3)B, (6)C, (10)B, (4)C, (1)B
Row 113&114 (R) (24)B
Row 115&116 (R) (12)B, (1)A, (8)B, (2)A, (1)B
Row 117&118 (R) (12)B, (3)A, (8)B, (1)A
Row 119&120 (R) (12)B, (2)A, (1)B, (1)A, (7)B, (1)A

Row 121&122 (R) (5)B, (2)D, (5)B, (2)A, (1)B, (1)A, (7)B, (1)A
Row 123&124 (R) (5)B, (2)D, (5)B, (2)A, (2)B, (2)A, (5)B, (1)A
Row 125&126 (R) (5)B, (2)D, (5)B, (2)A, (4)B, (6)A
Row 127&128 (R) (2)B, (2)D, (1)B, (2)D, (1)B, (2)D, (3)B, (2)A, (9)B
Row 129&130 (R) (2)B, (2)D, (1)B, (2)D, (1)B, (2)D, (14)B

Row 131&132 (R) (5)B, (2)D, (17)B
Row 133&134 (R) (5)B, (2)D, (15)B, (2)A
Row 135&136 (R) (22)B, (2)A
Row 137&138 (R) (22)B, (2)A
Row 139&140 (R) (9)B, (4)C, (9)B, (2)A

Row 141&142 (R) (8)B, (7)C, (7)B, (2)A
Row 143&144 (R) (8)B, (2)C, (4)B, (2)C, (6)B, (2)A
Row 145&146 (R) (8)B, (1)C, (3)B, (1)C, (2)B, (1)C, (6)B, (2)A
Row 147&148 (R) (9)B, (1)C, (2)B, (2)C, (2)B, (1)C, (7)B
Row 149&150 (R) (13)B, (4)C, (7)B

Row 151&152 (R) (2)B, (2)A, (1)B, (2)A, (17)B
Row 153&154 (R) (2)B, (2)A, (1)B, (2)A, (5)B, (1)A, (11)B
Row 155&156 (R) (2)B, (2)A, (1)B, (2)A, (4)B, (2)A, (5)B, (5)A, (1)B
Row 157&158 (R) (2)B, (2)A, (1)B, (2)A, (3)B, (2)A, (6)B, (1)A, (2)B, (2)A, (1)B
Row 159&160 (R) (2)B, (2)A, (1)B, (2)A, (3)B, (1)A, (7)B, (1)A, (2)B, (2)A, (1)B

Row 161&162 (R) (2)B, (2)A, (1)B, (2)A, (3)B, (1)A, (6)B, (2)A, (2)B, (2)A, (1)B
Row 163&164 (R) (2)B, (2)A, (1)B, (2)A, (3)B, (2)A, (5)B, (2)A, (2)B, (2)A, (1)B
Row 165&166 (R) (11)B, (7)A, (3)B, (2)A, (1)B
Row 167&168 (R) (24)B
Row 169&170 (R) (24)B

Row 171&172 (R) (24)B
Row 173&174 (R) (12)B, (1)D, (7)B, (1)D, (3)B
Row 175&176 (R) (7)B, (1)A, (4)B, (2)D, (5)B, (2)D, (3)B
Row 177&178 (R) (8)B, (1)A, (4)B, (3)D, (1)B, (3)D, (4)B
Row 179&180 (R) (8)B, (2)A, (5)B, (4)D, (5)B

Row 181&182 (R) (3)B, (1)A, (4)B, (2)A, (4)B, (4)D, (6)B
Row 183&184 (R) (3)B, (2)A, (2)B, (3)A, (4)B, (2)D, (1)B, (2)D, (5)B
Row 185&186 (R) (2)B, (2)A, (1)B, (4)A, (4)B, (2)D, (3)B, (3)D, (3)B
Row 187&188 (R) (3)A, (9)B, (2)D, (5)B, (2)D, (3)B
Row 189&190 (R) (24)B

Row 191&192 (R) (24)B

TECHNIQUES

Peyote Stitch

Peyote stitch (also known as gourd stitch) is a very versatile and widely used beading technique. Peyote has been used for centuries and was historically used to decorate the implements of the tribal peyote smoking and gourd containers.

There are many variations of peyote stitch, including flat, even or odd count, tubular, single to multiple "drop," circular, triangular, and shaped. The "drop" refers to the number of beads picked up in one traditional peyote stitch. A good way to think about multi-drop peyote is to think of each "unit" of beads as one bead. For example, in a two-drop peyote pattern, each "unit" consists of two beads.

Reading a peyote pattern

The projects in this book provide annotated patterns. This section describes how the patterns are labeled and how to follow them.

The first rows of an annotated pattern are shown in **Figure 1**. Each block represents one bead. The color of the block and the letter in each block indicates the bead color. The letters with bead descriptions (color and size) and number of beads required for each color are provided in the materials list for each project.

The patterns in this book may also have markings on or outside the pattern like the black dots at the top of the piece in **Figure 1**. These particular markings are for reference in placing a clasp or a fold. Their specific use is described in the individual project instructions.

Examples of row numbers for traditional peyote patterns are shown in **Figure 2**. The fast peyote instructions will follow the same convention. In both traditional and fast peyote, the first two rows are picked up together. Fast peyote is picked up in one direction—two rows at a time. (However, in traditional peyote, rows 3 and higher are stitched back and forth, one at a time, in numerical order.)

For the patterns in this book, always start reading at the upper right corner (row 1). Pick up the first two rows, following the pattern from **right to left**. Then pick up rows 3 and 4, reading from **left to right**. Those rows (3 and 4) will then be secured to the previous rows by weaving from **right to left** (no new beads are added). This concept will become more clear in the fast peyote instructions (p. 94).

Some instructions will refer to an "up bead" and a "down bead" — the "up bead" is simply the bead or beads on the row that are higher than their neighbors. For example, in **Figure 2**, the beads in row 2 are "up beads" and the beads in row 1 are "down beads".

The end of the piece is parallel to the thread path (along the rows, in **Figure 2**, beads numbered 1 and 2 are the end). The edge of the piece is perpendicular to the thread path as shown in **Figure 3**. The drop is the number of beads per unit. **Figure 1**, **Figure 2**, and **Figure 3** show four- drop.

Tip

If following the word charts rather than the bead patterns, be sure to read the following information on word charts before continuing.

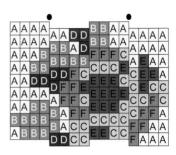

Figure 1

Figure 2

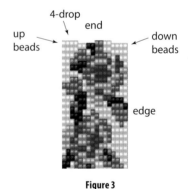

Figure 3

Tips

• There are a number of ways to keep track of progress as you follow a pattern. You can make a copy and use a pencil or color pen to draw a line through each completed row; this is my preferred method.

• If making multiple pieces from the same pattern, you can make a copy of the pattern, laminate, and use dry-erase markers. Then, you can erase and reuse the pattern many times.

Reading a word chart

Many beaders prefer following a peyote word chart. (Word charts are written or generated for traditional peyote to help keep track of the direction of the weave.) This book provides word charts *exclusively for fast peyote*.

Both traditional and fast peyote word charts are written using row numbering as shown in **Figure 2** (p. 93). In addition, the stitching direction is also given. Fast peyote word charts number the rows as in the traditional style and list the beads as they are sewn: two rows at a time and (after rows 1 and 2), always **left to right**.

The following example shows the first rows of a fast peyote word chart (for the pattern shown in **Figure 1** (p. 93). The row numbers are given first and each row of text represents two (traditional peyote) rows of beads. The direction you are picking up the beads is given in parentheses after the row numbers. In this case, the first two rows are picked up from *right to left (L)*. The remaining rows are picked up from *left to right (R)*. The rows are then secured by weaving back through the beads in the "odd" numbered row.

Row 1&2 (L) (6)A, (2)B, (2)D, (6)A
Row 3&4 (R) (4)A, (2)B, (1)A, (1)D, (2)B, (6)A
Row 5&6 (R) (3)A, (5)B, (3)F, (1)C, (1)A, (1)E, (2)A
Row 7&8 (R) (2)A, (2)B, (2)D, (1)F, (4)C, (1)E, (1)C, (2)E, (1)A

Fast Peyote Stitch

In traditional peyote stitch, the beads are picked up back and forth (right to left, then left to right) across the piece. The rows in a peyote pattern are numbered accordingly. However, with fast peyote, two rows of beads are picked up at once, and the Fireline is then woven back through the previous row. This technique, aside from being faster, has the advantage that after the first four rows, the beader is always stringing in the same direction—making it easier to follow a pattern.

1 Gather the required materials and tools, plus enough beads to finish the project. Next, prepare your workspace. (A specific materials and tools list is given for each project.)

2 Examine the pattern provided and read any special instructions. If you would like to modify the pattern in some way, make note of any changes before starting.

3 Cut a comfortable length of 4- or 6-lb. Fireline. To determine a comfortable length, remember that beads will be picked up and woven through the piece multiple times. If it is too long, it can get knotted and tangled; if it is too short, Fireline will need to be added more frequently. I typically use a half an arm span (from my chest to one extended hand).

Tip

When the thread is long, pulling it through each section of the row can slow things down. To speed up a little, do not pull the thread all the way through until the very end of the row. That is, while the newly strung two rows are being secured to the previous row, thread through each unit with just enough slack to string through the next unit of beads. Take care not to cross threads, as that will form a knot. Once the edge has been exited, pull all the slack through, tighten, and straighten the rows.

4 Thread the Fireline through a beading needle. If necessary, the end of the thread can be flattened with fingernails or pliers so that it is easier to pass through the eye of the needle. If you prefer, a needle-threader can be used.

5 Select a single bead to use as a *stop bead*. It is helpful if this bead is a contrasting color that is not in the pattern so that it does not get mistaken for part of the piece. (This bead is to stop your first rows from sliding off the end of the thread and will be removed later.) Pick up the stop bead, sew around the bead, and then sew back through the same end, as shown in **Figure 4**. Pull tight and leave a 6-in. tail.

6 Pick up the first two rows of beads, working from the right side of the pattern towards the left side as shown in **Figure 5**.

7 If using a word chart, always pick up the beads in the order listed in the chart, reading from right to left.

8 Pick up the next two rows of beads, working from the left side of the pattern **Figure 6** toward the right side as shown in **Figure 7**.

Tips

• If the thread is pulled too tightly, it can become difficult to tell where one row begins and the next row ends; also, the piece can twist. On the first four rows, keep the thread fairly loose, with the piece laid out on a beading mat. When the last bead of row 4 is exited on the left, the thread tail and the needle end of the thread can be pulled to tighten.

• Periodically roll the beads between your two fingers. This will help to align the rows so they lay alongside each other and so the edge beads are parallel and don't tilt toward each other.

9 Weave through the first unit of beads on row 4 from right to left; then through the first unit on row 2. Continue this alternating pattern until rows 3 and 4 are secured to rows 1 and 2 in **Figure 8**.

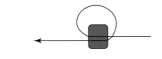

Figure 4

Figure 5

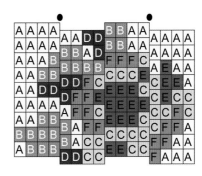

Figure 6

Figure 7

Figure 8

Tip

Frequently compare your work to the pattern to catch any mistakes. If there is a mistake, don't worry! Simply pull the thread out to undo the offending row or rows and pick up the process from there. If the mistake was picking up an extra bead, isolate the extra bead from its neighbors. Gently grab it with a chainnose or similar pliers and squeeze until the bead cracks. (Be careful not to grab any of its neighbors.) Discard the pieces and continue (no one will ever know!). If you progressed past the extra bead, unstring just to that point if the bead count was off due to the extra bead.

10 Repeat steps 7 and 8, picking up two rows as indicated in the pattern and word chart **Figure 9**, and securing them to the previous rows **Figure 10**, until done. When approximately 6 in. of Fireline remains, add more Fireline (Techniques, p. 97).

11 Because the ends and closure will endure the most wear, at the end of the piece, be sure to weave back through the last several rows to reinforce so your work will not fall apart. (I generally weave through the last four-eight rows if using 4-lb. line and two-four rows if using 6-lb.)

12 Add any fringe, trim, or embellishment. Follow the instructions for and examples of various types throughout the projects.

13 If required, add a closure. Follow the instructions for and examples of various types throughout the projects..

14 When the closure is complete, weave back into the piece. When you are several beads away from the end/edge, add finishing knots to secure. Repeat until you are comfortable that the piece is secure. (Test the end of the piece by rolling the beads in your fingers and tugging gently on the ends/edges to make sure the beads will not come loose and that all the rows are parallel to each other.)

15 Sew through one or two more beads. Trim the thread close to the piece and tuck the end into a neighboring bead to hide it.

Figure 9

Figure 10

Knots

Adding Fireline

1 Cut a new, comfortable length of Fireline.

2 Align the end of the new Fireline with the end of the working tail (that is coming out of the piece) and tie an overhand knot **Figure 11**.

3 Tighten the knot. Separate the two tails and tie them together with a half-square knot **Figure 12** or a surgeon's knot **Figure 14**. Pull tight to ensure that the knot will not slip and that it is as small as it can be. (If using a 6-lb. thread, the knot may need to be gently squeezed with chainnose pliers to make it small enough to go through the remaining beads.)

4 Trim the short ends, leaving a scissor width of thread. This little extra will be hidden in the beads and will keep the knot from pulling apart.

Tips

• After tying the overhand knot, but before tying the half-square knot, make a guess as to where the knot will fall within the bracelet to avoid having a knot on the edge. To do this, lay the thread back and forth across the piece to estimate where the knot will fall. Pull the two threads to move the knot several bead lengths away from an edge and then tie the half-square or surgeon's knot.

• Another way to hide a knot is to tie an overhand knot and pull the ends until the knot is flush against the bead that was just exited. Tie the half-square knot or a surgeon's knot. Trim and continue working, tucking the knot and short ends into the beads just strung.

Finishing knots

A series of half-hitch knots is used to finish the piece.

1 Sew down through the piece between two beads, as shown in **Figure 13**, then back up on the other side of the Fireline. Pass the needle through the loop that is created and pull tight; this will make a knot.

2 Sew through several beads and repeat a number of times for security.

3 Sew through a few more beads, trim the Fireline close to the piece, and tuck the end into a bead.

Surgeon's knot

A surgeon's knot starts as an overhand knot, and then the thread is passed through the loop one more time, thus making it less likely to slip **Figure 14**. (A surgeon's knot is a little bigger than an overhand knot, so check the size compared to the bead holes to make sure it will fit.)

Removing a knot

Sometimes the Fireline will get knotted. If using 4-lb. Fireline, the knot can easily be tightened and work continued, though the Fireline will be a little weaker at that point.

To untie the knot, place the knot on a bead mat and insert a needle or a fine beading awl through the center of the knot, taking care not to split the thread. Rock the needle/awl back-and-forth and side-to-side to work open the knot.

If the knot does not open, put a second needle or awl into the opening (again, being careful not to split the thread) and gently spread the two tools apart to open the knot. If the knot cannot be untied, trim the Fireline before the knot, add more Fireline, and then continue.

Figure 11

Figure 12

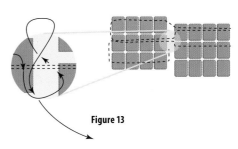

Figure 13

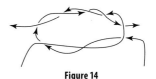

Figure 14

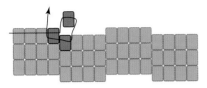

Figure 15

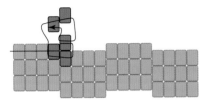

Figure 16

Figure 17

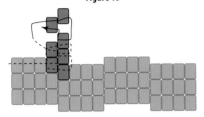

Figure 18

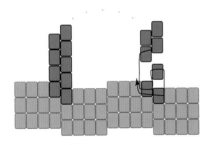

Figure 19

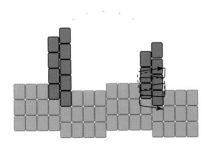

Figure 20

Loops

Many closures require a loop. Before adding a loop, decide what the other end of the closure will be. It may be a peyote toggle, a bead, a button, or another finding of choice. (Determining the complete closure will help you decide which loop will be best for your piece.) Before beginning the loop, reinforce the end of the piece so the closure will stay together over time.

Flat peyote loop

A flat peyote loop can be any width, depending on the desired effect. Most flat peyote loops in this book are two beads wide.

1 After reinforcing the last rows of the band for strength, estimate where the ends of the loop will lay (dark beads in **Figure 15**) and exit an up-bead on the end of its row.

2 Pick up one bead and sew through the bead immediately below it and its neighbor **Figure 15**. Exit the neighbor bead as shown.

3 Now create a fast peyote, two-column band: pick up two beads, sewing through the right side of the bead that was added in the previous step. Sew through the right side of the first bead just picked up, exiting on the left of the other bead as shown in **Figure 16**. Tighten the Fireline so the two beads lie flush with the end of the band.

4 Continue picking up and securing two beads **Figure 17** as in step 3 until the length of the loop is reached. If using a button or a larger bead as the toggle, test the loop opening frequently to make sure it is big enough for the button/bead **Figure 18**. For example, in **Figure 18** an octagonal vintage button from Germany that is approximately 14mm diameter is used and the loop is approximately 23 beads long.

Tip

Depending on the thickness of the button, the loop is generally twice the diameter plus two or three beads long; a thicker button might require a few more beads. Check several times before finishing.

5 When the loop is the correct length, exit the loop band on the left side. Sew through the left side of the up bead on the band where the loop will be attached **Figure 19**. Then pick up one bead and sew through the right side of the down-bead on the band where the loop will be added. Next, sew back through the up-bead, pulling the end of the loop flush to the end of the band.

6 Sew through several of the beads on the band and then around the areas where the loop ends to secure **Figure 20**.

Brick stitch loop

A brick stitch loop can be preferable if the loop is to span the entire length of a multi-drop piece.

1 To add a brick stitch loop two beads wide, first reinforce the end, and then exit the last row at the edge.

2 Pick up a unit of two beads and sew back through the previously exited unit, sewing in the opposite direction **Figure 21**. Pull tight and sew back through the unit of two beads just added **Figure 22**.

3 Pick up a unit of two more beads. Sew through the previous two beads and then through the beads just strung and pull tight **Figure 23**. Continue until the loop has the desired length. To estimate the loop length, test it with the toggle, bead, or button **Figure 18**.

4 Weave back into the piece at the opposite end. Secure the end of the loop to the base of the piece **Figure 24** using brick stitch. Reinforce the beads just picked up. Weave back into the piece and knot, repeating as desired for strength. Trim the Fireline close to the piece and tuck the end into a bead.

Simple peyote loop and round peyote loop

A round peyote loop lays differently and may be preferable to a flat loop, depending on the desired closure.

1 Exit the piece between two beads that are on the same level **Figure 25**, for example: two up-beads or two down-beads. Pick up the required number of beads, two at a time (to maintain an even count). Test frequently to make sure the opening is big enough for the button/bead, but not so big that it will easily slip out.

2 Enter the piece near the opposite edge, the same distance away from the edge as the starting point. **For a simple round loop, stop beading at this point.** Reinforce the beads just picked up and weave back into the piece and secure with finishing knots (Techniques, p. 97). Repeat as desired for strength.

3 To continue with a thicker, **round peyote loop**, add a third row with traditional peyote: Exit the up-bead at the base of the loop and pick up one bead to the outside of the loop. Skip a bead in the loop and then sew through the next bead in the loop.

4 Continue this single-drop, traditional peyote stitch, until one bead has been added between all the beads in the loop, and then weave back into the piece **Figure 26**.

5 To make the loop thicker, add a fourth row by exiting the piece one bead away from the base of the loop. Add one bead to the outside of the loop and sew through the next bead in the loop. Then pick up two beads, thread through one, and pick up one bead—alternating as you go.

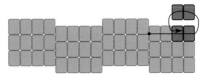

Figure 21

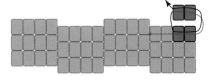

Figure 22

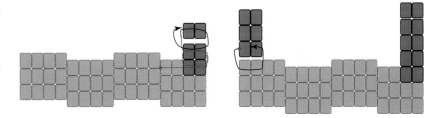

Figure 23

Figure 24

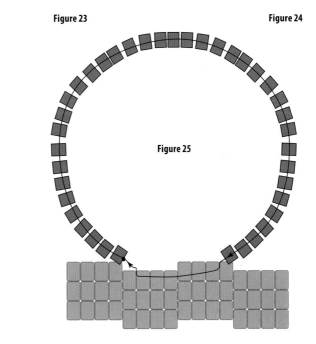

Figure 25

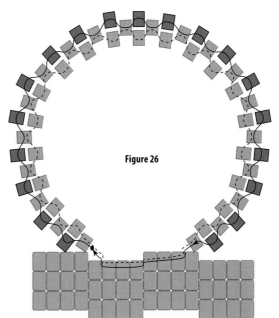

Figure 26

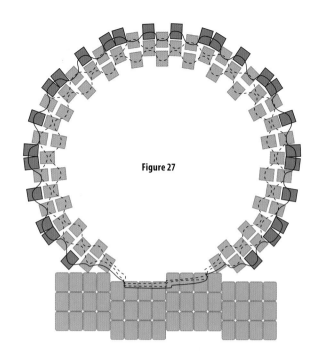

Figure 27

Tip

Depending on the size of the loop, some "gaps" may require an extra bead. (As in **Figure 27**, where the top of the loop has two single beads filling in spaces. This is a judgment call, depending on the desired "ruffle" or flatness.)

Trim for round peyote loop

Trim can be added to give a round peyote loop a more finished (even lacy) look. One option, shown in **Figure 30**, is alternating one and two 15º beads to "fill in" the spaces between the beads on the outer loop.

Exit the piece one bead away from the base of the loop, alternately adding one and two (or more for a lacier look) 15º beads between the beads on the outer edge. When complete, weave back into the piece and use finishing knots to secure by reinforcing a number of times.

Adjusting a loop

If the loop is too big, it can be made smaller by adding one or more rows of beads to the base of the bracelet between the loop ends. To do this, add some Fireline a few beads away from the base of the toggle loop (black dot on the left in **Figure 28**).

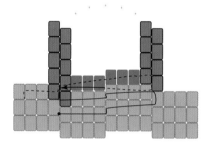

Figure 28   **Figure 29**

Sew through several beads and exit the inside base of the toggle loop just above the end of the piece. Pick up the same number of beads as between the toggle loop ends. (See the blue beads in **Figure 28**.)

Sew through the other base of the toggle loop so the beads just added fit inside the loop along the base. Sew through the up-beads at the base of the piece and then through the first beads picked up. This will secure them to the base inside the toggle loop **Figure 29**. Reinforce, finish, and trim the thread.

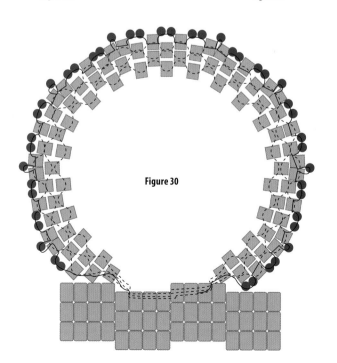

Figure 30

Reinforce a loop

1 Once the loop is connected on both ends, sew into the piece through the last two rows of beads and then weave back into the other connection point of the loop. Weave back through the loop one full time.

2 Weave back into the piece and through and around several beads at the base of the tail.

3 Place several finishing knots at various locations in the piece. I usually space these out by 1-3 units of beads and put 3-5 knots. (That way if one knot fails, there are several others to keep things together.)

4 Weave into the neighboring unit of beads, then trim the Fireline and weave the tail back into the piece.

Buttons

An alternative to a loop is a buttonhole. Then a button, bead(s), or a peyote tube can be used as the toggle.

Tip

If modifying a pattern, you can draw a rectangle with the same dimensions as the piece on paper. Make any desired modifications, then cut out the piece and use the paper pattern to make any further adjustments before starting. If using Delicas, use the tables in the Appendix to estimate the number of beads needed. Don't forget to size the buttonhole to your closure.

Add a button

1 To use a button as a closure with the loop or buttonhole at the end of the toggle tail, pick up several beads (three or more), making sure the button will not sit too tightly against the tail **Figure 31**.

2 Pick up the button, then the same number of beads as on the other side **Figure 32**. (At this point, a few extra beads may be required if the beads are small enough to move inside the shank of the button.)

3 Weave through the last two beads of the tail, then back through the beads and button for reinforcement. Weave through the tail into the base of the bracelet.

4 Reinforce and knot a number of times to secure; trim the remaining Fireline and tuck the tail into a neighboring bead.

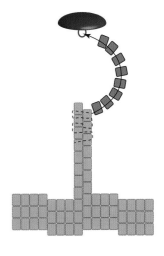

Figure 31

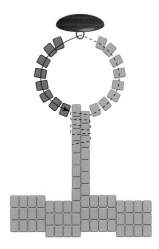

Figure 32

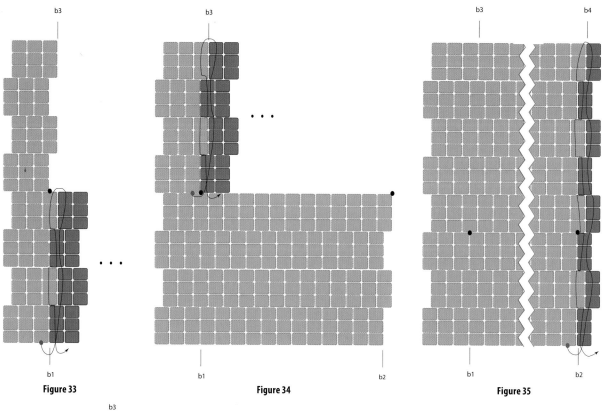

b3

Figure 33

b3

...

b1   b2

Figure 34

b3   b4

b1   b2

Figure 35

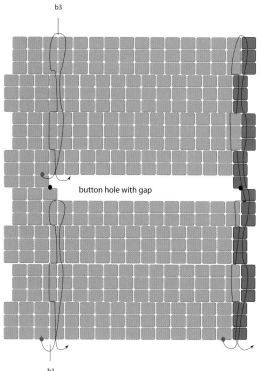

b3

button hole with gap

b1

Figure 36

Create a buttonhole

1 Follow the pattern to where the buttonhole begins near the line marked **b1** in **Figure 33**. Exit the edge and begin the next rows, but only pick up half the beads to the location on the pattern marked with a black dot.

2 Continue half the pattern until the location where the buttonhole ends is reached near the line marked **b2** in **Figure 34**. Leave the Fireline hanging.

3 Add Fireline to the other half of the pattern near the black dot in the center. Exit at the last bead near the black dot **Figure 34**. Continue the other half of the pattern until the location where the buttonhole ends is reached. Leave the Fireline hanging.

4 Return to the first piece of Fireline and pick up the two rows (the full width of the bracelet) after the marks **b2** and **b4** in **Figure 35**. Work fast peyote to "close" the buttonhole. Complete the pattern: Finish, reinforce, knot, and trim the Fireline.

5 Return to the second piece of Fireline near the line marked **b4** in **Figure 35**. Weave it back into the piece and reinforce around the buttonhole. Weave back into the piece and knot a number of times, then trim the thread.

Tip

Note the patttern of beads to the left and right of the center of the buttonhole in **Figure 36**. If adapting a pattern to use a buttonhole instead of a loop or clasp, the bracelet needs to be made long enough to overlap at the end. The buttonhole location must be marked on the pattern prior to starting the project. It is best to decide how to adjust the size of your bracelet before beginning,and then clearly mark the changes on the pattern.

Toggles

Toggle tail

If using a bead, button, or toggle to secure through the loop (or buttonhole), add a toggle tail as follows.

1 At the end of the piece, opposite the loop or buttonhole, remove the stop bead and add Fireline (Techniques, p. 97).

2 Weave back through the piece to reinforce and hide the knot, then exit between the up-bead in the center and the next up-bead **Figure 37**.

3 Pick up one bead and enter the opposite end of the bead below as in **Figure 38**. Then sew through the bead immediately to the right of it and exit the end of the band.

4 Pick up two beads and sew through the side of the bead added in the previous step **Figure 39**, creating the base of the toggle tail. Continue picking up beads, two at a time to create a two-bead, single-drop peyote tail until the desired length is reached **Figure 40**. This length should be at least half the diameter of the button, bead, or toggle, but can be longer to lengthen the bracelet, if desired.

Toggle bar / Peyote tube

A toggle bar can be constructed from a tube of peyote and can be embellished. Depending on preference, it can be a single color or it can be a small section of the pattern. The toggle bar's length should be at least 12 beads for most bracelets, but it can be as long as the bracelet is wide. The loop (Techniques, p. 98) should be sized accordingly: smaller for a shorter toggle bar and larger for a longer toggle bar.

1 To create the toggle bar, follow the fast peyote instructions (Techniques, p. 94), using two-drop unless otherwise specified, and make a band six beads long (12 rows) and the desired width **Figure 41**.

Tip

One- or two-drop stitch is preferred for a toggle bar, as the tube will not keep its shape as well with three-drop or more.

2 Roll the band into a tube and sew through the bead(s) that align with the beads just exited **Figure 41**.

3 Continue sewing through alternate bead(s) until the tube is closed **Figure 42**. Knot the two pieces of Fireline together, then sew down through the toggle. This is referred to as "zipping up the tube."

4 If embellishing the toggle bar, see the instructions (Techniques, p. 104). To attach the toggle bar to the tail, exit the toggle bar in the center **Figure 43**. Weave through the required number of beads for the toggle tail and attach it to the center of the peyote band.

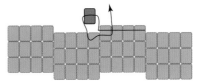

Figure 37

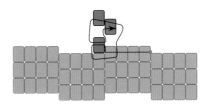

Figure 38

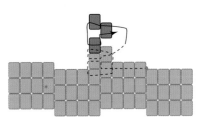

Figure 39

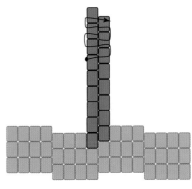

Figure 40

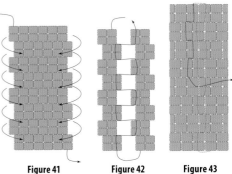

Figure 41　　Figure 42　　Figure 43

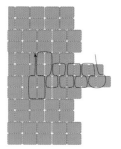

Figure 44

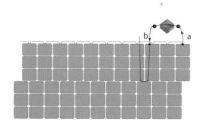

Figure 45

Reinforcing the toggle

1 Sew through the last beads in the same direction. For example, if a button was picked up, sew back through the button and the beads before and after the button two or three times.

2 Once you weave through the toggle, weave back through the tail one full time.

3 Weave back into the piece, then through and around several beads at the base of the tail as shown in **Figure 44** for peyote.

4 Follow the instructions (Techniques, p. 97) to make several finishing knots to secure the toggle. That way, if one knot fails, there are several others to keep things together.

5 Sew into the neighboring unit of beads, trim thread, and tuck end into a neighboring bead.

Embellishing a toggle bar

After zipping up a toggle bar (Techniques, p. 103), exit the edge. Two types of embellishments are described below and can be used to decorate the edge of a toggle bar.

Trim
Picot trim

A picot is a "half round" stitch that is often used in beading to make an edge. Picot fringe along the edge of a peyote band gives a more finished look to the edge where a small amount of thread may show. A picot stitch typically consists of three beads, but it can be more.

1 To add a three-bead picot fringe to the edge of a peyote band, weave back through the piece so the Fireline is coming out of the last (or first) row on the edge (point **a** in **Figure 45**).

2 Pick up the three beads that will make the picot: in **Figure 45** it is a 15º seed bead, a 4mm bicone, and a 15º. The bicone can be substituted for any seed bead up to 4mm beads. (Picot trim can be done with other size beads. If using smaller beads, do not skip a row in step 3, but enter/exit every other bead.)

3 Skip one row of beads, enter the edge bead marked point **b** in **Figure 45**, and sew through a unit of beads in that row (here, three beads, because it is three-drop).

4 Sew back up through the neighboring row of beads, then exit the edge and repeat until the other end of the piece is reached. Weave through to the opposite edge and repeat until the edges are covered in picots.

5 Weave back into the piece, knotting a number of times for security. Trim the Fireline and tuck it into neighboring beads.

Anemone or straight trim

1 To add straight trim to the edge of a peyote band, weave back through the band so the thread is coming out of the last (or first) row on the edge (point **a** in **Figure 46**).

2 Pick up the beads that will make the trim: in **Figure 46**, it is a 15º, a 4mm bicone, and a 15º. The bicone can be substituted for just about any number or size of bead, depending on the desired effect.

3 Sew back through the bicone and the seed bead. Then enter the edge bead (next to point **a** in **Figure 46**) and sew through the unit of beads in that row (here, three beads, because it is three-drop).

4 Stitch up through the unit of beads in the neighboring row; exit the edge and repeat until the other end of the piece is reached. (For a fuller trim, sew back along the same edge in the opposite direction to add another layer of trim.) Weave through the opposite edge and repeat until the edges are covered in trim.

5 Weave back into the piece, using finishing knots to secure. Trim the Fireline and tuck it into neighboring beads.

Twisted trim

A twisted trim is similar to a picot trim, but it uses more beads and overlaps to give it a twisted or rope-like edge.

1 To add a twisted trim to the edge of a peyote band, weave back through the band so the Fireline is coming out of the last (or first) row on the edge (point **a** in **Figure 47**).

2 Pick up five 15º seed beads.

3 Skip one row of beads and enter the edge bead (marked as point **b** in **Figure 47** and sew through the unit of beads in that row (here, three beads, because it is three-drop).

4 Stitch up through the skipped row of beads. Exit the edge and repeat, making sure to always exit on the same side of the previous five beads so the "twist" will be consistent **Figure 48**. Continue until the trim is complete at the other end of the piece. If there is only one row left at the end, pick up two or three beads in order to finish at the end.

5 Weave through to the opposite edge and repeat until the other edge is covered with twisted trim. Weave back into the piece, using finishing knots to secure. Trim the thread and tuck it into neighboring beads.

Picot embellishment

1 Pick up the three beads that will make the picot: for example, a 15º seed bead, a 3 or 4mm bicone, and a 15º seed bead. The bicone can be substituted for any other 2–4mm bead.

2 Skip one row of beads. Enter the edge unit of beads and sew through the unit of beads in that row.

3 Sew back up through the neighboring row unit of beads; exit the edge and repeat twice to complete the picot on the six-row toggle.

4 Weave through to the opposite edge and repeat.

5 Weave back into the bar and exit the toggle bar in the center. Pick up the required number of beads for the toggle tail and attach it to the center of the peyote band.

Straight or anemone embellishment

1 Pick up the two (or more) beads that will make the fringe: for example, a 4mm bicone and a 15º seed bead. The bicone can be substituted for similar size bead(s), depending on the desired effect.

2 Sew back through the bicone. Then enter the same edge bead unit that was exited and sew through the beads in that column.

3 Sew back up through the neighboring column of beads. Exit the edge and repeat six times for a six-row toggle bar.

4 Weave through to the opposite edge and repeat.

5 Weave back into the bar and exit the toggle bar in the center. Pick up the required number of beads for the toggle tail and attach it to the center of the peyote band.

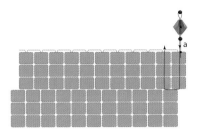

Figure 46

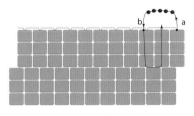

Figure 47

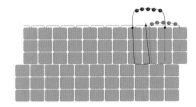

Figure 48

Figure 49

Fringe

Pendant fringe

Pendant fringe uses the same technique as a straight (or anemone) trim (Techniques, p. 105), but instead of adding the fringe along the edges of a peyote band, it is added to the end and often consists of many more beads.

1 Sew into one bead at the base. Exit between the end bead and its neighbor point **a** in **Figure 49**.

2 Pick up the beads listed in the first row of the fringe bead list. In the opposite direction, sew back through all but the last bead. (This makes the last bead, usually a seed bead or drop bead, the anchor).

3 Sew into the bead at the end of the piece (next to where you originally exited for fringe) and its neighbor. Exit two beads away from where the first fringe strand comes out of the piece. Repeat step 2 using the beads listed in the next row **Figure 50**. (If the fringe has an inverted "V," it will look like **Figure 51**).

Tip

A "v" or inverted "v" fringe comes from stepping up or stepping down the number of beads to the center. Then continue the step pattern in the opposite direction.

4 Repeat until the first strands of fringe are added **Figure 50** or **Figure 51**.

5 To create dimensional fringe, add another layer or layers of fringe. To do this, sew back into the piece and exit between two beads—between the existing fringe and/or on the ends; see point **c** in **Figure 52**. (This can also be one bead up from the base, depending on the desired effect and the types of beads.)

6 Follow steps 2–4 to complete the next row of fringe.

7 Weave back into the piece and use finishing knots in several locations to secure. Trim the thread and tuck the tail into a neighboring bead.

Tip

These instructions are done using two-drop peyote, so the fringe lies between each two-drop pair. For three- or other drop peyote, keep the spacing of the beads consistent so the strands are evenly placed. Count the beads first and plan where the strands of fringe will lie. (The center will not be directly in the center [as in these instructions] due to an even number of beads. Keep this in mind if modifying the fringe.)

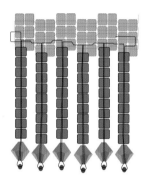

Figure 50

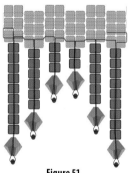

Figure 51

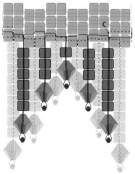

Figure 52

Tufted fringe

Similar to anemone trim, this fringe provides a fuller look by beginning the fringe along the edge of the band, instead of at the end.

1 Exit the bead at the end of the edge, point **a** in **Figure 53**.

2 Pick up the beads listed in the first row of the fringe bead list (a seed bead, a bicone, a seed bead). Sew back through the bicone and the other seed bead in the opposite direction. (This makes the seed bead the anchor.)

3 Sew into the bead at the end of the piece (next to where the fringe was originally exited) and its neighbor. Then exit one bead away from the end. Repeat step 2 using the beads listed in the next row (seed beads, a bicone, a seed bead), skipping two beads in the base to begin the following row.

4 Repeat until the first six strands of fringe have been added.

5 Exit at the end of the row. Add the last strand (a seed bead, a bicone, a seed bead). Sew back through the bicone and the other bead in the opposite direction (This makes the seed bead the anchor.)

6 Weave back into the base through one bead and exit at point **c** in **Figure 54**.

7 Follow steps 2–4 to complete the next row of fringe. Weave back into the piece and use finishing knots to secure. Trim the thread and tuck the tail into a neighboring bead.

Draped fringe

Top-drilled beads such as daggers, Rizos, teardrops, and magatamas can be used to make a draped fringe.

1 To add draped fringe to the end of a peyote band, weave through the band so the thread is coming out of the last (or first) row on the edge (point **a** in **Figure 55**).

2 Pick up the beads that will make the trim. In **Figure 55**, it is five 15º seed beads, then alternating a dagger and a 15º seed bead, then five 15º seed beads.

3 Sew back into the edge bead on the opposite side of the piece, point **b** in **Figure 55**. Then sew through the beads in the last two rows, exiting where the fringe started at point **a** in **Figure 55**.

4 Repeat for the desired number of fringe layers, stepping up or stepping down the seed beads closest to the edges for varied drape.

5 Weave back into the piece, knotting and weaving a number of times for security. Trim the thread and tuck it into neighboring beads.

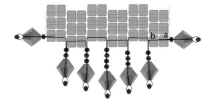

Figure 53

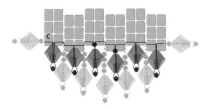

Figure 54

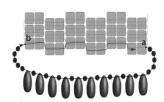

Figure 55

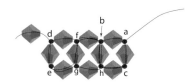

Figure 56

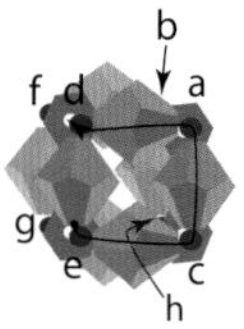

Figure 57

Figure 58

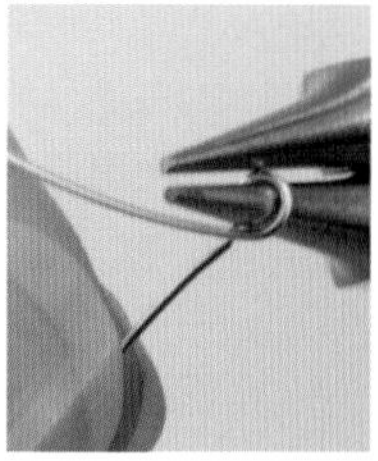

Figure 59

Figure 60

Figure 61

Figure 62

Adding a slide end tube

A slide end tube is a great option for ending a peyote piece or providing a bail for a pendant or earring.

1 Exit along one edge of the end of the piece. With a long needle, pick up the last rows of 11º seed beads. (The slide end tube used here is for 11º beads.)

2 Weave into the other edge of the piece. Work VERY LOOSE fast peyote to secure the beads, but do not tighten.

3 Use chainnose pliers to fold down one flap on the end of the slide end tube.

4 Slide all the loosely secured beads onto the other end of the slide end tube.

5 Carefully pull the Fireline tight until the beads pull the slide end tube snug along the end of the piece.

6 Weave back through the base row, including the beads inside the tube and through the beads along the end of the piece, to secure the slide end tube to the piece.

7 Carefully fold the flap at the other end of the slide end tube closed. You can also lightly tap it with a smooth mallet to close the flaps tighter along the edges.

8 Weave back into the piece and finish knotting in several locations to secure. Trim the thread and tuck the tail into a neighboring bead.

Beaded bead

A beaded bead made of right-angle weave makes a nice option for a toggle.

1 On a new length of Fireline, pick up a seed bead, a bicone, then repeat three more times until there are four pairs of beads.

2 Tie a double overhand knot at point **a** in **Figure 56** to secure the beads into a circle. Weave back through the three bicone/seed bead pairs and exit a bicone at point **b** in **Figure 56**.

3 Pick up a bicone, a seed bead, a bicone, a seed bead, and a bicone (total of five beads). Sew back into the other end of the bicone just exited to form another circle.

4 Repeat step 3 until there is a strip of three connected circles. The next step is to close this strip into a cylinder. Exit the seed bead marked point in **Figure 56**.

5 Pick up a bicone and sew into the seed bead at point **a** in **Figure 56**. Then sew out of the seed bead at point **c** in **Figure 56**.

6 Pick up the last bicone and sew into the seed bead at point **e** in **Figure 56**. Then sew around the circle to close the cylinder that is made up of four "rings" of bicones.

7 Close the top and bottom of your cylinder by sewing through **d, f, b, a**—then through **c, h, g,** and **e** as in **Figure 57**. Use a few finishing knots to tighten and to finish the bead, then trim the Fireline or leave it to secure to the toggle tail.

Wire-wrapped loops

Wire-wrapped links can be used for a variety of jewelry items. In this book, they are primarily used for connecting chain or clasps for the pendant projects.

1 Cut a 12- or 18-in. length of 24-gauge tarnish-resistant wire.

2 Hold the wire with a roundnose pliers and fold to make a 90 degree angle **Figure 58**.

3 Move the roundnose pliers to the other side of the angle just made and wrap around to form a loop **Figure 59**. Change the position of the pliers as needed to make a round loop **Figure 60**.

4 Grasp the loop with the pliers and fold the wire tail around the base of the wire to wrap the loop closed **Figure 61**.

5 Pick up the bead, making sure it is flush against the wrapped wire.

6 Repeat steps 2 and 3 on the other side of the bead to create the link.

7 If adding this link to another, add the link onto the loop just created **Figure 62**.

8 Repeat step 4 to close the link.

Opening and closing a jump ring or loop

1 To open a jump ring, hold the ring firmly on either side of the opening with two pairs of pliers **Figure 63**.

2 Carefully move one side up and one side down to "twist" the ring open. Do not "pull" the ring open, as it will become misshapen and make it difficult to close securely.

3 Add the desired component (clasp, link, ring, etc.).

4 To close the ring, repeat the twist in the opposite direction until the ring "snaps" closed **Figure 64**.

Finishing a cord

1 Trim the cord to the desired length, keeping in mind that the clasp will add $3/4$-1 in. to the total length.

2 Hold one of the fold-over cord ends, open side up by the ring or place it on a rough work surface—that is a surface that will not be ruined by a bit of glue. (A bit of wax paper or cellophane makes a nice cover for your normal bead mat.)

3 Gently squeeze a small drop of glue (Loc Tite, E6000, etc.) into the channel of the open end **Figure 65**. Lay the cord on the glue, align it properly, and make sure there is no glue on the outside that will make it stick to the work surface **Figure 66**. Allow it to dry for a short time. (Read the glue instructions. It does not have to be fully dry before proceeding.)

4 With chainnose pliers, squeeze one flap of the cord end until it is against the cord **Figure 67**. Repeat at the edges of the flap so the whole flap is flat. Repeat on the other flap **Figure 68**.

5 Repeat for the other cord end.

6 Follow the procedure for opening and closing a jump ring (Techniques, p. 109) to add a ring on either side and a clasp on one side.

Figure 63   **Figure 64**

Figure 65   **Figure 66**

Figure 67   **Figure 68**

APPENDIX

Delica Seed Bead Information
Compiled by Josie Fabre

11° DB
200 11° delicas per gram

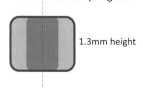

1.3mm height

1.6mm (diameter)
hole is ~.8mm .83mm

Size of piece created with beads side-by-side

1.00 inch	15.875 beads	25.4 mm
0.94 inch	15.0 beads	24.0 mm
1.01 inch	16.0 beads	25.6 mm

Size of piece created with beads end-to-end (along thread)

1.00 inch	19.538 beads	25.4 mm
0.94 inch	19.0 beads	24.0 mm
1.01 inch	20.0 beads	25.6 mm

Bracelet Dimensions

5.5" length (for 6.5" bracelet)	88 beads
6.5" length (for 7.5" bracelet)	103 beads
7.5" length (for 8.5" bracelet)	134 beads

1.5" width	24 beads
2.0" width	32 beads
2.5" width	40 beads

15° DBS
380 15° delicas per gram

1.15mm height

1.3mm (diameter)
hole is ~.65mm .7mm

Size of piece created with beads side-by-side

1.00 inch	19.5 beads	25.4 mm
0.97 inch	19.0 beads	24.7 mm
1.02 inch	20.0 beads	26.0 mm

Size of piece created with beads end-to-end (along thread)

1.00 inch	22.1 beads	25.4 mm
0.99 inch	22 beads	25.3 mm
1.04 inch	23.0 beads	26.5 mm

Bracelet Dimensions

5.5" length (for 6.5" bracelet)	107 beads
6.5" length (for 7.5" bracelet)	127 beads
7.5" length (for 8.5" bracelet)	166 beads

1.53" width	30 beads
2.0" width	40 beads
2.5" width	48 beads

10° DBM
109 10° delicas per gram
2.2mm height x 1.7mm diam
hold is .95-1.0mm

1.00 inch side-by side	~12 beads
1.00 inch end-to-end (strung)	~15 beads

Bracelet Dimensions

6.5 inch length	~75 beads
1.5 inch width	~18 beads

http://www.miyuki-beads.co.jp/english/seed/09.html
http://fusionbeads.com

ACKNOWLEDGMENTS

A special, heartfelt thank you to my family and friends, who give me encouragement, support, and feedback on everything I create and put up with my hours on the computer and at my bead table.

I sincerely thank the fabulous professionals of Kalmbach Publishing, especially Dianne Wheeler, who made this process enjoyable and successful. Thank you to Jane Cruz, former Associate Editor with *Bead&Button* magazine who introduced me to Dianne and made this whole dream possible.

Thank you to all my beading friends at *Meme's Beads and Things* (especially Michelle and Shirley) and to the members of the Slidell Bead Society: I enjoy learning from and spending time with all of you wonderful people.

The patterns in this book were generated by BeadTool4 and modified with Adobe Illustrator. I truly appreciate the capabilities of this software.

About the Author

Josie Fabre has lived in Slidell, La. most of her life. She is a scientist with an artistic side, who has been crafting, beading, and taking photos for many years. She loves to design and make jewelry and is inspired by the unique and beautiful natural areas and wildlife of the Southeast US (or wherever her travels take her), and by art and architecture.

She got hooked on creating peyote patterns and jewelry in 2012 when she designed and stitched squares for the Bead-it-Forward Breast Cancer Fundraising project.

When she is not beading, she enjoys spending time with her wonderful husband, two fabulous sons, close family, and friends.